Constructing the Enemy

Rajini Srikanth

Constructing the Enemy

Empathy/Antipathy
in U.S. Literature and Law

TEMPLE UNIVERSITY PRESS
Philadelphia

TEMPLE UNIVERSITY PRESS
Philadelphia, Pennsylvania 19122
www.temple.edu/tempress

Excerpts from Mitsuye Yamada, "To the Lady," and "The Night before Good-bye" are reprinted from Mitsuye Yamada, *Camp Notes and Other Writings* (New Brunswick, NJ: Rutgers University Press, 1998). Copyright © 1998 by Mitsuye Yamada. Reprinted by permission of Rutgers University Press.

Excerpt from Brian Turner, "In the Leupold Scope," is reprinted from Brian Turner, *Here, Bullet* (Farmington, ME: Alice James Books, 2005). Copyright © 2005 by Brian Turner. Reprinted with the permission of Alice James Books, www.alicejamesbooks.org.

Excerpt from Adrienne Rich poem reprinted from Adrienne Rich, *Your Native Land, Your Life: Poems* (New York: Norton, 1986). Copyright © 1986 W. W. Norton and Company. All attempts were made to contact the copyright holder.

Excerpt from Osaba Abu Kabir, "Is It True?" reprinted from Marc Falkoff, ed., *Poems from Guantánamo: The Detainees Speak* (Iowa City: University of Iowa Press, 2007). Reprinted with permission.

Excerpt from Chris Schatz poem reprinted from Mahvish Rukhsana Khan, *My Guantánamo Diary: The Detainees and the Stories They Told Me* (New York: PublicAffairs, 2008). Reprinted with the permission of Perseus Books Group.

Excerpt from Frank Bidart, "Curse," reprinted from *Threepenny Review*, no. 89 (Spring 2002). Copyright © 2002 *Threepenny Review*. All attempts were made to contact the copyright holder.

Excerpt from Naomi Shihab Nye, "Red Brocade," reprinted from Naomi Shihab Nye, *19 Varieties of Gazelle: Poems of the Middle East* (New York: HarperCollins, 2002). Text copyright © 2002 Naomi Shihab Nye. Used by permission of HarperCollins Publishers.

Library of Congress Cataloging-in-Publication Data

Srikanth, Rajini.
   Constructing the enemy : empathy/antipathy in U.S. literature and law / Rajini Srikanth.
      p. cm.
   Includes bibliographical references and index.
   ISBN 978-1-4399-0323-0 (cloth : alk. paper) — ISBN 978-1-4399-0324-7 (pbk. : alk. paper) —
ISBN 978-1-4399-0325-4 (e-book)
   1. American literature—History and criticism.   2. Law and literature—United States.
3. Empathy in literature.   4. Aversion in literature.   I. Title.
   PS169.L37S69   2012
   810.9'3554—dc23
                                                                    2011016212

♾ The paper used in this publication meets the requirements of the American National Standard for Information Sciences—Permanence of Paper for Printed Library Materials, ANSI Z39.48-1992

Printed in the United States of America

2 4 6 8 9 7 5 3 1

For Rudra, Sahana, and Anaga
Living empathetically, reshaping their futures

Contents

Acknowledgments

I owe an enormous debt of gratitude to the anonymous reviewers who read the manuscript exactingly and offered invaluable suggestions that strengthened its theoretical foundations and to the lawyers who agreed to be interviewed about their pro bono defense work for Guantánamo Bay detainees. I cannot adequately thank the reviewers and the lawyers for their invaluable contribution, without which this book would have been significantly diminished.

My thanks go as well to the many friends and colleagues who helped me keep faith in the project even through the most challenging times—Monica Chiu, who first invited me to the University of New Hampshire to present my ideas in the early days of their formulation; Larry Blum, who insisted that I persist in my endeavor even when it was becoming increasingly difficult to make progress; Samina Najmi, who generously read an early draft and drew my attention to unsupportable leaps of logic; Sunaina Maira, who made it possible to present my work on the Guantánamo lawyers at the 2010 American Studies conference; and Vik Muiznieks, whose interest in my research gave me hope that there would be an audience for this work beyond academe.

As always, I am indebted to my students at the University of Massachusetts Boston, who help me in my effort never to forget to ask, "So what?" about the research I pursue.

Constructing the Enemy

Introduction

The Landscape of Empathy

This book presents and charts the fraught terrain of empathy—in U.S. literature and law—specifically as it relates to "the enemy" at two historical moments: the Japanese Americans after the December 1941 bombing of Pearl Harbor, and the Muslim men captured and detained in various locations in the current U.S. "global war on terror." It poses the question "What will it take to generate a national ethos in which our construction and identification of 'the enemy' is carefully considered rather than hasty, informed by empathy rather than driven by unexamined antipathy, accompanied by scrupulous interrogation of our assumptions and actions rather than based on complacent faith in our institutions?" Empathy combines affective and cognitive components; in empathy one does not simply *feel for* (as in sympathy) but rather one *feels with* another individual or group.[1] One recognizes the complex realities of others' lives and subjectivities and the inextricability of one's world with theirs.

The Japanese American internment of the 1940s and the current indefinite detention of Arabs, South Asians, and Muslim Americans are similar in their violation of basic constitutional guarantees. The targeted groups (based on race for the former and religion for the latter) in both instances have been constructed as national threats and their detentions justified by questionable applications and interpretations of existing laws.[2]

The examination of empathy that follows in these pages serves two purposes: first, to move readers to appreciate the intricacies of empathy's emergence and manifestation, and second to encourage an application of this heightened appreciation for and knowledge of the complexities of empathy in the specific particulars of lived realities and in law and policy.

The literary analyses in this book illuminate the crevices and deep histories in the landscapes of empathy; the discussions of law foreground the ways in which lawyers have understood and drawn on (or not drawn on) empathy in the service of their clients (Japanese American internees and Muslim detainees). The language of law, once erected, can become formulaic, can become enshrined and dominate one's thoughts and actions in much the same way that built structures can eclipse the unbuilt structures that could have occupied the same space and which, perhaps, were strongly desired by certain populations whose voices were not heard. The unbuilt, says Arjun Appadurai, could be regarded as "once futures"; I submit that when we forfeit opportunities for empathy we regrettably reject possible desirable futures.[3]

Empathy requires significant imaginative labor. The representations of and actions in behalf of interned Japanese Americans and detained Muslims and Muslim Americans by creative writers and lawyers is a central concern of this book. The literary writers discussed do not necessarily *advocate for* the targeted groups; rather, the value of their writings lies in the texture and complexity they provide to deepen the public's understanding of these groups. Similarly, the lawyers working in behalf of the detainees may or may not be responding empathetically to their clients; their involvement in these cases may be a matter of principle—their commitment to certain inviolable, as they perceive it, norms of due process. The *consequence/outcome* of their adherence to ideals may be that their clients benefit, but my discussion does not take as its starting point any presumption of empathy on the part of the attorneys. In fact, the relationship between the lawyers' decision to offer their services pro bono and the sentiment of empathy is precisely what I seek to examine. Creative writers and lawyers occupy antipodal positions on the spectrum of participatory democracy: in the privacy of the creative mind versus the public space of a courtroom; in the unofficial medium of literary expression versus the official language of legal decisions.

I explore whether lawyers' felty to legal language yields a textured terrain of humanity. How does their labor of employing the letter of the law compare with the eloquent description that Richard Wright gives of the act of writing and the empathetic energy creative writers call into play as they imagine themselves into the consciousness of their characters and into the contours of their varied lives? In "How Bigger Was Born," Wright (1989a) explains his process:

> It was an act of concentration, of trying to hold within one's center of attention all of that bewildering array of facts which science, politics, experience, memory, and imagination were urging upon me. . . . I was pushing out to new areas of feeling, strange landmarks of emotion, cramping upon foreign soil, compounding new relationships of perceptions, making new and—until that very split second of time!— unheard-of and unfelt effects with words. . . . That is writing as I feel it, a kind of significant living. (xxx)

A kind of significant living. I am interested in understanding this phrase and in seeing how creative writers and lawyers perform a kind of significant living as they connect empathetically with their characters/clients through a vital grappling with language, albeit different kinds of language.[4]

In May 2009, President Barack Obama introduced the notion of empathy into general and widespread circulation by describing a key quality his nominee for the Supreme Court would possess: "You have to be able to stand in somebody else's shoes and see through their eyes and get an idea of how the law might work or might not work."[5] But as Ronald Dworkin (2009) observes in his analysis of the confirmation hearings of Judge Sonia Sotomayor (Obama's nominee), neither the public nor the senators on both sides of the political spectrum nor the nominee herself had the courage or honesty to acknowledge that the law (i.e., the Constitution) does indeed require interpretation and that this interpretive act is rooted in every judge's philosophical orientation to the Constitution. Sotomayor's emphatically declared "fidelity to the law" is, argues Dworkin, an "empty statement," which "perpetuate[s] the silly and democratically harmful fiction that a judge can interpret the key abstract clauses of the United States Constitution without making controversial judgments of political morality in the light of his or her own political principles."[6] The public, Dworkin argues, has a right to know the parameters of a judge's constitutional philosophy (for instance, what the judge understands by *due process* or *cruel and unusual punishment* or *equal protection of the law*), and confirmation hearings are a rich opportunity for the people to engage the abstract principles of the Constitution to see how they apply to current realities. The principles of the law, particularly constitutional law, were left deliberately abstract by the framers precisely so that subsequent generations could arrive at their meaning for their specific historical context through a process of deliberative exchange of ideas and shared discourse.

Dworkin holds that empathy is a desirable quality in a judge. The value of his explanation is that it illuminates the nexus between the individual and the institutional (in this case, the legal) and shows how a practice of empathy can be negotiated within established social and political structures. He argues:

> It plainly helps a judge not only in finding facts but in formulating law to be able empathetically to understand the law's impact on people of different kinds. . . . [B]eing a woman helps a judge understand the horror of a strip search for a teenage girl. Being a Latina may give a judge a better understanding of the crucial moral difference between racial discrimination poisoned by prejudice and race-sensitive policies aimed at erasing that prejudice. A judge with that understanding would reach a better interpretation of the Constitution's equal protection clause than a judge without it. (2009)

In light of this complex relationship between the empathetic individual and structures of institution, Candace Vogler's (2004) question is particularly apt:

"Given a shared practical orientation that treats the individual person as the fundamental unit for ethics, how ought one to respond to a man-made injustice that is neither any one person's fault nor the sort of thing that any one person can remedy?" (32) She reminds us that "It is hard to navigate the ethical from the first-person perspective when you are registering horrors (however inchoately, however unwillingly) that can be neither laid on any individual's doorstep nor laid to rest by any individual's act" (40). Further, one might ask, what is the individual's responsibility not just in responding to injustice but also in ensuring that injustice does not occur in the first place? Put another way, how do corrective and preventive empathy look, and where and how do they originate?

By invoking Vogler, I do not mean to privilege the individual as the site of transformative action or preventive posture against injustice. I heed, too, Wendy Brown's (2002) caution that a preoccupation with the individual (the bastion of liberalism) facilitates the emergence and hegemony of structural injustice and inhibits our awareness of "what liberalism cannot deliver, what its hidden cruelties are, what unemancipatory relations of power it contains in its sunny formulations of freedom and equality" (420–421). And, finally, I register my agreement with Lauren Berlant's suspicion of a politics of private feeling. Nonetheless, I refuse to abandon the individual as a valuable terrain of analysis: private feeling is worthless only if treated as isolated and discrete; however, it can provide the ground for a necessary and urgent understanding of the national ecosystem—the formal institutions (including legal, educational, economic, political, religious, and domestic), cultural forums, and informal social customs—and multiple contextual webs in which this private feeling is situated and implicated. Precisely because we fail to study the complicated and contested dynamics within which empathy lies latent, we are unable to facilitate its emergence and dissemination.

My engagement with empathy insists that we be cognizant of asymmetrical power relations. Empathy cannot simply be a sentiment to be dispensed (along with self-congratulations) by the group or individual in power to a subordinate individual or group. I explicitly reject the sort of empathy that functions as tawdry feel-good sentimental armor and a guilt-absolving palliative that inhibits and substitutes for necessary action. James Baldwin's (1953) scathing critique of Harriet Beecher Stowe's *Uncle Tom's Cabin*—that it enables delicate and well-meaning (white) women to cleanse themselves with a good cry—is not altogether unfair. Though Baldwin rather unjustly links the "wet eyes" of sentimentality, which he describes as "the ostentatious parading of excessive and spurious emotion" (326), with an "aversion to experience" and "fear of life" (326), his trenchant distrust of empathetic *display* is worth heeding.

The speaker of Mitsuye Yamada's poem "To the Lady" (1998, 40–41) responds forcefully to an interlocutor in San Francisco who wonders why the Japanese Americans did not protest or resist when they were led off to internment camps in 1942 (following the Japanese army's bombing of Pearl Harbor) and imprisoned until the end of World War II. The speaker's address to the "lady" of the poem's title is sorrowful, bitter, enraged, and deeply despairing. One can "hear" the frustration and imagine the clenched teeth as the speaker hurls at the woman a response that excoriates the thoughtlessness of her question. The speaker's anguish at the lady's ignorance and her inability to empathize is palpable.

Yet in fairness, one must also acknowledge that the woman, in wondering why the Japanese Americans did not resist their forced removal, displays a rudimentary empathy in that she imagines Japanese Americans as possessing a self-worth and dignity akin to hers. The implication of her question is that *she* would have protested such treatment. But beyond this granting of their similarity to her, there is little evidence of the lady's capacity to apprehend the vast difference between her sociopolitical position and that of the internees, a significant difference that kept most Japanese Americans from challenging the government's arbitrary abrogation of their constitutional rights. Moreover, even if the woman had been able to understand the asymmetrical power between them, her empathy would still be deficient, because it is devoid of action. Yamada's poem makes the point with forceful sarcasm that good sentiments cannot stand alone. Empathy, to be worth anything, must be accompanied by meaningful intervention. The speaker's assertion to the lady in San Francisco—"YOU would've / come to my aid in shining armor / laid yourself across the railroad track / marched on Washington / . . . / written six million enraged / letters to Congress" (41)—might be more correctly read as an implicit challenge in which the unspoken question to the lady is, "Would you have come to our aid, and, if yes, then what form would this aid have taken?" In the chasm between the perspectives and experiences of the poem's speaker, on the one hand, and those of the lady, on the other, unfolds the complex landscape of the intersection of empathy and power in the United States.

In the early years of North American settlement, the Native Americans were considered dangerous; the next group to be characterized in this way were the "resistant" or "rebellious" slaves; following them were various groups of Asian immigrants, culminating in the 1942 internment of 120,000 Japanese Americans; then there was the Communist scare of the 1950s fanned by Joseph McCarthy (whose anticommunist legacy lived on in the decades of Cold War politics through the 1980s); today the group deemed the enemy includes Muslim Americans and foreign nationals of identifiable Muslim descent. This list of groups deemed to be threats is by no means exhaustive, but these specific groups have constituted the *principal* source of danger at the historical moments noted. The absence of empathy for these groups, at the moments when it mattered the most and would have had the most impact, resulted in courses of legal action and formulations of policy that in later years we have come to reconsider and even, in the case of the interned Japanese Americans, apologized for and compensated monetarily for losses the victims suffered.[7] However, even delayed empathy is by no means easy to stimulate, particularly if it necessitates self-interrogations or a national probing of assumptions about attitudes and behaviors we consider valuable.

Why We Need Empathy

A focus on empathy may seem misplaced at this historical moment of heterogeneous subjectivity and postmodern rejection of the Western enlightenment notion of the primacy of the rational individual. Skeptics of my project would assert that the priorities of diverse peoples differ vastly and are shaped by the very particular social, cultural, economic, and historical forces that operate where they live. However, like Jürgen Habermas (1993), I hold that empathy is desirable; it is essential, urgent, and imperative, particularly now, when we recognize the existence of multiple value systems and the plurality of contexts within which individuals construct their subjectivities. The more divergent the sociocultural and political contexts that generate values, "the more sharply do forms of life and life projects become differentiated from one another" (90), and thus the more critical it becomes to "coexistence, and even survival, in a more populous world" (91) that we engage in a communicative discourse leading to "shared interpretations." The kind of empathy that this book advocates requires hard work—unflinching introspection, honest interrogation, complex analysis, and courageous risk-taking. Habermas describes the ideal situation leading to shared understanding: "The fusion of interpretive horizons at which . . . every communicative process aims should not be understood in terms of the false alternative between an assimilation 'to us' and a conversion 'to them.' It is more properly described as a convergence between 'our' perspective and 'theirs' guided by learning processes" (105).

But what Habermas takes as a fundamental starting point (i.e., *symmetrical relation*) of the "learning processes" that lead us toward one another is precisely what I caution we cannot and should not assume. The failure of "discourse-ethics" and the floundering of empathetic exercises occur precisely because of the *asymmetry* in the positions of the actors involved. The individual or group or nation in the position of greater power does not recognize the other actor(s) as equal in the exchange, and so the adjustment of perspectives and the reassessment of positions is not undertaken with full commitment or a genuine desire to come to a shared understanding.

How, then, does one bring to bear on an asymmetrical relationship the necessity of a full communicative discourse? Slavoj Žižek (2005) insists that the "first ethical gesture is . . . to abandon the position of absolute self-positing subjectivity" (138) and to acknowledge that we are always constituted by our relationship with the Other. Both Žižek and Habermas exhort us to realize as well that we and Others are shaped by the contexts in which we exist; the implication, particularly with Žižek, is that the individual be willing to acknowledge that "I am already nontransparent to myself, and I will never get from the Other a full answer to 'who are you?' because the Other is a mystery also for him/herself" (2005, 138). He stresses the vulnerability and fragility of our humanness and the humanness of Others. Žižek's appeal is compelling:

> What makes an individual *human* and thus something for which we are responsible, toward whom we have a duty to help, is his/her very finitude and vulnerability. Far from undermining ethics (in the sense of rendering me ultimately nonresponsible: "I am not a master of myself, what I do is conditioned by forces that overwhelm me."), this primordial exposure/dependency opens up the properly ethical relations of individuals who accept and respect each other's vulnerability and limitation. . . . Confronted with the Other, I can never fully account for myself. (138)

Yet over and over again, individuals and groups with and in power have shown themselves unwilling and unable to envision themselves in humble and vulnerable relationship to those over whose lives they exercise control. They persist in self-assured certainty and see no reason to alter their perspective. I would agree that we ought to "be" the way that Habermas and Žižek urge us to be; but there is no formulaic way of achieving that end. Rather, each situation requires its own delicate choreography of interaction of persons and exchange of ideas.

Our truncated forms of discourse (televised election debates, judicial confirmation hearings, and campaign commercials, for example) do not enable any meaningful give-and-take of perspective; what is required is a radical extension of what Ronald Dworkin recommends as a long-term corrective to our defensive insularity as a nation and our complacent and uninterrogated comfort in our democracy: namely, the overhaul of our high school classrooms and how we teach the urgent issues of deliberative democracy. I have argued elsewhere that we need to reimagine the United States as an integral part of a community of nations;[8] American individualism and American exceptionalism are seductive narratives, but they have blinded us to our vulnerabilities and allowed us to persist in our delusional certainties not only about ourselves but also about Others. In the spaces of democratic discourse (including classrooms, neighborhood gatherings, town meetings, places of worship), we would do well to cultivate the attitude Žižek (2005) describes of acknowledging one's own "impenetrability" and recognizing the Other not as a fully known or knowable being but "in the abyss of [his or her] impenetrability and opacity. This mutual recognition of limitation thus opens up a space of sociality that is the solidarity of the vulnerable" (139).

Two Airport Stories: The Political Architecture of Empathy

Martha Nussbaum (2001) explains empathy as an exercise of "the muscles of the imagination, making people capable of inhabiting, for a time, the world of a different person, and seeing the meaning of events in the world from the outsider's viewpoint" (431). In any situation, these imaginative muscles are differentially exercised, and the outcomes can vary dramatically, depending on who exercises them, to what extent, and when. I begin my discussion of literary texts and their treatment of empathy with two brief memoirist accounts of airport experiences. Through these vignettes, one becomes aware of the supplications that certain players must undertake to elicit empathy and the postures of indifference and/or inflexibility that other players can persist in maintaining. One also sees how the individual and the institutional intersect.

In the first, "Gate 4-A," Palestinian American poet/essayist Naomi Shihab Nye (2007) narrates a hopeful resolution to an airport situation in which an Arabic-speaking elderly woman is distraught because she mistakenly believes that the flight she is scheduled to take has been canceled. The author-narrator is at Albuquerque International Airport awaiting the departure of her delayed flight when she hears an announcement over the PA system: "If anyone in the vicinity of Gate 4-A understands any Arabic, please come to the gate immediately."[9] Arriving there, the narrator finds that "an older woman in full traditional Palestinian embroidered dress, just like [her] grandma wore, was crumpled to the floor, wailing loudly." In her halting Arabic, the narrator quickly determines from the woman the reason for her distress; then, launching into full empathetic mode, the narrator clarifies to the older woman that the flight's departure has simply been delayed and that she will eventually get to her destination (El Paso) in time for a scheduled medical procedure; she then calls and assures the woman's son (who awaits her in El Paso) that she will stay by his mother for the rest of the time. In the two hours that they spend waiting together at the gate, they call the woman's other sons, the narrator's Palestinian father (who speaks to the old woman in Arabic), and several of the narrator's Palestinian poet friends. By now, the elderly woman is comfortable, happy, and expansive, and she distributes Palestinian cookies to all the women sitting at the gate. The airline officials bring out free beverages, intensifying the air of goodwill and camaraderie. The narrator glows with optimism about the possibility of a "shared world."

The arc of this short anecdote moves from difference to sameness, from distance to nearness, from incomprehension to understanding. The Arabic woman's strangeness morphs into hospitality, as she distributes the cookies to the women and encounters no refusals. From being the outsider, she becomes the caring host; from being the unfamiliar figure of the "wailing" Arab, she becomes the recognizable figure of the caring grandmother. Her transformation is made possible by the Palestinian American narrator, who facilitates the Arab woman's relabeling as a familiar type and enables the temporarily disoriented Arab woman to return to balance and calmness and reenter the universally recognizable role of grandmother.

What is most noticeable about this shared airport community is that it foregrounds women. The elderly Arab woman offers her cookies to the women at the gate, and none of them refuses: "not a single woman declined one. It was like a sacrament. The traveler from Argentina, the mom from California, the lovely woman from Laredo." In addition, two young girls also traveling on the same flight bustle about distributing the apple juice that the airline makes available to the waiting passengers. The narrator describes an idealistic female community free of suspicion, all covered in the sweetness of "powdered sugar." The only hint she gives of a flawed world beyond this idyllic gate community is contained in the line "Not a single person in this gate—once the crying of confusion stopped—seemed apprehensive about any other person." What is left unsaid is that the Arab woman's age and her being female soften the strangeness with which she might have initially been viewed by the other passengers at Gate 4-A.

Also left unnarrated are the details of how the narrator succeeds in dispelling the apprehension of the other waiting passengers and creating the link between them and the older woman. That the narrator helps the elderly Arab woman is clear. She succeeds in changing the woman's demeanor from nervousness to comfort, from anxiety to laughter. We do not learn what the narrator said to the other waiting passengers to soften their initial apprehension, whether in fact she said anything at all, or whether her presence and her obvious comfort with both the Arab woman and the gate personnel gave her a certain kind of authority and made her acceptable as the bridge between the waiting female passengers and the older Arab woman.

We know that the narrator actively creates a virtual community for the older woman through the many phone calls she makes to various Palestinians, including the woman's sons. Through these calls, the narrator reminds the Palestinian woman that she is not alone. The phone calls transport a familiar community into the airport space and perhaps give the woman confidence that she is surrounded by a protective and welcoming network. Her offering of traditional Palestinian cookies is perhaps a manifestation of this confidence and comfort.

Nye paints a romanticized portrait of the airport space. There is no criticism of the other passengers' initial insularity, no commentary on the power dynamics and regulations that contribute to the travelers' inability to see the possibilities of transforming the impersonal space of an airline gate into an opportunity for rich cultural exchange and human connection. The paradox of airports is that though they bring together in close proximity an impressive array of diverse peoples from diverse cultures, they are not designed to encourage these diverse peoples to engage in any kind of meaningful interaction. Rather, as Mika Aaltola (2005) points out, "an airport is a place where one goes to collect a sense of identity. A vital ingredient of the airport experience is that one goes there to see who one is in the worldwide Who's Who" (274). And the more subordinate one's position in the "hierarchical world order-imagination of the airport" (275), the more attentive one must be to fulfilling carefully one's part in the "morality play" of the airport and "demonstrate faithful adherence to procedures, signs, orders, and types" (269).

As Aaltola (2005) observes, "the airport turns into a place of reverence" (269), and the "political pedagogy inherent in airport performance" (270) requires one to execute faithfully the script that reinscribes local, regional, and global hierarchy. Within the context of expected performance, the older Arab woman's gesture of outreach and friendship in distributing the cookies is understandable. She, the outsider, has to be the supplicant and prove that she comes in friendship. Especially as an Arab woman, she is expected to deliver a certain kind of conciliatory performance. And she complies. It is she who wishes to put the other passengers at ease, she who seizes the opportunity to enlarge her embrace and expand her community to include not just the Palestinians she reaches through the phone but also these cultural strangers. Even if one were to defend the other passengers' hesitation to initiate contact with her as stemming from their lack of familiarity with her customs, one cannot deny that their privilege (whether of race, language, social class, or national origin) frees them from the expectations of performance.

By contrast, the elderly Palestinian woman does what none of the other passengers contemplates or even feels moved to do: she offers a part of herself to the others. The narrator's use of the word *sacrament* to characterize the woman's giving of cookies and the other female passengers' acceptance of them is significant. By consuming these cookies, they incorporate this Palestinian woman into their own beings and briefly awaken to their and her humanity. The empathetic effort in this situation has been almost entirely one-sided— from the Arab woman to the other female passengers. Granted, there is no antipathy on the part of the other waiting passengers, but there is also little they do beyond passively accepting her efforts at connection.

The second essay is by Indian American Varun Sriram, a twenty-something former television sports broadcaster who worked in Missoula, Montana, for three years. He explains that his skin color and physical features are such that people perceive him to be a member of several ethnic groups, including Brazilian, Arab, Italian, and Mexican. Sriram writes of his experience at the Ronald Reagan airport in Washington, D.C., in April 2009.[10] As in the Nye piece, the specific airport location is the airline departure gate; Sriram, too, has been informed that his flight to Denver, en route to Missoula, has been delayed by ninety minutes. He takes a seat in the waiting area by the gate and smiles at two women—one black, the other white—whose seats are near his. He notices that the gate is crowded, and he notices as well that there are a number of "unattended" bags, whose owners are not in obvious sight. Feeling hungry and not inclined to board the aircraft on an empty stomach, Sriram is tempted to get a pizza at the stall he sees nearby, and he contemplates whether he should pick up his bag and walk with it to the pizza stall or leave his bag behind and quickly purchase the pizza and return. He is aware of the constant warning announcements: "Please do not leave your bags unattended at any time. Please report any suspicious looking items to security." At this point, Sriram decides on the following course of action: "I take a look around and see two bags on top of a seat a few feet away from me, their rightful owner nowhere in sight. 'No big deal,' I think to myself. Rules are meant to be broken. I put my book back in the bag, place the bag on my seat, and walk no more than 100 yards to get myself a slice of pizza." When he returns to his seat, he finds his bag missing. He looks at the white woman to find out what has happened, and she says, "I called security to take your bag because I didn't think you were coming back." Sriram informs us that the other unattended bags he has noticed earlier are all still where they were when he left. With ten minutes to go for his flight's departure, he is panicked. Then he sees a security guard walking away from the gate carrying his bag. Sriram hurriedly yet respectfully approaches him, apologizes for having left his bag unattended, and describes its contents to the satisfaction of the security guard who, fortunately for Sriram, returns the bag to him.

Thus far, Sriram adheres to a familiar script. The white woman "reads" him with his four-day unshaven brown face as potential terrorist, sees his bag as a potential weapon, and notifies the security guard, singling out his unattended bag from all the others in plain sight at the gate. But at this point, Sriram launches into a surprising act of empathetic identification with the white woman even though, he says, he felt both "anger and embarrassment" for the brief panic he suffered as a result of her thoughtless prejudice:

> Was she watching without me noticing, studying my every move? Did she consult the other people sitting around me before having my bag removed? Were they threatened by me too?
>
> As I thought more and more about it, I began to wonder if I was assigning prejudices to people that didn't actually exist. After all, I did leave my bag unattended, which is an airport no-no. What if there actually *was* something dangerous in my bag. Isn't it better to avert disaster at the risk of offending one person? Yes—there were other unattended bags in the area that did not get picked up, but maybe she didn't notice them when she called security to take mine away. I guess I will never know.

Sriram both acknowledges his "minor" transgression of leaving his bag unattended and makes a genuine effort to imagine the white woman's position. One could read this empathetic identification in one of two ways—as a genuine complexity and maturity of perspective indicative of his humility and thoughtfulness. Or one could read it as an act of psychological survival and a desire to confirm his full membership in the nation-state: perhaps he needs to see her action as rationally determined rather than motivated by irrational prejudice against the color of his skin and his unshaven face so that he can continue to have faith in "his" nation, seeing in her act not the manifestation of its institutional structures of racial profiling but the misguided act of one individual. The security guard's act of returning his bag without undue fuss also facilitates his sense of essential fair play by the nation's agent of power.

Sriram not only tries to diminish the larger implications of the white woman's action; he also diminishes his own injury by placing it alongside the more damaging instances of racial profiling that others have suffered. In this invocation of other acts of racial profiling (against Arabs and Muslims and anyone "looking like them") and other groups (African Americans) who have suffered egregious forms of discrimination, he historicizes and politicizes his experience, moving it beyond the microcosm of personal injury to the macrocosm of systemic injustice.

I discuss this incident in class and invite students to comment on Sriram's empathy for the white woman, comparing it to her seeming lack of empathy for him. Immediately, I am challenged. One student, a white male, interjects, "You can't know that she wasn't empathetic. How can you say with certainty that she wasn't 'cut up' about having to inform the security guard about the unattended bag? Maybe she really debated with herself before she called the guard. Maybe she weighed the option of ignoring the bag and considered the possible outcomes and only then informed the security guard. It could have been something she did only after a fierce internal debate. Maybe she even thought about how prejudiced she might appear." I concede the student's perspective and acknowledge that I have been insufficiently complex in my understanding of the situation and in reading the landscape of empathy. I had not attended to the gaps and silences in the narrative. But at the same time, despite the validity of the student's challenge, I am left with a nagging feeling of having allowed myself and the students to retreat to the terrain of individual injury (the damage to the white woman's sense of herself as a fair and just person, in this case), leaving behind the far more complex "imperial" geopolitical landscape of the post-9/11 international airport that Aaltola describes. The white woman who called the security guard and informed him of the unattended bag was exercising her power over a brown man even as, in the exercise of this power, she was projecting herself as a possible victim (of potential terrorism) and, one could argue, empathizing with all the other potential victims.

In this morality play, the true "hero" is the security guard who returns Sriram's bag without further fuss. As the agent of state power, he could have made things particularly difficult by penalizing Sriram for having broken the rule of never leaving one's bag unattended. Several factors may have contributed to his exercise of prudent judgment and display of basic trust: perhaps he empathized with Sriram's youth and gender, understanding the harmless carelessness and recklessness common to the twenty-plus male; perhaps he felt affirmed in his power by Sriram's contrition; perhaps he had developed expertise in "reading" people and felt confident that Sriram posed no threat; perhaps his conversation with the white woman who reported the bag led him to believe that she was not entirely convinced that the bag represented any danger but felt obliged to report it nonetheless; perhaps there was something about the manner of her drawing attention to Sriram's bag that sat uneasily with the guard, who may have seen her action as motivated by prejudice rather than caution (and this last supposition rests on the assumption that the guard was not himself quick to make hasty assumptions about people based on their race). Whatever the reason, the security guard's act of returning the bag to Sriram is noteworthy for opening up an unexpected zone of flexibility in the otherwise rigid edifice of state power.

That Sriram himself does not speculate on the reasons for the security guard's uneventful return of the bag is also significant. Perhaps it provides evidence of one's tendency to accept the arbitrary workings of the power of the state and its agents. The machinery of state is ubiquitous, its displays of power capricious, and Sriram in his supreme sense of relief may have simply not wanted to attempt a rational analysis of the outcome. Or he may have wanted to preserve the fiction of the benign and just state and not wanted to shatter that presumption.

The security guard is the human face of state power; mapping the various acts of empathy or antipathy onto him enables an engagement with compassion on two levels: "the level of individual psychology and the level of institutional design" (Nussbaum 2001, 403). Nussbaum reminds us that "institutions can either promote or discourage, and can shape in various ways, the emotions that impede appropriate compassion, shame, envy, and disgust" (405).

By comparison, Adam Smith's understanding of justice is inadequate. In his *Theory of Moral Sentiments* (first published in 1759 and modified through six editions, with the final edition appearing in 1790), he treats justice in isolation from power. The absence of power in Smith's disquisition on justice is unfortunate, because Smith understands the centrality of justice to the smooth coexistence of diverse peoples. He posits that justice is a highly complicated social virtue that should have no connection to feelings of positive affect. One ought to contemplate justice for a person or a group even when one has no feelings of "friendship, charity, or generosity" toward that person or group. He observes:

> Society may subsist among different men, as among different merchants, from a sense of its utility, without any mutual love or affection; and though no man in it should owe any obligation, or be bound in gratitude to any other, it may still be upheld by a mercenary exchange of good offices according to an agreed valuation. . . . Beneficence . . . is less essential to the existence of society than justice. Society may subsist, though not in the most comfortable state, without beneficence, but the prevalence of injustice must utterly destroy it. (Smith 1976, 86)

That justice should prevail even in the absence of positive feelings toward another is an issue I take up in my discussion of *Snow Falling on Cedars* in Chapter 3. Smith presumes an equality of relationship in his articulation of the "mercenary exchange of good offices" that regulates the interaction of those who may not necessarily harbor beneficent feelings toward one another. The kind of considered exchange of good offices that Smith describes can occur only when both parties perceive each other to be relative equals, with each standing to lose significantly if anything in the balance goes awry. He has little to say about situations in which one party is in a subordinate relationship to the other (this silence probably stems from his being influenced by the Stoics and, therefore, believing that every man is equipped with the dignity and self-command to assert his full worth).[11] The absence of power in Smith's framework significantly limits its application to perceiving "the difference between the vulnerabilities common to all human beings and those constructed for the powerless by the empowered" (Nussbaum 2001, 431). The question Smith does not pose, but one that I seek to address, is, "In situations of asymmetrical power, what is the interplay between empathy and justice?"

Language as the Site of Inquiry

Though empathy can be evoked by visual images (photographs and cinema) and music/dance, I maintain (along with psychologist Jerome Bruner and neurologist Oliver Sacks) that underlying all these situations is the use of language by which we "explain" our actions and our feelings to ourselves (what Bruner calls "self-making" through "self-telling" [2002, 70]) and Shoshana Felman describes as "gaining semantic authority" (2001, 127) over oneself and others. With regard to empathy, I am principally interested in the intensity of the psychic labor we invest and the intellectual complexity with which we approach "self-making" through "self-telling. Language enables the efficient portability of experience and therefore allows for "remoteness of reference." Language, Bruner reminds us, "equip[s] us to talk of things not present, to do so without reenacting their scale or shape, and to mark the flow of human ongoing action" (2002, 96–97). (However, see the discussion later in this Introduction for Amy Shuman's valid problematizing of this too-easy portability of experience through narrative.) Undeniably, our modes of interacting with one another are increasingly visual these days, and our capacity to absorb multiple stimuli from diverse media increasingly sophisticated; nonetheless, as even an encounter with the graphic novel underscores, images are decoded and absorbed through our familiarity with "narration" and patterns of knowing that are constructed through language (Bruner 2002, 65–70).

The field of *narrative medicine* has developed in response to the realization that doctors can more readily and meaningfully empathize with their patients when they listen to their patients' stories of illness—that is, when they are more than just expert clinicians. Rita Charon's *Narrative Medicine: Honoring the Stories of Illness* is a powerful testament to the compelling value of narrative and the use of language in the service of empathy. Doctors are now encouraged to become storytellers themselves, to practice the art and craft of narrating so that they can better understand what their patients endure emotionally, not just physiologically. Just as physicians are learning to engage their patients beyond the particulars of the clinical chart and beyond the discourse of illness, so also, this book shows, lawyers are venturing out beyond the legalisms that typically structure their interactions with clients to a more "risky" and unstructured relationship that is guided by a desire for genuine connection.

There is by now a highly developed field called *literature and law* that for more than two decades has theorized about the links between these two areas and the function of language in each. Bruner (2002) explains the relationship between law and literature as the "dialectic of the established and the possible" (13), with law using language to fix and keep within "recognized bounds" the immense complexities of human experience, and literature using language to defy predictability and go beyond the familiar "into the realm of the possible, the might-be, could have been, perhaps will be" (13). Trauma and Holocaust studies theorist Shoshana Felman (2002) observes that "Literature is . . . a language of infinitude that, in contrast to the language of the law, encapsulates not closure but precisely what in a given legal case refuses to be closed and cannot be closed. It is to this refusal of the trauma to be closed that literature does justice" (8). Felman defines *trauma* as a "wound" and "a shock that creates a psychological split or rupture, an emotional injury that leaves lasting damage on the psyche" (171). Though empathy is more likely to emerge in the realm of the literary than that of law, my book complicates the simple dichotomy between the rich textures of literature's imaginative language and the carefully crafted prose of legal formulations. Legal language is constraining, yet it can provide the means to enter a wider imaginative space; lawyers, too, have used the "safety net" of law to take risks with their imaginations and enter into the complexity of their clients' experiences and emotions.

Yet there is no guarantee of empathy's emergence, no matter how compelling a narrative of trauma. Consider the case of the five Uighur (ethnic Chinese Muslims) detainees who have been at Guantánamo Bay since early 2002. The five are the last remaining of an original group of twenty-two Uighurs who were apprehended in Afghanistan in 2002, in the "early" days of the U.S. response to the attacks of September 11, 2001. The government and military officials today agree that the Guantánamo Bay Uighurs are not terrorists; they pose no danger and have no connection to al-Qaeda. They simply were in the wrong place at the wrong time. Most of the released Uighurs have been unable to return to China, because they will be persecuted there. But despite their innocence, no community in the United States is ready to accept them within its midst, which leaves the remaining five in a state of limbo.[12] The state of Virginia, where a Uighur community already exists and so would be the logical place to send the Uighur detainees once they are released, is unwilling to have them. Most other nations have been equally reluctant; their precondition is that the United States first accept a few, and only then would they be willing to consider providing a home for the others. However, four countries have volunteered to provide homes for some of the Uighurs, largely as a result of behind-the-scenes deals with the United States. Of the twenty-two Uighurs who were brought to Guantánamo Bay, five were relocated to Albania in 2006, and twelve to Bermuda, Switzerland, and Palau in 2009. The United States, however, has been steadfast in its refusal to admit any Uighurs within its borders. The *Washington Post* editorial of March 3, 2010, comments appropriately, "Congress should rethink its wrongheaded determination that no detainees be allowed on U.S. soil. The Uighurs are not ultimately at fault in this sad situation, and it is the height of hypocrisy to ask of allies what Congress is unwilling to do."[13] Had it not been for Albania, Bermuda, Palau, and Switzerland, the 17 released Uighurs would in all likelihood still be at Guantánamo Bay, like the remaining 171 detainees, facing a frightening and uncertain future, barren and bleak, a "living death."

Internment and Detention: Manifestations of Twin Antipathies

Numerous legal scholars have considered the relationship between the Japanese American internment and the administration's detention policies since the launching of the U.S. "global war on terror."[14] "Military necessity" and "national security" (respectively, the reasons offered by the Franklin Delano Roosevelt administration for its treatment of Japanese Americans during World War II and by the George W. Bush administration for its launching of the "global war on terror" and its detention of Muslim men) are similar alarmist signals of danger to the nation-state. They both have generated attitudes and conditions in which particular populations become targets of antipathy and hatred. The World War II racialization of Japanese Americans as the enemy (the racist cartoons by Dr. Seuss, for instance, that appeared in newspapers and *Life* magazine's "tutorial" on how to tell the difference between the Chinese and the Japanese)[15] and the racialization and religious profiling of Arabs and Muslims today reveal the obvious parallels between the 1940s and the post-2001 period (Moustafa Bayoumi [2008] and Leti Volpp [2002], among others, write of the racialization of Arabs and Muslims). It has become easy to excise Arabs and Muslims from the realm of common humanity and to confine them to an ambiguous space, in much the same way that it was easy to target the Japanese Americans and denationalize them. The commonality lies in both groups'—the internees and the detainees—being stripped of their human complexity and becoming reduced to the reductive categories of "enemy" and "terrorist."

There are, of course, differences in how the public learned of conditions in the Japanese American internment camps and how we today become informed of conditions at Guantánamo Bay, in detention centers on the mainland, and in "American" prisons of the "global war on terror" in locations outside the United States. Despite the strict restrictions on what newspaper reporters can gain access to and what they are allowed to reveal about the Guantánamo

Bay facility, in particular, "informal media" such as blogs and YouTube images provide us greater and faster access to information about conditions in these restricted and hidden places than was the case during the 1940s, when there was both less available information about the internment camps for the public to consume and slower circulation of that information. Yet the immediacy of the dissemination of images today versus the slower circulation sixty years ago does not necessarily invalidate reading these two moments side by side in order to understand the forces that affect empathy. The elusiveness of empathy is common to both historical moments.

The abundance of visual images of inhumane incarceration and torture in circulation (via the Internet) today does not necessarily heighten empathy for those affected by these practices. Susan Sontag (2006) has argued that photographic images of pain and bodily violation can "arouse a prurient interest" and can "also allure" (95). We may seek out such "atrocious" images not to stimulate and fortify our empathy but to "steel oneself against weakness. To make oneself more numb. To acknowledge the existence of the incorrigible" (98). Further, the ready availability of these images of violation of the body and the resulting increase in public viewing and discussion of them can heighten controversy and therefore *decrease* empathy. A recent study (published in April 2010) conducted by law students at Harvard examined the readiness with which four major newspapers (the *New York Times*, the *Wall Street Journal*, the *Los Angeles Times*, and *USA Today*) in the United States used the word *torture* to describe the practice of waterboarding.[16] What they found was that for seventy years before 2004, waterboarding was "almost uniformly" described as "torture." However, after 2004, when the practice became politically charged, the same news outlets refrained from calling the practice "torture," seemingly so as "not to prejudge" a controversial topic (according to the response of the *New York Times* to the study). This attitude of "journalistic objectivity" exists at a time of readily available videotapes on YouTube showing graphic simulations of waterboarding (lending further confirmation to my earlier argument that though visual images may be powerful in their ability to evoke emotion, we ultimately process our emotional response through language). The Harvard study shows that the practice of waterboarding has become wrapped up in politically volatile semantics; as a result of the controversy surrounding waterboarding—"Is it or is it not torture?"—the major print media are hesitant to describe it outright as "torture." Stripping language of its ability to communicate the pain and injury inflicted by the practice of waterboarding restricts those who receive this pruned language from fully apprehending the trauma of those who are subjected to the practice.

Though empathy for the Japanese Americans was in short supply during the internment years and empathy for the detainees is relatively scarce today, it is imperative that we not forget the few significant voices of protest against and challenges to the official narratives and policies of suspicion and antipathy. Though the impact of empathy may be slow to materialize, every instance of empathy's occurrence is a crucial reminder to those who are the targets of hostility that they have not been abandoned, that there are still individuals and organizations in the larger population who recognize their humanity and labor to preserve it. In the 1940s, the nation did not by any means universally and unquestioningly accept the internment of Japanese Americans. At the time of the internment many sectors of the American public—churches, charitable organizations, and at least one chapter of the American Civil Liberties Union (ACLU)—strongly condemned what was happening (see Chapters 2 and 3). Today, the Center for Constitutional Rights and several hundred pro bono lawyers are serving as the conscience of the nation (see Chapter 4).

Empathy is the state of mind that results from the (Hans-Georg) Gadamerian sense of conversation, in which "To be in a conversation . . . means to go beyond oneself, to think with the other, and to come back to oneself as if to another" (Gadamer 1989, 110). Meaningful empathy cannot rest on momentary contact and cannot simply involve two similar persons/groups. Similarly, Amy Shuman (2006) critiques a too-glib quest for empathy in storytelling. She reminds us that "people who suffer an experience are presumed to understand it best. When stories travel far from their owners, the distant tellers and listeners can still presume to understand; empathy provides one means for understanding across disparate differences. But empathy is a weak claim to entitlement; in fact, empathy is almost always open to critique as serving the interests of the empathizer rather than the empathized" (153).

The Limits of Empathy as Individual Gesture

George Irani (1999) implies in his discussion of conflict resolution techniques in the Middle East that responding to another's grief or loss in many cultures of the Middle East is channeled within prescribed rituals and established ceremonies. To imagine empathy as an act of individual goodwill is to ignore the powerful hold of "ethnicity; the relevance of identity; the nature of tribal and clan solidarity; the key role of patron-client relationships; and the salience of norms concerning honor and shame" (1). Speaking specifically of Lebanon, a society of multiple religious groups and ethnic affiliations, Irani elaborates:

> Rather than a cohesive group of individuals bound together by an agreed-upon set of rights and obligations, (i.e., citizens), the Lebanese instead comprise an agglomeration of competing communities, each of which requires absolute allegiance and obedience from its members. Every one of these communities feels that the others have victimized it, so the process of acknowledgment, forgiveness, and reconciliation has to begin at the community level, rather than at the individual level. (5)[17]

Even in societies like the United States that valorize the individual and enshrine in theory the essential equivalence of every member of the nation-state, feminist and multicultural scholars have shown that empathy is not readily forthcoming across the barriers of gender and race (see Lynne Henderson later in this Introduction).[18] Thus, to speak of empathy as though there were a common set of universal priorities governing people's actions may be profoundly naïve at best, unforgivably ignorant at worst. Within and between societies, negotiations and accommodations must necessarily take place if there is to be a viable, even if not vibrant, coexistence among individuals and groups with differing ideals and aspirations. Empathy, therefore, does not require that we ignore the unbridgeable differences among those who hold disparate visions of humanity. At a minimum, empathy is the *willingness* to concede that some other person's or group's priorities require attention.

Consider this vignette from Amitav Ghosh's memoir *In an Antique Land* (1992). Ghosh, an Indian of Hindu background, is spending a few months in an Egyptian village during the 1980s. He has been welcomed warmly by the inhabitants and accepted with affection into their homes. Yet they are puzzled by his reluctance to adopt Islam, and they continually badger him about converting. Ghosh is firm in his resistance, but he does not wish to insult his hosts, of whom Ustaz Mustafa is one. The manner in which he and Ustaz Mustafa come to an understanding reveals that it is indeed possible to be empathetic despite the persistence of fundamental schisms between people's ideals. Though Ustaz Mustafa is deeply disappointed that Ghosh will not convert, once he realizes that by converting to Islam Ghosh would be going against his father's wishes, he relents: "Well it would not be right for you to upset your father. That is true" (52), Ustaz Mustafa concedes. Ghosh writes, "After that the heart went out of his [Ustaz Mustafa's] efforts to convert me: he had a son himself and it went against his deepest instincts to urge a man to turn against his father. And so, as the rival moralities of religion and kinship gradually played themselves to a standstill within him, Ustaz Mustafa and I came to an understanding" (51–52).

The accommodation that Ghosh and Ustaz Mustafa arrive at is the potential that William Spanos (2005) envisions and defends in his call for a restoration of notions such as "humanism," "care," and "sensitivity" (259). In turning to concepts that seem outmoded and perhaps even ludicrous in a post-9/11 world, Spanos draws on the inspiration provided by Edward Said's famous observation that exile is the preeminent condition of a responsible and ethical way of being in the world. For it is only when you cannot arrogantly declare that you are completely "at home" that you realize what it is like to be vulnerable. This is the "inside-outside (exilic) condition of always *being-in-the-midst* of time and history . . . that instigates *care* and the *interrogative mood*" (Spanos 2005, 246). I would assert that empathy is intimately related to the interrogative mood, to the ability to acknowledge alternate interpretations of a given situation and to entertain the possibility of frames of understanding that are different from one's own. Thus, the precondition of empathy is the recognition of a heterogeneous world. It is not, as the skeptics assert, commitment to a uniform sense of humanity.

Paradoxes, Ironies, and Aporias of Empathy

At the level of personal action as well as at the institutional level of creating law or constructing policy, attention to the paradoxes, ironies, and aporias of empathy is imperative. Without such awareness, there is little hope for meaningful and long-term justice. One of the paradoxes of empathy is that it can sometimes more easily emerge for peoples physically distant from us or "removed" in some other way, rather than for those with whom we share physical and social space. This tense relationship between proximity-antipathy and distance-empathy underscores the difficulty of cultivating and maintaining genuine concern for the well-being of those unlike us with whom we must coexist in close quarters. In the discussion of empathy that follows, I use the terms *proximate* and *distant* in both a concrete spatial and an abstract intellectual/emotional sense.

One is reminded of James Weldon Johnson's (1995) observation in 1912 that "Northern white people love the Negro in a sort of abstract way, as a race; through a sense of justice, charity, and philanthropy, they will liberally assist in his elevation. . . . Yet generally speaking they have no particular liking for individuals of the race" (80), and of Elaine Scarry's (1996) trenchant assessment of literature's effect on us: "the very imaginative labor of picturing others that we ought to expend on real persons on our city streets, or on the other side of the border, instead comes to be lavished on King Lear or Tess" (104). Johnson's perceptive observation cautions us to the allure of theoretical empathy; Scarry reminds us of literature's limited usefulness in evoking empathy for "real persons."

There are additional caveats to consider in regard to empathy. The first is to be cognizant of the ephemerality of empathy stemming from a brief encounter. Luc Boltanski (1999) reminds us of the relative ease of the onetime empathetic response and aid to a stranger. In such a situation, there is no expectation of an extended relationship, no call to readjust the rhythms or the routine of one's life or to alter the familiar dynamics of one's social networks to accommodate this stranger's distress (10). If anything, the service one renders enhances one's sense of self as a charitable human being. The second caveat is to recognize that empathy for a similar (along the lines of race, gender, nationality, religion, ethnicity, sexual orientation, or class) person or group requires relatively little intellectual or emotional effort. Žižek (2004) declares that a politics that privileges "the neighbor" who is the mirror image of oneself is limited and not sufficiently committed to justice. It is the neighbor who remains "an inert, impenetrable, enigmatic presence" (502) who challenges us to enter the territory of the divine and engage with the Other.

The principal difference between the kinds of empathy discussed in this introductory essay and the situation of the Good Samaritan—which is the classic situation most frequently referenced in any study of empathy—is that the empathies I seek to examine are framed and complicated by extended contact between the parties concerned. This contact has placed the would-be empathizer and the intended recipient in a web of relationships enmeshed in power, privilege, and hierarchical difference. The situations that I focus on are those in which empathy, when it emerges, is steeped in a history of relationships between the empathizer and those with whom one seeks to or believes one ought to empathize. This historical connection profoundly affects the nature of the empathic contact. Thus, generosity or empathy to a stranger, while certainly a sentiment worthy of praise, is not the same as empathy for the person or group with whom one is in an asymmetrical relationship of power with the advantage decidedly in the empathizer's favor.

The Soldier in Iraq "Confers" Empathy

I turn now to Brian Turner's (2005) poem "In the Leupold Scope" to tease out the entangled issues of empathy, power, distance, and nearness embedded within this literary artifact. In "In the Leupold Scope," the speaker is an American soldier in Iraq looking through the scope of his or her (there is no specific gendering of the speaker) rifle at a rooftop two thousand meters away. The soldier sees on the distant rooftop a woman hanging garments to dry, and the poem records the richness of the soldier's imagination as he or she describes the woman dressed "in sparkling green" and her laundry comprising "dresses in tangerine and teal, / woven cotton shirts dyed blue" (7). To the soldier, physically distant from the woman, the laundry line is "invisible," and this optical fact allows the soldier to imagine her movements with tender significance: "She is dressing the dead, clothing them / . . . She waits for them to lean forward / into the breeze, for the wind's breath / to return the bodies they once had" (7). This poem lends itself handily to engaging the relationship between distance and connection. The soldier who peers through the rifle's scope and sees the woman brought up close is removed from her both culturally and physically. The role in which the soldier occupies the woman's space and sees her is that of the aggressor. It is through the scope of the rifle that the soldier is accorded a vision of her. It is in this asymmetrical relationship of power that the soldier glorifies the woman's domestic action of hanging laundry, investing it with the sacredness of reanimating dead companions and family members. The lyricism with which the soldier imagines the woman's generous and resurrective gesture of "welcoming them back," the swell of the soldier's empathetic attachment in conferring on her task the quality of ritual and ceremony, all take place through the scope of the rifle, a lens that at once signals the soldier's physical remove from the woman and at the same time enables the connection. The clothes she hangs are more than just clothes; they are transformed into garments for the dead, as she invites the ghosts to inhabit the tangible materiality of the clothes and become reborn. The paradox of the vision the soldier has of these newly reanimated beings—"women with breasts swollen by milk, / men with shepherd-thin bodies, children" (7)—is that now the target that the rifle is trained on is suddenly multiplied in number. These reborn ghosts, with their newfound tangibility, are all "running hard into the horizon's curving lens" (7); they live again in the soldier's Leupold scope, in the eye of the rifle directed at them.

The soldier holds power—ultimate power—over the woman in the sight of the scope. The soldier could shatter the woman's momentary serenity and invade her ephemeral respite from the turbulence of war. This position of power enables the soldier to suspend temporarily, and on his or her terms, the advantage he or she has over the woman and imagine her reality as she might see it. Perhaps the soldier seeks an empathetic connection with the woman, and in this sense the poem functions as evidence of that desire. But through its title, "In the Leupold Scope," the poem reminds us that the impulse to empathy is ultimately intertwined with power, made possible by the scope of one's rifle aimed at the target of one's empathy. The woman is distant, and so the soldier's empathy is an outcome of her safe remove from him or her. The soldier's faux proximity, effected through the instrument of the scope, encloses the complicated relationship between distance/proximity and empathy/antipathy.

The African American Woman Inhibits Empathy

Alice Walker's short story "Advancing Luna and Ida B. Wells" (1981) delineates further the complex and unpredictable terrain of empathy. Walker's story serves as a compelling warning against a too-hasty celebration of empathy without an adequate understanding of the many variables that cohere around its emergence and manifestation. She provides a valuable complication on the issue of power and its manifestation in the field of empathy and situates the variables of distance and proximity within the intersection of race and gender.

Briefly, the two protagonists in Walker's short story are the black female narrator and her white friend, Luna, who is the daughter of an affluent Cleveland suburban family. As young women, both meet in the summer of 1965 when they are civil rights workers in the American South; after that tumultuous period, their lives diverge as they pursue different interests. The story picks up in New York a year later, where they share an apartment, having discovered each other's presence in the city. (The Ida B. Wells of the title refers to the famous black journalist of the late nineteenth and early twentieth centuries whose fierce crusade against lynching demonstrated the injustice of the unfounded accusations of rape against black men.) The climax in Walker's narrative occurs when Luna informs the black narrator that she had been raped in the summer of 1965 by Freddie Pye, a black civil rights worker, when they had all been in the South trying to change the world. Luna makes the disclosure not to initiate any action on the part of the narrator but merely to share with her a significant personal moment in a historically critical period. At the time she was raped, Luna had made a conscious decision not to divulge the violation, knowing the consequences to Freddie Pye and to the struggle for civil rights of her disclosure. Luna's restraint and silence signal empathy; she subordinates her own interests to the welfare of Freddie Pye and the cause for which they were fighting.

The black narrator's reaction to Luna's delayed disclosure is noteworthy for the tangle of emotions it brings to the surface and for its illumination of the extremely complicated politics of empathy. The narrator fumes:

> I was embarrassed. Then angry. Very, very angry. *How dare she tell me this!* I thought.
>
> Who knows what the black woman thinks of rape? Who has asked her? Who *cares*? Who has properly acknowledged that *she* and not the white woman in this story is the most likely victim of rape? Whenever inter-racial rape is mentioned, a black woman's first thought is to protect the lives of her brothers, her father, her sons, her lover. A history of lynching has bred this reflex in her. (A. Walker 1981, 93)

The narrator is not unaware of the historical implications of Luna's silence. Luna is being true to the legacy of Ida B. Wells, the narrator's hero and role model, in knowing that her declaration of being a rape victim cannot be isolated from the hundreds of false accusations of rape that led to the lynching of black men. At the same time, the black narrator is acutely conscious that Luna's decision to withhold information and then to release it to her at this particular moment signals the power of the white woman over both the black man's fate and the black woman's image of the black man: "whether Luna had been raped or not—it had always been so; that her power over my life was exactly the power *her word on rape* had over the lives of black men, over all black men, whether they were guilty or not, and therefore over my whole people" (A. Walker 1981, 95).

"Is the narrator's anger justified or unreasonable?" is the question that one is compelled to ask, or that Walker appears to pose for us. Should one applaud Luna's decision to subordinate the violation of her own body to the imperatives of history, or should one be outraged that she would choose to disdain the importance of her rights as a woman and by so doing minimize the struggle against patriarchy and sexism?[19] One also wonders whether the narrator's representation of Luna's motives (or purported motives) in disclosing the rape to her is entirely accurate. It is clear that the narrator is somewhat contemptuous of Luna—in particular, for the emptiness of her economically privileged family that is lacking in purpose, her search for meaning and substance that leads her to join the civil rights struggle, and, finally, the weakness and lack of character (in the narrator's view) that would have made her vulnerable to Freddie Pye. Thus, one must be somewhat skeptical of the narrator's attributing to Luna less than savory motives for divulging the rape. Further, one must ask whether the narrator's anger at Luna is not unrelated to two other factors: (1) that she has to acknowledge the fact that a black man *did* indeed rape or *could indeed* have raped a white woman, and that though this violation does not in any way negate the legitimacy of Ida B. Wells's fierce crusade, it nevertheless complicates for the narrator the monolithic narrative of the victimized black man, and (2) that she finds herself and other black workers in the civil rights struggle with the necessity of having to acknowledge, albeit retrospectively, their indebtedness to a white woman whom she, the narrator, has come to see as an unprepossessing specimen of womanhood.

In the narrator's reaction to Luna's disclosure, racial solidarity trumps gender solidarity, or, put another way, the narrator cannot empathize with Luna as a woman. Her empathy is for the *black* woman who always has to live in fear of the white woman's power over the black man's fate. The fact that Luna can always exercise control over, or choose, when she will or will not disclose her rape confirms for the narrator that fundamentally nothing has changed with regard to power. Thus, Luna's empathy in silencing herself at the time of the rape has been rendered meaningless to this narrator, who sees in Luna's selective and delayed disclosure full evidence of white power and privilege—despite the fact that the revelation is made only to the narrator. The narrator sees the disclosure as Luna's power over her and through her over Freddie Pye, specifically, and over black men generally.

Whether or not one finds the narrator's protestations against and hostility toward Luna despicable and unreasonable, the great value of Walker's story is that it reminds us of the enormous nuances of power as these are manifested within the complex landscape of history. Luna may have relinquished control over her body by refusing to scream rape in the 1960s, but in the eyes of the narrator she could not ever entirely relinquish her power over the black man or black woman. Luna's word, whenever she *chooses* to utter it, would effectively condemn/damn the perpetrator and not just the perpetrator alone but an entire group of people. Luna's silence regarding her violation is a classic empathetic act, but if one subscribes to the black narrator's perspective, then Luna's empathy at the time of the rape does not diminish or erase her power beyond the moment of the rape.

One could see in the rage of Walker's black female narrator yet another dimension of Luna's power, over and beyond that of the word *rape* that is Luna's to utter at any time of her choosing. This other power to which Walker's narrator gestures is the utility of Freddie Pye in Luna's self-construction as empathetic, ethical, and admirably self-abnegating. Freddie Pye serves Luna, this narrator would argue, to negotiate a moral dilemma—"*whether, in a black community surrounded by whites with a history of lynching blacks, she had a right to scream as Freddie Pye was raping her*" (A. Walker 1981, 101)—and conclude that it was ethical to remain silent at the time. We get little sense of how the rape has affected Luna, other than to see it as her moment of moral crisis grounded in the exigencies of history. That her emotions are treated so cursorily may be Walker's way of turning attention away from the white woman's body, where it is usually focused in cases of interracial rape, toward the black woman's heart and mind. The narrator's anger does not grant to Luna the comfort of her own nobility, does not confer on her a deserved gratitude for her strategic silence. The narrator aborts, as it were, the process by which Freddie Pye's act of violence becomes the measure of Luna's morally and historically enlightened civic consciousness. Luna's empathy comes ultimately, the narrator would contend, from knowing at a basic level the power she holds over Freddie Pye's life. The narrator's lack of empathy for Luna lies in her perception (justified or not) that Luna will always have power over her history and her people.[20]

"Taxonomy" of Antipathy and Empathy

Walker's narrator's refusal to empathize with Luna is an external manifestation of the entrenched wounds that persist within the American racial landscape. Obama's March 2008 speech about race gestured at some of these injuries, sentiments felt on both sides of the black-white divide, in particular, but his discussion of race touched only the surface of this very charged subject. The deep excavation that might yield meaningful discussions could come only from a form of national truth telling akin to the South African Truth and Reconciliation Commission (TRC). Though the South African TRC received vehement and valid criticisms (which I discuss in Chapter 3), its value lay in its forcing a nation to confront its flawed and complicated past. The United States has not engaged in a comparable form of national truth telling, despite the creation of the U.S. Commission on Civil Rights in the 1960s. Sanford Levinson's (2000) useful assessment of the gains and limitations of the U.S. Civil Rights Commission helps us understand that there is still much unfinished introspection to be done with regard to the country's history of slavery, segregation, and systemic disenfranchisement of African Americans.

In *Country of My Skull*, Afrikaner poet and radio broadcaster Antjie Krog writes of her confrontation with the atrocities of the apartheid government through the TRC hearings. Krog expresses her growing horror as she realizes that she and every other white South African, including her brothers, other family members, and friends, are implicated in this dark history, even if they have not themselves personally committed the crimes. Krog's painful absorption of these hearings into the bone and muscle of her body (she does not flinch from the assault to her ears and psyche) is an act of ingesting and claiming as her own deeds the abductions, killings, and tortures of the actual perpetrators. Kay Schaffer and Sidonie Smith (2006) note that what makes Krog's narrative compelling is that she comes as a supplicant beneficiary, asking for forgiveness. She does not shy away from her part in the country's history and claims no special status separate from the perpetrators: "Krog, presenting herself as a white Afrikaner beneficiary of apartheid, imagines the landscape of her narrative, the country of her skull, as an in-between, transitional space in which her place is uncertain. She can no longer claim South Africa as her beloved ancestral homeland, the landscape of her past, and she has not yet been invited into the postapartheid South Africa that is becoming" (1579).

There has been some talk of a truth commission (see, for example, the *Washington Post* editorial of February 21, 2009) to unearth the abuses of the Bush administration in its "global war on terror"—in particular, the establishment of the Guantánamo Bay detention facility and other prison sites outside the United States, the process by which detainees were rounded up, and the use of torture—but these initial speculations have not borne results. Empathy for the detainees is sparse, as is evidenced in the entrenched assumption that all the men still at Guantánamo Bay are dangerous terrorists bent on destroying the United States. That the Senate is unwilling to give the president the necessary funds to close the facility (and disperse the detainees to maximum-security prisons in the United States or return them to their native countries or to other allied nations) reveals both fear and hatred of the detainees on the part of the American public.

Marc Falkoff's well-intentioned collection, *Poems from Guantánamo: The Detainees Speak* (2007), in which he gathers twenty-two poems (through great difficulty as a result of the Pentagon's strict rules about what information is permissible to be cleared for public consumption), appears to have had little effect in influencing public opinion or creating empathy for the detainees. The same could be said for the play *Guantánamo: Honor Bound to Defend Freedom* (2003), constructed by Victoria Brittain and Gillian Slovo from official speeches, legal rulings, and personal letters: these creative interventions, though powerful as artistic performances of voice, have had little tangible or material benefit. As of June 2011, there are still 171 prisoners who remain in Guantánamo Bay. The 600 or so who were sent back to their home countries, or to other nations who would accept them or were coerced into taking them, were able to leave Guantánamo Bay largely through the intervention of lawyers and politicians.[21] There is weak public support for a ground-up examination of the culture of fear and antipathy that appears to pervade the nation.

Writing about human rights violations that frequently accompany counterterrorism policies, Jonathan Marks (2006) argues, "We know now that our behavior, both individual and collective, in a heightened emotional state can appear incomprehensible to us once we have cooled off. Acknowledging this 'empathy gap' within ourselves is the first step towards addressing it" (563). What recourse, then, does the concerned individual have? What would be an equivalent response to Guantánamo Bay by a U.S. resident that would parallel Antjie Krog's opening of consciousness to the violations of apartheid and her interrogation of the past verities by which she lived? Chapters of the national ACLU organized readings in various states (Massachusetts, New York, Connecticut, Illinois, Florida, and Oregon, to name a few) of the Brittain and Slovo play, akin to holding town meetings, to generate discussion of important issues of national character. These readings were held in 2006 and 2007. The attendance was mixed, and the impact of these performances was, at best, minimal. There has been no groundswell of clamor for a national engagement with the fundamental and urgent questions that the play raises. Should there be neighborhood discussions of torture? Preventive detention? Indefinite detention? These matters are being considered by President Obama. If the nation were to have grassroots-level discussions of these issues, who would organize them? Representatives of town government? The neighborhood social activist?

The South African TRC hearings were mandated from the top down, through a structure put in place by an act of Parliament following an official declaration by newly elected president Nelson Mandela. But despite their imposed structure, they enabled a national voicing of experiences—of both victims and perpetrators—on a scale that made it impossible for anyone, particularly white South Africans, to say that they did not know what had transpired under the apartheid government. Alex Boraine (2000), one of the TRC commissioners, comments on the pervasiveness of the TRC hearings in the lives of all South Africans, bringing into being a collective national memory of a disgraceful period of history:

> A remarkable feature of the commission was the media coverage of its progress. There was hardly a day since the beginning of 1996 to late 1998 when newspapers did not feature the TRC either on their front pages or in editorials and feature articles. As far as television was concerned, hardly a day went by without the life and work of the TRC being featured on its major news bulletins, over and above a highly professional and effective one-hour weekly program on a major television station. But radio probably had a greater impact. Not only were hearings broadcast live throughout South Africa for four hours per day, but broadcasts, commentaries, discussions, and debates featured prominently in all the eleven languages used in South Africa so that even those unable to read or write participated in the developing story emerging from the work of the TRC. (155)

Would it be possible to imagine the United States engaging in a similar national conversation generated from the grassroots level about the consequences of the nation's "global war on terror"? A national discussion on detention policies and torture must, in order to be truly meaningful, originate in the ethical act of deep recognition of the link between self and Other that Judith Butler (2001) describes:

> Recognition becomes the process by which I become other than what I was and, therefore, also the process by which I cease to be able to return to what I was. . . . I am compelled and comported *outside myself*; I find that the only way to know myself is precisely through a mediation that takes place outside of me, exterior to me, in a convention or a norm that I did not make, in which I cannot discern myself as an author or an agent of its making. (23)

Butler insists on the internal transformation that must accompany any genuine desire to engage with the Other. Stereotypes and reductive descriptors inhibit one's capacity both to give a full "account of oneself" and to recognize the Other as he or she gives a full account of himself or herself. Any national conversation must begin with the precondition that Butler articulates.

Tristan Anne Borer (2003) provides us with a taxonomy of perpetrators and victims with respect to the South African situation, a categorization that helps in understanding the extent of various people's involvement in and victimization from the system of apartheid. There are the direct perpetrators and the indirect perpetrators; the direct victims and the indirect victims; the perpetrators by default (or, as Mahmood Mamdani calls them, "beneficiaries"—see Chapter 3) who did not oppose the system of apartheid because they gained from its assumptions; those who were guilty of bystander complicity; and individual perpetrators and institutional perpetrators. Likewise, she distinguishes between individual victims and communities that were victimized through the recruitment by the apartheid government of collaborators. Borer's taxonomy is not just a matter of assigning labels. She stresses that only through a nuanced understanding of people's diverse and differentiated reactions to their racial privilege and subordination can a society begin to assess appropriate accountability, recover from the haunted past, and move forward to build a more transparent and just future. She observes:

> In the midst of conflict, it is easier and more satisfying for people to think in terms of absolutes. . . . And so, under apartheid, people were either victims or they were perpetrators, and the reality of a much more complex relationship between the two was buried. One's life might depend on having a clear distinction between enemy and ally. However, in post-apartheid South Africa, the search for and process of reconciliation may well be better served by moving beyond the black and white of victims and perpetrators to a more nuanced understanding of a landscape painted in shades of gray. (1116)

The value of Borer's classification is that it takes us beyond static description to consider the various avenues through which individuals and groups, victims and perpetrators in all shades of gray, can engage in a whole range of responses: for example, apologize for wrongdoing to families who have suffered as a result of one's actions, rediscover self-dignity by testifying in public about the specific wrongs one has suffered from the machinery of the apartheid state, provide monetary compensation, or take an active role in redressing the asymmetry of opportunity that was part of apartheid. Every member of society then feels a responsibility to engage actively, in the most appropriate fashion, in the project of building the democratic multiracial state.

Within the context of the United States, such a taxonomic exercise could be useful in identifying precisely how one's action or inaction led to the conditions in which Guantánamo Bay was established and hundreds of Muslim men were detained, tortured, and deported, or face the prospect of remaining in captivity indefinitely. The level of involvement of John Yoo, one of the attorneys in the Bush administration's Office of Legal Counsel (OLC) who authored the legal justification for Guantánamo Bay and the "torture memos," is different from that of a senator in the U.S. Congress who did not sufficiently interrogate the argument for Guantánamo Bay, and this level of engagement (or disengagement) is different still from the print and broadcast media who presented the OLC justification as evidence of the careful application of the law in a "state of exception" (the "war on terror").

Paralleling the different levels of culpability, one could envision the various types of possible responses to the violations of the "war on terror." The response of the individual who reads or hears of the hundreds of men held in Guantánamo Bay could range from articulated outrage (in the form of a letter to one's elected representative), to mobilizing a group of friends and allies and hosting a public discussion or some other form of dialogue, to organizing or participating in a march on Washington or implementing some visible form of protest. Interventions could be local, state-level, or national. They could be individual or collective; they could be artistic or pedagogical, material or symbolic. To be engaged in some way to keep the situation of the detainees in the forefront of the national consciousness is an act of necessary empathy. The range of possible and useful responses grows out of a spectrum of types of empathy.

I place the empathetic reactions that I discuss in this book into three broad categories: compassionate, strategic, and ethical—and these arise under different circumstances and produce different results. *Compassionate empathy* is what we ought to experience when we see an obvious injustice suffered by someone; it is a condition in which we recognize the shared humanity between ourselves and the sufferer/victim, when the differences of background cease to matter and when we are moved to acknowledge that, yes, we, too, participate in the grief and loss. This is the kind of empathy that practically all nations felt for the United States immediately after the attacks of September 11, when even the officials and general populace of Iran, a nation not usually sympathetically inclined toward the United States, declared that the wound to the United States was a wound to all peoples and nations. This is the kind of empathy that followed the 2004 ravages of the tsunami in the countries of Indonesia, Sri Lanka, and India. From everywhere in the world, it was clear that people understood what it was to lose one's home and one's family to a natural disaster of enormous magnitude.

Though compassionate empathy can frequently cross boundaries of race, gender, ethnicity, religion, and class, its most ready emergence takes place *within* these groups. One is more likely to be readily compassionate to an individual of similar socioeconomic, racial, religious, and ethnic background than to those who are differently placed. Both the empathizer and the recipient of empathy can benefit from compassionate empathy—the former, from the self-satisfaction that comes from knowing that one has performed a worthy act (assuming that the feeling is followed by some concrete action that goes beyond a verbal acknowledgment of the other's difficulty); the latter, from the mitigation of pain and suffering that results from the empathetic act. However, compassionate empathy may also be accompanied by the complicating forces of guilt, shame, and anger (guilt on the part of the empathizer, and shame or anger on the part of the recipient, who may resent having to accept the much-needed empathy); I discussed some of these forces earlier in the analysis of Alice Walker's story "Advancing Luna and Ida B. Wells."

Martin Hoffman (2000) explains five empathy-arousing modes, the most relevant of which is role-taking. Through role-taking, the empathizer constructs an imaginative "reality" in which he or she locates himself or herself in the same circumstances as the group or individual in need of empathy. Hoffman distinguishes between self-focused role-taking and other-focused role-taking, noting that the former, though arousing more intense empathic responses than the latter, can also paradoxically contribute to the "egoistical drift" that leads one to forget about the particular situation of the person needing empathy and become preoccupied instead with oneself and one's own feelings were one to be similarly placed.

> Self-focused role-taking may have its limitations . . . [A]n observer feels empathic/sympathetic distress . . . , but when he starts ruminating about a similar perhaps more traumatic experience in his own past . . . , he begins to feel a more personal distress; the empathic pain remains, but the image of the victim recedes into the background. . . . Ruminating about his painful past, he becomes lost in egoistic concerns and the image of the victim that initiated the role-taking process slips out of focus and fades away, aborting or temporarily aborting the empathic process. (56)

During the congressional discussions in the summer of 2006 leading up to the now discredited Military Commissions Act (MCA), egotistical drift may have influenced the insistence by Senators John McCain (R-AZ), Lindsey Graham (R-SC), and John Warner (R-VA) that the United States honor Article 3 of the Geneva Convention (specifically banning cruel and inhumane treatment). Their stand was likely not based on empathy for prisoners who would be apprehended in the U.S. "war on terror." Rather, their rhetoric reflects that their concern for the humane treatment of prisoners was ultimately about the humane treatment they desired for American soldiers (i.e., individuals like themselves) in the event of their being captured by enemy forces. McCain, who was himself tortured as a prisoner of war of the North Vietnamese Communist forces, argued, "Weakening the Geneva protections is not only unnecessary, but would set an example to other countries, with less respect for human rights, that they could issue their own legislative 'reinterpretations.' . . . This puts our military personnel and others directly at risk in this and future wars" (qtd. in Riechmann 2006, A25).

One could read their antitorture position as a form of strategic empathy, as well. *Strategic empathy* is the kind of accommodation for or understanding of an Other that one calls into play, even when the Other may be an adversary, because there is the expectation that empathy will ultimately redound to one's own benefit. That empathy is not necessarily prompted by goodwill alone is an important perspective that Martha Nussbaum (2001) provides. She argues that empathy is by itself a value-neutral state of mind that could lead to such divergent emotions as compassion, indifference, or cruelty. Merely being able to imagine the plight of another or the circumstances contributing to the other's suffering does not guarantee goodwill or compassion to that other, she observes, pointing to torturers and sadists who are fully aware of the details of how and why their victims suffer but do not therefore feel any compassion for them (327–335). For instance, Alfred McCoy (2006) speaks of "empathetic interrogation" as a practice employed by the FBI in order to secure the cooperation of apprehended suspects:

> There is, in fact, a well-established American alternative to torture that we might call empathetic interrogation. U.S. Marines first used this technique during World War II to extract accurate intelligence from fanatical Japanese captives on Saipan and Tinian within forty-eight hours of landing, and the FBI has practiced it with great success in the decades since. After the East Africa bombings of U.S. embassies, the bureau employed this method to gain some of our best intelligence on Al Qaeda and win U.S. court convictions of all of the accused. (23)

Orin Starn, Peter Suzuki, and Caroline Chung Simpson, among others, decry the government's enlistment of anthropologists during and at the close of World War II to understand the Other so as to anticipate and shape behavior (see Chapter 3). Specifically, they critique the social scientists' complicity in supplying cultural information that was then used by the government to regulate life in the Japanese American internment camps and facilitate the U.S. occupation of Japan. During the Cold War, social scientists provided insights to the attitudes and predilections of the peoples of Eastern Europe and other nations likely to come under the influence of the Soviet Union. Such cultural expertise was deemed essential to constructing the decades-long campaign against Communism that the United States launched in order to counteract the Soviet Union's influence and substitute it with the attractions of capitalism.

Empathetic identification leading to cross-cultural expertise is a strategy that has been resurrected by the U.S. military in its efforts to take on the violent insurgencies of radical Islamic movements. Anthropologists such as

David Kilcullen (who is an officer in the Australian army on loan to the U.S. State Department) and Montgomery McFate emphasize to the U.S. military the need for a nuanced understanding of Islamic societies and recognition of the many different types of insurgencies across countries as diverse as Iraq, Indonesia, Pakistan, and Somalia. The biggest mistake of the United States has been its monolithic response to what is essentially a multitude of different situations and scenarios, says Kilcullen: "Actually, there are sixty different groups in sixty different countries who all have different objectives" (qtd. in Packer 2006, 63). For her part, McFate insists that the U.S. government acquire a "'granular' knowledge of the social terrains on which it is competing" (qtd. in Packer 2006, 65).

McFate and Kilcullen are returning to a military-academic cooperation of earlier times, a relationship that fell into disfavor as a result of the Vietnam War and U.S. abuses of power in the context of nation-building imperatives. McFate acknowledges that many of her academic colleagues disdain her working with the military, but she and Kilcullen insist that social scientists are essential to providing "a complex human understanding of societies at war" (qtd. in Packer 2006, 65). That the arguments of anthropologists are having an impact on the U.S. military is evident in the Pentagon-conceived project called "Cultural Operations Research Human Terrain," which uses social science data collected in Iraq, such as "an analysis of the eighty-eight tribes and subtribes in a particular province" (qtd. in Packer 2006, 65). In 2006, the project involved "recruiting social scientists around the country to join five-person 'human terrain' teams that would go to Iraq and Afghanistan with combat brigades and serve as cultural advisers on six-to-nine month tours" (Packer 2006, 65).[22]

Whether such strategic knowledge of the Other in order to serve one's own ends can strictly be called empathy is debatable. And yet if a complex understanding of unfamiliar societies resulting from empathetic identification within the context of strategic imperatives leads to a lessening of tension and easing of destructive conflict, then is one justified in categorically dismissing the empathy as tainted and manipulative? An anthropologist who was hired to work for the Cultural Operations Research Human Terrain project observes that she was ambivalent about her assignment: "I see there could be misuse. But I just can't stand to sit back and watch these mistakes happen over and over as people get killed, and do nothing" (qtd. in Packer 2006, 66). It is not clear whether her lament is for the loss of Iraqi (and Afghani) lives or those of American soldiers or both. If her empathy is principally for the American soldier, and through her desire to protect the American soldier she engages in understanding the Iraqi insurgents, then one could say that she employs two different types of empathy: a compassionate empathy for the American soldier and a strategic empathy toward the Iraqi insurgent. (Akbar Ahmed [2003], in a somewhat tongue-in-cheek fashion, claims that the discipline of anthropology, which had fallen into disfavor in the 1970s and 1980s because of its imperialist excesses and Orientalist perspective, has found new life after the attacks of September 11, 2001. He observes, with validity, "The main interests of anthropology—ideas of ethnicity, group loyalty, honor, revenge, suicide, tribal code, the conflict between what anthropologists call the Great Tradition of world religions and their local practice or the Little Tradition—[are] being discussed everywhere" [23–24].)

The third kind of empathy this book takes up—*ethical empathy*—is characterized by a reaching-out to an unfamiliar Other on the basis of principle (i.e., because the empathizer believes that some fundamental value that he or she treasures has been violated and this violation threatens the integrity of the empathizer's worldview and experience). Ethical empathy is the kind of empathy exhibited by William Faulkner's (1990) protagonist Isaac McCaslin, who relinquishes his plantation heritage because he realizes that his inheritance has been amassed through the oppression of an entire group of people (see Chapter 1). Ethical empathy is what initially prompts many of the lawyers from private law firms to come forward to take up the cause of the Guantánamo Bay detainees; the lawyers feel that fundamental principles of the U.S. Constitution have been violated: the separation of powers and the right of an individual to challenge his or her detention in court. Wayne Collins's defense of the Japanese American renunciants who gave up their U.S. citizenship was also prompted by ethical empathy (see Chapter 2).[23]

Law and Literature—A Rocky but Meaningful Partnership

The nexus of literature and law has long been recognized as a terrain rich for the study of our capacity for humanity or inhumanity to one another, and the social and political implications of such a capacity. Typically, scholarship that is located at the intersection of literature and law touches on one or more of the following contact zones: (1) depictions of lawyers and trials in literature (e.g., Aeschylus's *Oresteia*, Shakespeare's *The Merchant of Venice*, Herman Melville's *Billy Budd*, Albert Camus's *The Stranger*, Franz Kafka's *The Trial*, Richard Wright's *Native Son*, Harper Lee's *To Kill a Mockingbird*, Nadine Gordimer's *House Gun*); (2) the deployment of rhetoric in both the construction of a literary world and the construction of a legal argument; and (3) the parallels between literary interpretation and adjudication—for instance, between literary interpretation that focuses closely on the text (formalist and structuralist approaches, for example) and adjudication that turns to precedent and established legal rules in preference to contextual and social/economic considerations (the distinction that Jean Stefancic and Richard Delgado explain in their book *How Lawyers Lose Their Way*).

At a very obvious level, this book may be said to occupy the space where literature and law intersect. Yet I am mindful of Peter Brooks's (2003) rather cutting assessment that "there is little indication that the movement generally known as 'law and literature' has made any difference to the practice of law. While it may provide law students with some interesting truffles in their education, it remains marginal, an exotic specialty of the academy rather than anything the litigator or the opinion writer has to think about" (245). However, Brooks's dismissal of literature's ultimate influence on the "resolutely hermetic" (245) domain of law rests on an outmoded notion of literary practices as applying only to verbal (principally written) texts. A more accurate conclusion about the relationship between law and literature is that offered by Julie Peters (2005), who observes that the practitioners of both law and literature are increasingly positioning their fields as cultural artifacts (451). Peters's recounting of the original mutual attraction of the two disciplines provides a valuable understanding of what lies at the heart of each domain's apprehension of the world: "Law seemed, to the literary scholar longing for the political real, a sphere in which *language really made things happen*. Literature seemed, to the legal scholar longing for the critical-humanist real, a sphere in which *language could stand outside the oppressive state apparatus*, speaking truth to the law's obfuscations and subterfuges" (448; emphasis added).

Empathy and Law

In appealing to judges, lawyers broadly employ one of two approaches, directed at either the judges' formalistic or humanistic predilections. Of course, the same judge may exhibit one predilection in one case, and the other in a different instance, but in general it is fair to say that judges' decisions show them as falling into one or other category. Formalist judges seek refuge in the structures and written text of the law—the Constitution, legal precedents, and other coded and enshrined practices. They rely more heavily on the established text of the law than on fluctuations of social and cultural forces. Humanist judges are more open to envisioning the unpredictable and tumultuous world outside the courtroom and legal texts, a world that resists neat descriptions, where human behavior is frequently inexplicable and cannot be understood by recourse to stock stories and predetermined patterns.

Lynne Henderson (1987) observes that formalist judges eschew the "moral anxiety" (1590) that ensues from sensitivity to the complexities and amorphousness of lived reality. Thus, the language and rhetorical devices lawyers use are determined by whether they seek to make formalist or humanist appeals—in other words, whether they seek to evoke empathy for their clients with the judges or whether they wish to keep the judges' focus on the text of the law. Writing on the complicated relationship between legality and empathy, Henderson notes that "fidelity to rules and to the autonomy of a legal system, and belief in its internal coherence, can support a judicial decision maker's avoidance of empathy and of his responsibility for human pain caused by law" (1590). Legal systems have come to take the place of religious systems in many societies; legality or legal rules fill the void left by the weakening controls of religious laws. But Henderson cautions that "legal categories can 'freeze' human experience and reality unreflectively" (1591). Taking refuge in legality, or adhering automatically and strictly to the text of the law, leads to the negation of the particularities of a defendant's situation and therefore to the risk of a decision that may be grossly unjust.

Similarly, Ian Ward (2003) discusses the need for formalist justice or positive law to be balanced by the notions of compassion, mercy, and friendship. Ward berates the present-day "brutal unsentimentality" of law (2) where reason or sense eclipses sentiment or sensibility. He does not argue for an absence of reason but rather for a return to a tradition in which "compassion and mercy are necessary constituents of justice" (4). It is the same argument Henderson makes. She writes that the Supreme Court justices deciding *Brown v. Board of Education* in 1954 or *Roe v. Wade* in 1973 could not empathize, in the first case, with the feelings of a black child in the United States who received the message that she was not worthy of being in the same school with a white child (Henderson 1987, 1596–1606), and, in the second instance, with a woman suffering an unwanted pregnancy and forced either to place herself in grave danger through a back-alley abortion or to have her entire life materially altered as a result of child care and motherhood (1628–1633). The lawyers arguing for the defendants in both cases had the challenge of evoking the judges' empathy. Thurgood Marshall, the National Association for the Advancement of Colored People (NAACP) attorney who pleaded before the judges in *Brown*, did precisely that. On the other hand, the lawyers in *Roe v. Wade* found that the justices were better able to empathize with the fetus than with the pregnant woman, resulting, therefore, in the "weak success" of legalized abortion. Some experiences cannot be lived; they can only be imagined. And to imagine with complexity and depth, with responsibility and care, one must be willing to step beyond the boundaries of the familiar and venture into the territory of the unknown.

However, as Toni Massaro (1989) cautions, an empathetic judge is not always an unalloyed blessing. One can be differentially empathetic, she warns, and judges are not exempt from this failing. Before we unthinkingly call for the diminishment of legal rules that we perceive to be rigid, let us not forget, she remarks, that these rules often guard against the possibility that certain defendants will enjoy the judges' favor while others receive harsh treatment. Massaro contends that precisely because "American society is pluralistic" and heterogeneous, if judges are allowed to use their personal discretion in rendering decisions rather than held to "abstract legal standards," we may find that the "large number of genuinely conflicting interests and views make official discretion *more* troublesome, not less. If our voices truly are different, then decisionmaker flexibility may lead more often to the suppression, rather than the release of some of these different voices" (2118). She concludes that "a judge or other law official likely will *not* hear those people who are culturally, morally, ethnically, or otherwise alien to that judge or official" (2118; emphasis added).[24]

Though one could argue that judges may be better trained than the rest of the population to examine or admit the influence of their biases, history has proven that individuals/groups/nations in power are not given to doubting their own perceptions. Although one can have mercy, compassion, and friendship for those whom one deems similar to oneself on a number of salient identity axes (gender, socioeconomic class, race, religion, and sexual orientation, for example), it is not a given that one can be empathetic or compassionate across all types of differences. Massaro (1989) offers a nuanced and thoughtful discussion to finding an equitable and humane balance in the courtroom between adherence to abstract rules and openness to the dynamic specificities of every individual's circumstance:

> Although we "know" at some level that we tend to treat people like ourselves better than those outside our spheres of familiarity, we often ignore this knowledge. If verbal reminders of this tendency are built directly into our legal discourse, they may stimulate legal decisionmakers to reach beyond those tendencies more consistently. . . . They also may foster a healthy, perpetual skepticism about prevailing categories and legal paradigms. Questions may be raised more often about which voices are tuned out, and which voices are given leading roles. Legal outcomes that wound may be harder to tolerate, and thus more susceptible to reform, if we routinely ask how we would feel if we were to suffer that same pain—whether it is the pain of job discrimination, segregation, termination of welfare benefits or some other form of loss or unfairness that the law seeks to redress. (2123–2124)

Massaro recognizes that bias does exist even in the most carefully constructed legal frameworks, and she does not deny that U.S. legal structures typically favor dominant groups (those that Lynne Henderson would identify as male, white, Christian, heterosexual, and socioeconomically privileged). But she does not therefore dismiss the usefulness of these laws. Her recommendation that legal professionals (whether lawyers or judges) acknowledge bias within the edifice of law and therefore pay particular attention to their arguments and dispensations, making the effort to empathize with the situation of the defendant, is an essential corrective. Empathy does not mean an abandonment of abstract legal principle; rather it means a conscious and deliberate adoption of ironic critique in the application of legal principles: a reflective analysis of one's subject position as a lawyer or judge—the extent to which one's identity and upbringing shape one's value system and the ways in which one's emotions and opinions are invariably influenced by forces of race, gender, religion, and class.

Though the balance between empathy and fealty to legal text that Massaro proposes is essential to a humane democracy, the use of the word *empathy* by President Obama in considering David Souter's replacement on the bench sparked fierce debate, as though he were proposing an unacceptable attribute. Something about the quality of empathy connotes vulnerability—both in the empathizer (who "opens" oneself up to receive pain and suffering) and in the one receiving empathy. And yet, as the discussions of the preceding literary texts have revealed, invariably a taint of power accompanies an empathetic gesture, with the empathizer frequently being in a position of privilege with respect to the recipient.

Disgrace: A Final Digression

However, if we see empathy not as the endpoint in a relationship of asymmetrical power but as the beginning of a connection that will, through genuine and meaningful engagement of the individuals and groups concerned, lead to a condition of true equity, then empathy would appear to be a posture worth cultivating and nurturing. In this context, permit me one final digression to discuss South African novelist J. M. Coetzee's highly provocative book Disgrace (1999). I focus on this text not because it offers an example of empathy to emulate, but rather because its complex presentation of empathy is both welcome and abhorrent at the same time. Welcome, because it foregrounds the centrality of humility to empathy, specifically the humility of the empathizer. Abhorrent, because it locates this humility-infused empathy in an emotional landscape of unimaginable and relentless bleakness, in which the empathizer is stripped of all self-worth and dignity, as if to suggest the ultimate futility of the empathetic life. This is not an empathy one can embrace, and it does a grave disservice to the possibility of a transformative empathy that has the potential to alter profoundly both the empathizer and the recipient of empathy without degrading either.

Disgrace was published shortly after South Africa's TRC hearings were concluded, and it addresses the fraught question of how to ensure a meaningful coexistence of different racial groups in a postapartheid South Africa. Coetzee was criticized by the African National Congress (ANC), the party of Nelson Mandela, for having written a racist novel in which there is no redeeming black character and where the white female protagonist, Lucy, is gang-raped by three black South Africans. Lucy chooses to keep the child from that horrific violation and to marry and be the third wife of her black South African neighbor, Petrus, despite the strong possibility that he is protecting one of the rapists. Lucy's father, David, is aghast at her decision, beseeching her not to assume the burden for her race's exploitation and oppression of black South Africans. She is unyielding in her determination, and the novel draws to a close with her acceptance of her condition. She tells her father, "Yes, I agree, it is humiliating. But perhaps that is a good point to start from again. Perhaps that is what I must learn to accept. To start at ground level. With nothing. Not with nothing but. With nothing. No cards, no weapons, no property, no rights, no dignity" (205). It is the bleakness of this prospect for white South Africans that the ANC protested, decrying Coetzee's implication that as a white South African the only possible way to survive in the new multiracial South Africa was to be stripped of every iota of self-worth.

Lucy's decision to stay, to remain in close proximity to a man who might have facilitated her rape, is curious and, one could argue, deeply problematic. She refuses her father's offer of sending her to Holland or of setting her up somewhere safer than her current situation. In her resolve and voluntary act of dispossession—"No I am not leaving. Go to Petrus and tell him what I have said. Tell him I give up the land. Tell him that he can have it, title deed and all. He will love that" (205)—Lucy has gone outside herself in an act of unimaginable recognition, fulfilling, as it were, Butler's (2001) exhortation, discussed earlier in this Introduction, that a genuine recognition of the Other requires a going beyond oneself to "become other than what I was and, therefore, . . . cease to be able to return to what I was" (23). Unwilling to leave South Africa, unwilling to leave the site of her violation, she seems to be saying that this is the only genuinely ethical and responsible act open to her—to live in the proximity of her trauma, just as black South Africans lived in the proximity of their sufferings and traumas for decades.

Perhaps Coetzee gives us this extreme portrait of vulnerability and empathetic self-degradation so that we may understand precisely what we take on when we commit ourselves to engage the Other deeply and wholly. But I would submit that Lucy's abject submission to the future does not grant to Petrus his full humanity. Her adopted posture suggests that this is the only kind of offering Petrus will accept as sincere and commensurate. And herein lies the problem with Coetzee's apocalyptic depiction of empathy—it is a corrosive vision of both she who gives and he who receives. In rejecting this vision and in examining various alternate depictions of empathy, I offer in subsequent chapters other paradigms of empathetic engagement, in which both empathizer and recipient (whether individual or group) are enriched by their interaction.

Overview of Chapters

Four chapters and a conclusion follow this introductory essay. Chapter 1, "Literary Imagination and American Empathy," offers a *broad sweep* of American empathetic writing, beginning with Mary Rowlandson in the seventeenth century, through Lydia Maria Child and William Apess in the first half of the nineteenth century, all of whom present the Native Americans as complex human beings rather than as hostile heathens; the chapter then moves to Harriet Beecher Stowe's *Uncle Tom's Cabin* (1851/2), Frederick Douglass's *The Heroic Slave* (1853), and Mark Twain's "War Prayer" (1904), bringing us up to the early twentieth century; from here, I take up Richard Wright's *Native Son* (1940) and William Faulkner's *Go Down, Moses* (1942); the chapter then moves to John Hersey's *Hiroshima* (1946). I leap ahead several years to Mohsin Hamid's *The Reluctant Fundamentalist* (2007) and H. M. Naqvi's *Home Boy*

(2009). Because this chapter is a survey, I do not offer an in-depth literary analysis of any of the texts; however, I do situate each within the context of empathy and its emergence in these writers at critical junctures in the history of the American colony and nation.

Chapter 2, "Deserving Empathy? Renouncing American Citizenship," features the lawyer Wayne Collins, from San Francisco, who single-hand-edly battled for twenty-three years to reinstate the citizenship of more than five thousand Japanese Americans who renounced it following the issuing of Roosevelt's Executive Order 9066 calling for the internment of individuals of Japanese descent. Collins took on this seemingly insurmountable challenge even as the national offices of the ACLU forbade him from doing so. He was fiercely committed to securing justice for the renunciants, who, he believed, had given up their citizenship under unnatural conditions of duress and psychological manipulation. This chapter draws on archival documents, such as letters and other communications to and from Wayne Collins (whose papers are housed in the Bancroft Library of the University of California, Berkeley), and on the extant literature of Collins's legal efforts on behalf of the renunciants (discussed in Michi Weglyn's, Peter Irons's, and Donald Collins's books). The chapter addresses itself to the question "What drives certain individuals to immerse themselves in the situation of others, even when the benefits to themselves are not obvious or immediate, even when they are made vulnerable by their pursuit of these causes, even when they are displaced from positions of comfort?"

Chapter 3, "Hierarchies of Horror, Levels of Abuse: Empathy for the Internees," focuses on a selection of literary texts that engage the Japanese American internment. Two novels have been published in the last twenty years: David Guterson's *Snow Falling on Cedars* (1995) and Julie Otsuka's *When the Emperor Was Divine* (2002). Both novels have received high critical acclaim. Combining the diverse tools of literary analysis and a cultural studies approach, I examine and critique the techniques these authors use to construct empathy for Japanese Americans. David Guterson is European American, and Julie Otsuka is a Japanese American whose mother, grandmother, and uncle were interned. Given that both novels were published long after the internment, I compare their techniques to those in works by writers who were themselves internees—the fiction writer Hisaye Yamamoto and poet Mitsuye Yamada. In addition, I discuss selected journalistic and anthropological writings of the 1940s and 1950s that helped construct the Japanese Americans—both favorably and unfavorably—to the majority population.

Chapter 4, "Guantánamo: Where Lawyers Connect with the 'Worst of the Worst,'" presents the voices of lawyers working in behalf of the Guantánamo Bay detainees. The superregulatory function of law, specifically with regard to its policing of the spaces in which we are most likely to come up against unfamiliar persons (along any number of axes but primarily those of language, race, ethnicity, and religion), facilitates a too-easy labeling of them as unwelcome and unwanted within our midst. In this chapter I argue that paradoxically the language of law enabled approximately three hundred lawyers (from both the public and private bar) to secure access to the more than seven hundred detainees in Guantánamo Bay and subsequently to dismantle the legal arguments made by the Bush administration to hold the men there indefinitely. The lawyers have been variously criticized, from both the right and the left. From the right, they have been attacked as naïve, opportunistic, misguided, and unpatriotic. From critics on the left, they have been disdained as too cautious, excessively idealistic, and insufficiently interrogative of power structures. However, using the tether of the law, the lawyers ventured out into the open waters of humanity and found a new way to encounter the unfamiliar Other. In the process, they have also become more willing to question the sanctity of the law and to recognize its constructed nature. I draw on my interviews of and conversations with seven detainee lawyers (five of whom are from the private bar). I treat, as well, two works of creative nonfiction: "Bottomless," by a detainee lawyer, and *My Guantánamo Diary*, a legal student's memoir of being a detainee translator.

The Conclusion poses several questions: What can the United States expect for itself? As a nation, will we adopt a strategic empathy because we recognize that it may be the only way to survive in a world of interdependent nations? Or will we opt for a less self-centered and ideologically grounded ethical empathy? A compassionate empathy may be difficult to achieve if we see ourselves as the world's "most hated" nation. Darfur, the global AIDS crisis, and global warming: these are immediate challenges that require from us an empathetic response. Naomi Shihab Nye's "Red Brocade" (2002) and Frank Bidart's "Curse" (2002) are two poems that offer us antithetical perspectives of a possible U.S. approach to the world; I wrap up the book with a discussion of these two texts, speculating on the choices we might make, terrified as we are that despite our military and economic power, we remain vulnerable to the unpredictable.

1

Literary Imagination and American Empathy

mpathy is a relationally imaginative approach to living that underscores interdependence—whether of individuals, communities, or nations—and has at its foundation the call to imagine our lives always in the context of similar and dissimilar others. A crucial aspect of this relational imagining is the recognition of power and how it operates, particularly the asymmetrical power that inhibits empathy. I discuss asymmetrical power in the Introduction to this book; here I take it up in greater detail. The literary texts that are the focus of this chapter are inhabited by two types of voices: (1) of those who have been or are the targets of antipathy, as they speak back to their ill-wishers, and (2) of those who attempt empathetic connections to misunderstood or marginalized groups. The earliest literary text I discuss dates back to 1682, and the most recent text was published in 2009. The texts span several genres—speeches, memoirs, and novels—and they reveal attempts by the misunderstood, maligned, and criminalized to present nuanced and complex portraits of themselves, and efforts by empathetic individuals to see things from the perspective of those who have been wronged. By reading both types of articulations, we can see the difficulty involved in establishing genuine connections between groups in positions of asymmetrical power. Through recognition of the challenges, we can gain heightened appreciation for the types of cognitive and emotional investments that must occur for antipathy to be kept at bay and for meaningful relationships to emerge between erstwhile adversaries or those who view each other with suspicion.

The literary texts I examine are not in any way meant to provide a comprehensive gamut of representations of empathy for and antipathy toward a constructed enemy. But the examples I offer are of sufficient range and complexity to suggest how high the stakes are for our collective survival. In these texts, the groups in positions of power receive exhortations to step beyond themselves and to engage in imaginative acts of occupying other realities where they cannot blithely assume the same levels of privilege and power they now enjoy. As Kimberly Davis argues, true acts of empathy are marked by recognition of one's privilege and power relative to those with whom we empathize as well as by an acknowledgment that one's privilege may come at the expense of others' deprivation (157). In most cases, it is relatively easy to identify where the power lies and to see why the person or group in power has difficulty acknowledging privilege and relinquishing power. However, in some instances the situation is not quite as straightforward, and power does not necessarily come with its full trappings. The complicated dynamics at play in Alice Walker's short story "Advancing Luna and Ida B. Wells," discussed in the Introduction, is a case in point. Walker's black narrator dismisses her white friend Luna's empathetic decision not to disclose her rape by a black civil rights worker. Luna's empathy appears tainted to the narrator, because of Luna's position as a white woman who can decide when to disclose her knowledge of his act of rape and when to withhold it. Though the black narrator is right about the power of Luna's word over Freddie Pye's fate, she, too, is guilty of a lack of empathy. Luna was violated, her body was assaulted, her consciousness was wounded. To acknowledge this fact is not to ignore Luna's power over Freddie Pye. The narrator's inability to extend a gesture of understanding toward Luna underscores both the supreme importance of the person-to-person dialogue (between the narrator and Luna) as the potential source of empathy and, at the same time, the impossibility of extricating this communication from the larger historical and political contexts that may inhibit empathy.[1]

I am not content that a heightened understanding of empathy should constitute the endpoint of this literary exercise. Rather, I would hope that our attention to the language of texts and to the articulated and unarticulated feelings within the texts leads to practical outcomes: a genuine understanding of the need for dignity of individuals, communities, and nations, and the *translation* of the recognition of that need into constructive engagement. The medical sciences now give attention to translational research—that is, clinical tests and other initiatives that translate or convert the findings from experiments on genes, cells, enzymes, and other chemical and organic agents into applications (pharmaceuticals or medical practices) that fight against disease and contribute to improved patient care. So too I would hope that literary engagement translates into visible and tangible improvements in how we communicate and live with one another, the laws we seek to establish, and the laws that we interrogate and have the courage to dismantle when they fail us.

Morality is always intersubjective, Tzvetan Todorov (1996) avers, in his study of human interaction in the Nazi concentration camps. "Morally, one can require something only of oneself; to others, one can only give" (288). The connection is between two human beings. Yet it is important to remember that though acts of intersubjective empathy can occur within exploitative and oppressive structures of power, they may do nothing to change the underlying situation. In fact, one could argue that empathetic acts serve as crucial release valves to the explosive pressure of resistance that is likely to build up within systems of oppression that provide no outlet for challenge. Thus, empathy that stays at the level of the intersubjective, while extremely valuable for the two individuals involved in the connection, is not necessarily something that we should celebrate unequivocally. Instead, we should ask what potential this intersubjective empathetic connection offers for mobilizing a widened force of resistance leading to ultimate equitable reconstitution of power relationships.

Widening the impact of a deep empathetic relationship across the chasm of fraught divisions is extremely difficult. Sandy Tolan's book *The Lemon Tree: An Arab, a Jew, and the Heart of the Middle East* (2006) provides a sobering study of the possibility for coexistence between Palestinian Arabs and Israeli Jews.[2] *The Lemon Tree* offers a useful vantage point from which to view both the value and the deficiency of acts of individual connections. In Tolan's book, the political situation is always in the forefront, dominating the personal narrative of the friendship between an Israeli woman and a Palestinian man. Bashir's family home in al-Ramla becomes Dalia's when the state of Israel is founded. Bashir's entire adult life (he is now a man in his sixties) is spent trying to resist the Israeli occupation so that he and his family can return to their home. Upon a visit in 1967 from Bashir and his cousins, who want simply to see this home they have lost, Dalia learns of the painful consequences of the founding of the state of Israel. She had, until that point, believed that the home was legitimately her family's because it had been abandoned by its previous (Arab) residents. A friendship develops between Bashir and Dalia that endures through his many imprisonments for suspected terrorism. *The Lemon Tree* is at once an illumination of the power of individual connections and a commentary on the cul-de-sac quality of such a friendship given the asymmetrical power between Israelis and Palestinians in the wider political context. Dalia's growing recognition of the injustice done to the Palestinians leads her to convert her home (which was once the home of Bashir's family) into a kindergarten for Arab, Jewish, and Christian children and a place for Arab-Jewish interaction. The "Open House" was Dalia's attempt to create a "shared legacy" of the home that her family had come to possess as a result of the creation of the state of Israel. "But she would go to great lengths to explain that this was a personal choice, not to be understood as an endorsement of a broader right of return for the Palestinians" (220). On the other hand,

> Bashir had always understood Dalia's gesture of sharing the house in al-Ramla, and making it into a kindergarten or Open House for the town's Arab children, as an acknowledgement of his right of return, and, by extension, of the rights of all Palestinian people, as enshrined by the UN, to go back to their homeland. Dalia, on the contrary, saw

Open House, with its programs of encounter between Arabs and Jews, as the result of one choice made by one individual. . . . This was her personal decision, Dalia would make clear, and not one that should be required of other Israelis. (261)

In the powerful story of the friendship between Dalia and Bashir, in the strength of their personal connection, one sees clearly the limits of such individual acts of reconciliation. Though Dalia belongs to the side with greater economic and political power, she realizes that she cannot single-handedly affect the political landscape to create the situation that would materially change conditions on the ground for the Palestinians. Bashir had written to Dalia at one point in their friendship, "*I wish . . . there had been a forest of Dalias*" (Tolan 2006, 262). But even a forest of Dalias would need to agitate for change and prevail against the institutions of the state before such a shift would occur. Individual acts of humanity are essential, even crucial, to the creation of collective movements and changes in power structures. But individual acts of redemption also run the risk of becoming self-contained and isolated gestures of humanity whose only value lies in their momentary sparkle amid an otherwise bleak and gray indifference and inhumanity.

And yet, before we dismiss altogether the value of such acts of person-to-person empathy, it is important that we consider Lawrence Blum's (2004) provocative assertion that not just acts of empathy but even *attitudes* of support can serve as significant mobilizing forces. Blum argues that Polish Catholics during the time of the Nazi occupation of Poland could have done much to help the Polish Jews even through simple *attitudes* of solidarity. "But *why* is it morally appropriate what people feel, not just what they do?" Blum asks (143). His answer is that "as human beings, we care not only about what people do for and to us, but how they feel about us; and their concern or its absence can be particularly heightened in certain situations" (143). To members of a stigmatized and persecuted group, the knowledge that even some individuals (no matter how few) regard them as fellow human beings or fellow citizens equal to themselves "can be deeply affirming, apart from any concrete actions they take on your behalf" (143). In fact, argues Blum, "a sharp distinction between action and emotion is not always possible. The actions of some are influenced by the attitudes of others. . . . The attitudes of those around us shape our sense of what is right and wrong, appropriate and inappropriate, what is to be expected and what is too much to expect" (144). If the actions of some are influenced by the attitudes of others, and if the acts of these some set in motion a snowball effect, then attitudes can become stimuli for action.

The literary texts I examine focus primarily on the individual empathetic connection. But they gesture in varying measure to the possibilities or impossibilities beyond this contained space of empathy. I turn now to examine how these texts invite us to reconsider the enemy as a possible friend and what further reorientations of our perspectives they urge us to make. I do not give equal analytical attention to all the texts; I spend greater energy on those texts that offer us an opportunity to explore a relatively unexamined aspect of empathy.

The Indian: Unexpected Friend, Eloquent Exhorter

Mary Rowlandson's 1682 narrative (considered by many to be the first truly *American*, as opposed to English, novel) relates her eleven-week captivity among the Narragansett Indians, who were part of the multitribe "organized" resistance to Puritan settlers. The tribes were exhorted to come together by Metacomet (also known as King Philip), the sachem of the Wampanoag Indians, who viewed with alarm the aggressive encroachment into Indian lands by the European settlers. Rowlandson's captivity narrative, *The Sovereignty and Goodness of God, Together with the Faithfulness of His Promises Displayed, Being a Narrative of the Captivity and Restoration of Mrs. Mary Rowlandson*, recounts her experience six years earlier, in 1676, when her home in Lancaster was attacked by the Narragansett and she was among several people taken captive.

In an earlier essay, I have argued that the captivity narrative provided Puritan women the opportunity to reconstitute their selfhood and to assert a voice that was typically denied them in the extremely patriarchal ethos of the Puritan colony. Upon their return from captivity, many of them wrote narratives in which, despite the authors' succumbing to the prevailing rhetoric of the barbarity and savagery of the Indians, there are unexpected moments of empathetic representation. Thus, Rowlandson records her captors' attention to her comfort "in 'The Fifth Remove' when they ensure that her feet do not get wet when they cross a river even though several of the Indians are themselves knee-deep in water; in '[T]he Eighth Remove,' when they comfort her, tell her that no harm will come to her, and offer her spoonfuls of meal; and also in 'The Eighth Remove,' when King Philip pays her for her seamstressing services and treats her with friendship" (Srikanth 2002, 96–97). She writes, as well, of King Philip's kindness to her when he learns that she has not had a chance to wash herself for a month: "he fetcht me some water himself, and bid me wash, and gave me the glass to see how I lookt and bid his squaw give me something to eat" (Rowlandson 1990, 42).

Ralph Bauer characterizes as "exculpatory discourse" Rowlandson's presentation in her narrative (in the section titled "The Twentieth Remove"), that "not one of the Indians 'ever offered . . . the least abuse of unchastity . . . in word or action'" (Bauer, 2003, 137). Though one might argue that the exculpation is meant primarily to establish her purity and chastity rather than to offer a positive portrayal of Indians, nonetheless, the insistence on the Indians' restraint with regard to her body, to be found in the phrases "not one of the Indians ever offered" and "least abuse," is of no small significance. For their part, the Indians may have wished her to be unharmed and in relatively good health because they intended to trade her for "powder" (guns), tobacco, and liquor.

It is not my intention to downplay the antipathy that Rowlandson exhibits toward her Indian captors, but rather to point out that despite expectations from her audience that her narrative would confirm the Indians as "savage" and "brutal," she succeeds in inserting descriptions of their acts of kindness to her. And though she often qualifies that kindness as evidence of God's favor upon her, at other moments she allows the import of their kindness to reach us unmediated by the rhetoric of Christianity. The complexity of her language and the language of other female European captives who return from their "ordeal" underscores the contested nature of the encounter between Indians and white women, in particular.[3] In the immediate context of captivity, the Indians obviously held power over their white female captives; however, in the larger context of the settlers' and colonists' actions against the Indians, the power balance tips heavily in favor of the Europeans, who arbitrarily imposed laws "regulat[ing] everything from thievery to blasphemy, Sabbath breaking, and property rights, . . . things that were foreign to the Indians" (Ludwig 1990, 5). Given these realities, Indians' kindness to captives might have been entirely strategic, a form of empathy predicated on their knowing that the only way they might win any concessions from the settlers was if they protected the European hostages.

The critique of Puritan patriarchy becomes less oblique in the writings of Lydia Maria Child and Catherine Sedgwick, who both published in the nineteenth century. Child was long predisposed to empathize with Africans and Indians; she was curious about other people's perspective and approach to the world and did not assume that hers or those of her community were necessarily superior. Child's 1824 novel *Hobomok* reveals an intermingling of radicalism and restraint in its presentation of the Indian protagonist Hobomok. This novel is set in seventeenth-century New England, at a time when the Puritan settlers were still learning how to survive in the New World. In appearance noble and impressive, Hobomok is also almost saintlike in his demeanor, sacrificing his happiness for that of his English wife and her lover. Child ventures into fraught territory, in that she has her female protagonist, Mary, become Hobomok's wife. But that union is presented as the result of Mary's mental "derangement" when she learns of her English lover's death and receives from her father little understanding of her sorrow. Mr. Conant, Mary's father, is an unyielding self-righteous Puritan who abhors any kind of ostentation and finery that reminds him of the corrupt and idolatrous England he has left behind. When he flings Mary's ornate Bible, a gift from her lover, Charles, who is presumed to have died at sea, she can no longer abide the thought of living with her father, and in rejection of his patriarchal insensitivity, she turns to Hobomok and becomes his wife.

In her narrative, Child presents this cross-racial alliance as the result of sorrow-induced derangement of senses and unbearable patriarchal control and oppression. Mary's mental condition at the time of her decision to marry Hobomok is described thus: "A bewilderment of despair that almost amounted to insanity" (Child 1991, 120); this confused state of mind and Mary's "deep and bitter reproaches against" (121) her father's emotional coldness and unyielding views lead her to declare to Hobomok that she will be his wife. Thus, Child appears to give the impression that a white woman could marry an Indian only if she were not quite in her right mind. Yet such a conclusion is too hasty, because Child complicates the outcome. When Mary's father urges her to return home to him given that her marriage to Hobomok is not lawful because it "had been performed in a moment of derangement" (136), she rejects this parental overture and resolves to remain with Hobomok for two reasons. One is her awareness that she would not be welcome among the colonists, and the other is her reluctance to take any less seriously her marriage vows to Hobomok simply because he is Indian.

Ultimately, however, Hobomok has to be marginalized and made to disappear or, as Mielke (2004) notes, the novel "asserts the inevitability of the races' dissociation after close contact" (174); the Indian is characterized by his eventual absence. Charles returns, encounters Hobomok, learns of his marriage to Mary, and is ready to relinquish the object of his love to Hobomok, but Hobomok emphasizes that Mary's first love is Charles and, in a grand gesture of sacrifice and selflessness, disappears into the woods after he has dissolved his marriage to Mary in the proper Indian way.

Child offers and then thwarts the one possibility of coexistence and intermingling between the two races—the son who results from the union between Mary and Hobomok. The young Charles Hobomok Conant gradually sheds his Indian identity and becomes cleansed of his Indian heritage. He becomes "a distinguished graduate" of Cambridge University in England; "his father was seldom spoken of; and by degrees his Indian appellation was silently omitted" (Child 1991, 150). One should not be too hasty in calling Child cautious, however; in subsequent years, her critique of attitudes demeaning African Americans and her call for doing away with laws that prohibited interracial marriages was sharp. Her empathy was costly, as she suffered hostile disparagement and the loss of her prestige as an author for young readers (Karcher, xiii).[4]

Catherine Sedgwick is frequently mentioned along with Child as providing a challenge to the early to mid-nineteenth century's ready acceptance of the Puritan depiction of Indians as hostile and savage. Her 1827 novel *Hope Leslie* carries Child's agenda of empathy for the Indians further, even presenting us with a strong and articulate female Indian protagonist, Magawisca. Sedgwick, like Child, sets her novel in an earlier time, during John Winthrop's governorship of Massachusetts Bay Colony (1630–1645). Magawisca, a stalwart representative of her tribe, fearlessly presents the Indian perspective of the attacks on the early settlers, showing them to be justifiable Indian responses to the aggressive intrusions of the settlers and to their arbitrary seizure of land and resources. Sedgwick goes further with her counternarrative, making her white female protagonist, Hope Leslie, help Magawisca escape from being imprisoned by the governor and his troops. The author also brings about the marriage between a white woman and an Indian, with the couple eventually settling among the Indian husband's tribe. But Sedgwick, too, does not bring to full measure her challenge to patriarchy and Puritan ethnocentrism. Faith, Hope Leslie's younger sister, marries Oneco, Magawisca's brother, but her marriage, too, is not presented as the rational choice of a strong and articulate white woman; rather, there is a childlike and undeveloped quality to Faith, as though she were not quite an independent-minded adult capable of making her own decisions.

One of the first Indian voices who published an autobiography (in 1829) and also became known for his speeches was the Pequod William Apess. Known for his skill at oratory, Apess, who became a Methodist minister, made a living by delivering sermons for the Methodists. In 1836, William Apess delivered a speech at the Odeon theater on Federal Street in Boston. He was likely invited by one of the groups involved in advocating for the rights of Indians. The speech was subsequently published at the author's own expense.

It is a passionate rewriting of the memory of King Philip, the Wampanoag sachem who had rallied a force of resisting Native American tribes in the latter years of the seventeenth century to take a stand against the settlers in New England who were exerting their power arbitrarily, or so the Native American tribes thought, on the original residents of the area. King Philip's War, as his revolt was called, was the first major organized campaign of hostilities between the white settlers and the Indian tribes of New England. The defeat of King Philip and his allies consolidated the Puritan settlers' dominance in New England and reinforced for them their sense of their own mission and destiny.

A large part of Apess's speech, which is titled "Eulogy on King Philip," is a rewriting of the events leading up to and during the war. Also, the speech sought to highlight precisely what was at stake for the Indian tribes—not just the appropriation of their natural resources but also the assault to their dignity and their humanity. Thus, the speech performs a dual function, in that it presents King Philip's War from the perspective of the Indians, and King Philip as the leader of this war, positioning him as the champion of his people worthy of the same type of honor and glory that the citizens of the young republic bestowed on George Washington. Apess makes it clear that there is every reason to honor King Philip in this way. The second function of the speech is to move the audience into acknowledging the hypocrisy of the settlers who profess to practice and adhere to the tenets of Christianity, by arguing that their behavior was anything but Christian. Apess had also already (in 1833) published a tract that he titled "The Indian's Looking Glass for the White Man," where he similarly exhorts the white settlers to examine their professedly Christian behavior and beliefs. Here, in this eulogy to King Philip, he asks the audience to go back and cast judgment on the actions of their predecessors and to concede that those acts were indeed unwarranted and highly questionable.

The speech is a lengthy redrawing of King Philip, providing the audience with a perspective on the chief as a person who was noble, kind, and deserving of the respect owed to the leader of a people. However, this eulogy had more than one function—it was meant not only to provide an alternate portrait of King Philip to those currently on record or in popular memory but also (equally) to serve as an indictment of the professed Christianity of the settlers and their current descendants. Apess's logic is simple and straightforward: if you are Christians, as you say, then pay attention to Christ's teachings that exhort you to be compassionate, just, and understanding. You are cruel in your treatment of the Indians; so either you are not Christians, or you do grave disservice to your religion and its teachings. To drive home the undeniability of the settlers' cruelty to Indians, Apess provides his audience with a detailed history lesson, this time presented from the perspective of an Indian:

> It is said that in the Christian's guide, that God is merciful, and they that are his followers are like him. How much mercy do you think has been shown towards Indians, their wives and their children? Not much, we think. No. And ye fathers, I will appeal to you that are white. Have you any regard for your wives and children, for those delicate sons and daughters? Would you like to see them slain and laid in heaps, and their bodies devoured by the vultures and wild beasts of prey? and their bones bleaching in the sun and air, till they moulder away, or were covered by the falling leaves of the forest, and not resist? No. Your hearts would break with grief, and with all the religion and knowledge you have, it would not impede your force to take vengeance upon your foe, that had so cruelly conducted thus, although God has forbid you in so doing. (Apess 1997, 136)

The most interesting aspect of his speech is that it is neither confrontational nor conciliatory, but veers a path between the two modes. Though his ultimate objective is to move the audience to consider the world from the perspective of an Indian, in other words to show empathy for the Indian, the appeal he makes to them is motivated less by his need for their compassion for the wrongs that the Indians have suffered, but rather is impelled by his desire that they acknowledge the humanity of the Indian as no different from their own. But, he cautions them, this acknowledgment, when and if it comes, will not immediately absolve them of their past wrongs. Their journey to winning back the trust or good opinion of the Indian will be difficult and long. (Apess is under no illusion that the white man or woman is hungry for the good opinion of the Indian because of any desire to create a connection with the Indian; his implication is that the white man wishes to be thought well of by the Indian because then it reinforces his own sense of himself as just, fair, and humane; in other words, white empathy for the Indian is a self-aggrandizing motivation.)

The Indian does not, for good reason, trust the white man, Apess asserts, though there are white people who have spoken up in favor of the Indians. But their number is very small; therefore, he is guarded in his interaction with white people and prepared for their betrayal:

> And although I can say that I have some dear, good friends among white people, yet I eye them with a jealous eye, for fear they will betray me. Having been deceived so much by them, how can I help it; being brought up to look upon white people as being enemies and not friends, and by the whites treated as such, who can wonder? (Apess 1997, 138)

Apess's sentiments are not unlike those conveyed by Frederick Douglass in his famous "Fourth of July" speech, which he delivered in 1852 in Rochester, New York. The title of Douglass's speech, "What to the Slave Is the Fourth of July," might have prepared the audience for what they would hear (the hollowness, from a slave's perspective, of the nation's celebration of its independence); but the title of Apess's speech leaves no doubt about what he will say: this is a eulogy for a man who has been condemned and hated by generations of New England settlers. Thus, Apess's audience would not have been entirely surprised by the thrust of his talk. However, they may very well have thought of themselves as removed in time from the duplicitous behavior of the earlier settlers and may have considered themselves to be enlightened and large-minded. One can only speculate on the reactions of those sitting in the audience. Likely, there was a full gamut of emotion; possibly, in the audience were individuals who thought, like the famous Lydia Maria Child, that the Indians had suffered most grievously and were entitled to the little they had remaining of their land and way of life. Child and her husband were active in 1828 in campaigning against the removal of the Cherokee from their land in Georgia (Karcher 1991, xi) and later protesting the aggressive federal policies against the Seminoles of Florida. To them and to others of their persuasion, Apess's speech would have reinforced their pro-Indian position and justified their involvement in the abolitionist and Indian rights causes. That raising awareness of the injustice to Indians was not a matter of irrelevance to New Englanders is made evident by Apess's speech and Child's activism. Though the New England Indian tribes had been decimated by the early 1800s, nonetheless New Englanders could influence the crafting of national policy about Indians. Apess's visibility as an orator was short-lived. He died in 1839, just three years after his speech at the Odeon.

Empathetic Freedom: "Precious and Priceless"

The most famous orator of the mid- to late nineteenth century was Frederick Douglass, who mesmerized audiences with the power of his language and the force of his delivery. John Stauffer (2005) argues that for Douglass the act of speaking in public was a crucial aspect of performing a liberated subjectivity that countered reductive and simplistic understanding about African Americans held by the white public, even those sympathetic to the abolitionist cause. The objection to slavery of some abolitionists was a matter of principle and not necessarily based on their appreciation for the slave as a full human who was every bit as complex as they in the range of his or her desires and the depth of his or her personhood. For Douglass, his speechmaking provided him the means to impress his listeners with the force of his mind and being. He weaves this power into the one work of fiction he wrote, *The Heroic Slave*.

Douglass's short novel *The Heroic Slave*, which was published in 1853, shortly after Stowe's *Uncle Tom's Cabin*, made a very different kind of appeal to the reader than Stowe's novel (which I take up shortly). In Douglass's text, the scope of the action is narrow and the focus is on the extraordinary connection forged between Madison Washington, an escaped slave, and his white interlocutor, Listwell, who until his encounter with Madison Washington has been a mere bystander in the fight against slavery.

Listwell, who is from Ohio, knows that the country is heavily engaged in debate about slavery, but he himself has not invested too much of his energy and thinking in the discussions. All of this changes when he hears Madison Washington inadvertently one morning as he is walking through the woods in Virginia. Washington, who is debating aloud as to whether he should attempt to escape, speaks powerfully and ultimately resolves that he will follow the example of a recently escaped fellow slave. The narrator tells us that Washington's "air was triumphant" (Douglass 1990, 28) He is no abject slave, cowering from the desperate hardships or anticipated punishments he is certain to experience if he should get caught. Rather, it is the magnificence of his demeanor and the power of his presence and voice that Listwell finds so irresistible. Listwell promises himself this: "From this hour I am an abolitionist. I have seen enough and heard enough, and I shall go to my home in Ohio resolved to atone for my past indifference to this ill-starred race, by making such exertions as I shall be able to do, for the speedy emancipation of every slave in the land" (30).

The opportunity to render assistance comes his way when Washington unexpectedly appears at his home as an escaped slave fleeing to Canada. Listwell gathers the courage it takes to enter into a space that has been deemed illegal, and he asserts that he will aid Washington though it exposes him to the danger of fine and imprisonment and possibly the destruction of his way of life. Listwell's decision causes him to feel the vulnerability that has been the slave's only reality since the day of his birth. He risks losing his privilege as a white man, and his willingness to subject himself to danger is not to be taken lightly. We learn that

> the laws of Ohio were very stringent against any one who should aid, or who were found aiding a slave to escape through that State. A citizen, for the simple act of taking a fugitive slave in his carriage, had just been

stripped of all his property, and thrown penniless upon the world. Notwithstanding this, Mr. Listwell was determined to see Madison safely on his way to Canada. "Give yourself no uneasiness," said he to Madison, "for if it cost my farm, I shall see you safely out of the States, and on your way to a land of liberty." (Douglass 1990, 44)

Though Washington does escape to Canada, he is recaptured when he returns to help his wife escape and placed aboard a slave ship. The uprising aboard the slave ship that Washington leads is the subject of a fascinating exchange between the shipmate, Tom Grant, and a Virginia seaman, Jack Williams. The conversation reveals not only the manner in which Washington successfully overpowered the crew and then took control of the ship but also how, despite the seaman's initial support for slavery and the treatment of slaves as property, Washington's words won him over to his cause. Williams is appalled that the captive slaves were able to get the better of the ship's crew. He accuses the shipmate of not having understood the essential weakness of the "Negro" and laments the shipmate's miserable inability to capitalize on the "Negro's" deficiency.

We learn from the shipmate's response that Washington had filed through his chains (with three files that Listwell had surreptitiously handed to him just before he boarded the ship in Richmond) and then also enabled eighteen other captives to file through theirs. So this group of nineteen had overpowered the crew and under Washington's expert leadership had exhibited remarkable good judgment in not killing the entire crew, though some members had been killed in the initial struggle. The shipmate recounts that Washington had spoken most powerfully and compellingly to refute the term *murderer*. In Grant's telling of the story, Washington declares:

> You call me a *black murderer*. I am not a murderer. God is my witness that LIBERTY, not *malice*, is the motive for this night's work. I have done no more to those dead men yonder, than they would have done to me in like circumstances. We have struck for our freedom, and if a true man's heart be in you, you will honor us for the deed. We have done that which you applaud your fathers for doing, and if we are murderers, *so were they*. (Douglass 1990, 66)

A short while earlier, the shipmate has made a most remarkable admission: he has vowed not to continue in this line of work anymore. "I'm resolved never to endanger my life again in a cause which my conscience does not approve. I dare say *here* what many men *feel*, but *dare not speak*, that this whole slave-trading business is a disgrace and scandal to Old Virginia" (Douglass 1990, 63). Yet when he is accused of being an abolitionist, he takes great objection and is ready to fight Williams. But at the same time, he acknowledges the profound impact that Washington has had on him:

I confess, gentlemen, I felt myself in the presence of a superior man; one who, had he been a white man, I would have followed willingly and gladly in any honorable enterprise. Our difference of color was the only ground for difference of action. It was not that his principles were wrong in the abstract; for they are the principles of 1776. But I could not bring myself to recognize their application to one whom I deemed my inferior. (68)

This admission by Grant is rather extraordinary: he is able to recognize his own limited perspective and racial socialization, and he readily acknowledges the power of Washington's words and eloquence. The ocean, with the unconstrained character of its terrain and its unpredictable natural elements, its remove from the laws of man, becomes the site of Tom Grant's reeducation.[5] That we get the power of Washington's words through Grant's retelling of the situation is perhaps strategic: Douglass knows that not everyone would be willing to receive a black man's language, however powerful, however compelling. And so he has Grant serve as Washington's mouthpiece.

Douglass foregrounds Washington's eloquence, his commanding presence, his determination to be the author of his own freedom, and his ability to influence his white listeners to believe that his endeavor is worthy and just and must be supported. The noticeable difference between Douglass and Stowe is that the former gives to the slave the capacity to be the prime mover in his own freedom and to be the voice capable of changing people's views about African Americans through the force of his example and intelligence. The empathetic link is established through the strength of language and demonstration of supreme assurance. Grant, the shipmate, does not wish to be called an abolitionist, and yet he admits that the force of Washington's personality is so powerful that were his mind able to acknowledge the equality of black and white, he would have gladly followed Washington's leadership. This admission of his own deficiency or adverse socialization is perhaps the beginning of his shift to another plane of thinking and doing. As it is, he resolves that he will no longer do the work of transporting slaves—he is convinced that such work is unconscionable. The label *abolitionist* is not one that he is willing to adopt, perhaps because of its association with the North and his reluctance to be seen as emulating northern sentiment. But as a man making his own decisions, and making it as a seaman who has been shown the meaning of liberty as akin to the movement of the oceans, he is firm in his resolve to reject the heinous task of transporting slaves.

Unlike Douglass's novel, which is focused tightly on utterance and storytelling (Madison Washington's and the shipmate Grant's), and action itself is kept to a minimum, Stowe's 1851 novel is panoramic in its spatial geography (covering a large region of the South) and action (the plot is complex, with a large cast of characters and many locations). Her attack on slavery is based on the un-Christian quality of the institution and its destructive impact on families—tearing apart mother and child and severing ties between husband and wife. The abolition that Stowe advocates springs from a sense of the moral wrongness of such a practice and the corrosion of one's own spiritual well being that ensues from one's complicity in the practice—either actively or as a passive abettor. Her challenge to slavery has less to do with her appreciation of the African in his or her complexity and more to do with her urgent need that the nation live up to its Christian ideals and preserve the sanctity of the family.

Two scenes in particular in Stowe's novel challenge the existing Fugitive Slave Law of the time and present whites with a moral dilemma: Should they uphold the law and return an escaped slave to her or his master, or should they obey a higher law, that of God's charity to a fellow human in distress, and flout the law of man? Senator Bird of Ohio, who has been a strong supporter of the Fugitive Slave Law, believes that one must have consideration for the neighboring state, Kentucky, and return the fleeing slave: "Our brethren in Kentucky are very strongly excited, and it seems necessary, and no more than Christian and kind, that something should be done by our state, to quiet the excitement" (Stowe 1981, 76). Here, of course, being Christian is presented as performing good offices for one's neighbor, "our brethren in Kentucky," and showing consideration for their interests. The senator has tried to persuade his wife that his support of the Fugitive Slave Law is done in the best interests of the public good, but his wife is having none of it and keeps bringing him back to consider the un-Christian spirit of the law. He futilely attempts to frame the law as a Christian gesture to a neighbor.

But the senator undergoes his own spiritual transformation when he encounters the fleeing Eliza and her son. Before this encounter,

> his idea of a fugitive was only an idea of the letters that spell the word,—or, at the most, the image of a little newspaper picture of a man with his stick and bundle, with "Ran away from the subscriber" under it. The magic of the real presence of distress,—the imploring human eye, the frail trembling human hand, the despairing appeal of helpless agony,—these he had never tried. He had never thought that the fugitive might be a hapless mother, a defenceless child. (Stowe 1981, 86–87)

What is particularly noticeable in this excerpt is the sheer abjectness of Eliza and her son's condition. Their helplessness, their complete dependence on the kindness of the Birds, is foregrounded. It is this defenseless condition, this complete capitulation to the mercy of the senator, that is most evident. His benevolence comes in the presence of her total deprivation. The power dynamics are entirely clear.

The Quaker settlement in the novel (Stowe 1981, chap. 13) provides us a first glimpse of the possibility of the escaped slave being made to feel the equal of a white man. George and Eliza are welcomed with sincere warmth and support by Simeon Halliday and his large bustling family. The important point about Halliday's resolve to break the Fugitive Slave Law is that he does so without any seeming rancor for those who crafted it. "Thee mustn't speak evil of thy rulers" (139), he admonishes his son. "I would do even the same for the slaveholder as for the slave, if the Lord brought him to my door in affliction" (139).

These two instances of Stowe's depiction of empathy both reveal her objectification of the slave as "victim" and, at the same time, show her ability to see the slave as an equal within the sanctity of the home where the conventions of Christian hospitality apply. Ultimately, however, her vision is problematic, and as some critics say, racist. The most objectionable of Stowe's recommendations regarding the future of freed blacks, which emerges in the novel, is that they should make for themselves a home in the West African country of Liberia. Even at the time of its publication, many abolitionists objected strongly to this proposal; Frederick Douglass, too, as Susan Belasco (2000) reminds us, though highly supportive of Stowe's treatment of slavery and its enormous capacity to arouse "sympathy" for the slaves' suffering, was troubled by her African solution (31). Elizabeth Ammons's (2000) criticism of Stowe goes one step further in its harshness: "There is no rationalizing the racism of Stowe's Liberian solution, which readers have rightly criticized from the beginning. . . . Stowe wants slavery to end and racial inequality to remain" (75), because she "dispatches every educated black American in her book to Africa" while keeping the unlettered newly freed blacks "on the Shelby plantation so grateful to their magnanimous young master that they vow never to leave the plantation" (75). Stowe's novel illustrates in compelling fashion that empathy carries within it the deeply problematic thread of power—the abjectness of the "victim" to which the empathizer responds from a position of privilege. To keep the empathetic connection intact, it appears that this dynamic cannot be disturbed too much. Stowe was strategic in her approach in that she enabled whites to enter into the black slave experience and see it as their opportunity to redeem themselves. The popularity of her book was astonishing: "In the first week of publication, the book sold over 10,000 copies; the numbers quickly rose to 300,000 by the end of the year" (Belasco 2000, 31); clearly, it had widespread impact and of a kind that was palatable to most of its readers.

Dinerstein (2009) reminds us that Richard Wright, Chester Himes, and Ralph Ellison all wrote their own "answers" to protest the politics of feeling and sentimentality pursued by Stowe. They were not content to let people "feel good" about their righteous outrage. Redemption of his white readers was definitely not what Richard Wright had in mind when he wrote *Native Son* in 1940. Scholars of American literature are familiar with his rejection of white redemption as having any part to play in the structural scaffolding of his work. Wright's protagonist is Bigger Thomas, a young black man who has murdered and disposed of the body of the daughter of a wealthy white philanthropist. *Native Son* was the calculatedly hard-hitting follow-up that Wright offered to the sympathetic tears that his earlier collection of stories *Uncle Tom's Children* had evoked in readers, particularly in white female readers. Disdaining such a response (in the same way that Baldwin disdained the response to *Uncle Tom's Cabin*), Wright was determined that his protagonist Bigger Thomas would not elicit simple sentimental sympathy but the horrifying recognition that Bigger's rage, bitterness, and hostility grew out of the society in which he lived, where his personhood was a mere object of control for those with the power to dictate the contours of his life. It was as though Wright meant to say, "If you want to understand what your racism and lack of empathy do, then look at Bigger and see what he has become." The essay "How Bigger Was Born" (1989a) can be read as Wright's manifesto of antipathy/empathy: These are the hard facts of Bigger's existence, and you (white America) are his creator. You cannot empathize with him through tears, because he is the product of your system. If you wish to the ensure that no more Biggers are born, then you must undo the system that makes it possible for him to come into being.

Wright's novel is a record of white antipathy toward Bigger; it is a record so destructive of the capacity for any meaningful relationship between a white person and a black person that even when a white person, Jan (Mary Dalton's boyfriend), makes an attempt to connect with Bigger, the gesture is entangled with the ingredients of its own collapse. Jan, kindly disposed to Bigger though he is, cannot see Bigger in all his complexity and understands him only as the unfortunate product of a racist and failed capitalist system. Jan wants to rescue Bigger, and his Communist sympathies settle on Bigger as the ideal "project" of a left politics. But the circumstances are too heavily weighted against Bigger's being able to pursue any path other than the one he seems destined to travel given his particular racial, social, and political position. Bigger's environment produces Bigger and his crime.

Bigger understands clearly and devastatingly how the dominant white community perceives him:

> It was not their hate he felt; it was something deeper than that. He sensed that in their attitude toward him they had gone beyond hate. He heard in the sound of their voices a *patient certainty*; he saw their eyes gazing at him with *calm conviction*. Though he could not have put it into words, he felt that not only had they resolved to put him to death, but that they were determined to make his death mean more than a mere punishment; that they regarded him as a figment of that black world which they feared and were anxious to keep under control. (Wright 1989b, 257; emphasis added)

The two phrases I have italicized indicate the degree to which the group in power has already made up its mind about the individual under its control. There is no room in their consciousness for self-doubt, no possibility that they would imagine themselves to be mistaken in their understanding of this person, and that there might be the opportunity to learn something meaningful and transformative about another human being. The group in power is in a condition of unyielding affirmation about its perspective.

Fear is a powerful motivator; the vulnerability that one experiences as a result of fear can lead to irrational action. It is when irrational action begins to parade as a rational response that the possibility of empathy becomes severely diminished. Thus, for instance, the justifications for torture so carefully constructed by the Bush administration's Office of Legal Counsel (see Chapter 4 for details)—which led George W. Bush to believe then and to say even as recently as November 9, 2010, in an NBC interview with Matt Lauer that waterboarding is legal because his legal advisors said it was so—present torture as a rational response authorized by the rational discourse of law. In this context, the title of Elaine Scarry's (2010) book, *Rule of Law, Misrule of Men*, is a particularly apt reminder that law can become "deform[ed]" (xv) to suit the aggressive tactics of those in power who allow their fear to become the primary driver of attitude and action. How to dismantle fear or how to deemphasize one's fear so that it is not seen as more imperative or more exceptional than the fear of others is a principal challenge to facilitating empathy.

The second passage from Wright's *Native Son* reminds us of yet another seemingly insurmountable obstacle on the path to empathy. Buckley, the state's attorney general, visits Bigger Thomas in his cell in order to get from him a statement about his actions leading up to and after his killing of Mary Dalton. Buckley's approach could be construed as strategic empathy—feigning understanding of Bigger's situation in order to make him pliable and willing to speak. It can also be understood as a manifestation of cognitive empathy *minus* positive emotional empathy. Buckley can comprehend the difficulty of being black, but this understanding does not translate into a genuine desire to establish a human connection with Bigger and so begin to chisel away at the racial barrier between them. In this passage, Buckley visits Bigger in prison and speaks with seeming concern for him, confusing Bigger with his faux empathy:

> "I know how you feel, boy. You're colored and you feel that you haven't had a square deal, don't you?" the man's voice came low and soft; and Bigger, listening, hated him for telling him what he knew was true. He rested his tired head against the steel bars and wondered how was it possible for this man to know so much about him and yet be so bitterly against him. "Maybe you've been brooding about this color question a long time, hunh, boy?" the man's voice continued low and soft. "Maybe you think that I don't understand. But I do, I know how it feels to walk along the streets like other people, dressed like them, talking like them, and yet excluded for no reason except that you're black. I know your people." (Wright 1989b, 286)

Buckley's attitude—his antipathy for Bigger—is at odds with his empathetic knowledge of Bigger's experiential reality. He illustrates perfectly the truth of Kimberly Davis's (2008) assertion that "knowing without feeling can result in distance and a complacent sense of mastery" (179). She cautions us that knowledge without feeling can be theoretical and cold, just as feeling without knowing can be paralyzing. Bigger's bewilderment regarding Buckley's attitude—how it was possible for Buckley to know so much about Bigger and "yet be so bitterly against him"—reveals the dark side of empathy: that it can be a manipulative instrument of power and control. And it is precisely because of empathy's manipulative capacity that recipients of empathy are frequently suspicious of the circumstances in which it is offered and so reject it.[6]

"The Bear": Empathy as Escapism

Faulkner's novel *Go Down Moses*, and in particular the section titled "The Bear," offers remarkably rich ground to examine empathy in the context of the economic privileges of whiteness. Empathy in "The Bear" holds radical promise for redistributing resources and restructuring privilege, but ultimately its impact is at best anemic. "The Bear" includes two empathetic acts that are central to its protagonist's coming of age into adulthood (his coming of age into adolescence has been marked by an initiation by the half-Indian half-Black Sam Fathers into the ways of the big woods, with respect for the untamable land and humility in one's prowess as a hunter). Ike McCaslin, born in the postbellum South in 1867, is the scion of a powerful slave-owning family, the patriarch of which is Carothers McCaslin, Ike's grandfather. There are two climactic moments in the text: Ike's sighting of the legendary bear in the wilderness and his relinquishment, at age twenty-one, of his plantation heritage. Both climaxes are intimately tied to the issue of power.

Through an extraordinary effort of imagination, Ike grasps the violation and pain that his grandfather's female and male slaves endured. The ledgers he finds in the commissary (the general store where the slaves and, after Emancipation, the sharecroppers make their small purchases) provide the means for his entry into the past, serve as his time machine, as it were, and become the stimulus for his reconstruction of his heritage and the discovery of his blood kinship with his grandfather's and father's slaves. Through reading imaginatively into the sparse and truncated ledger entries of his father and uncle, he realizes that his grandfather forcibly violated his female slave Eunice, who gave birth to Tomasina. Tomasina subsequently gave birth to a son, Terrel (also Tomey's Terrel or Tomey's Turl), in whose ancestry Ike surmises there already was some white blood "before his father gave him the rest of it" (Faulkner 1990, 259). Ike reads in the abbreviated ledger entries that on Christmas Day in 1832, Eunice drowned herself. His father and uncle cannot conceptualize that a slave would suffer such grief and despair as to commit suicide, and their staccato ledger dialogue communicates to us their utter lack of empathy. To

Ike's enormous credit, he stitches together the fragments of the ledger dialogue, providing the emotional and intuitive patches to cover the chronological gaps. He realizes, with horror, that his grandfather has forced himself upon his own daughter Tomasina, conceived on Eunice, and this act of incest has led to Eunice's suicide by drowning. *"His own daughter His own daughter. No No Not even him"* (259), Ike intones in incredulous outrage.

Ike's tutelage under Sam Fathers makes it possible for him to empathize with his grandfather's and father's slaves even though he knows that conceptually he could never be in an analogous situation. The reason for this capacity is that Ike gains from Sam humility and, with it, awareness of his own vulnerability. This recognition of his nonomnipotence enables Ike to imagine a situation in which he could be in the thrall of forces beyond his control. Ike has been in precisely such a situation, when he finds himself as a young boy face to face with the legendary bear of the big woods. What he learns from Sam is that by systematically stripping oneself of the appurtenances of power (in this instance, the watch, the compass, and the gun), one invites vulnerability, but one also gains something—a treasured insight not available to those who are unwilling to give up control. Ike's glimpsing of the bear is a climactic experience for him and an affirmation of the apprenticeship he has served under Sam. Ike learns how to open himself up to vulnerability, and this state of mind prepares him to imagine empathetically the horror of Eunice's and Tomasina's lives and the pride and bitterness in Tomey's Terrel's rejection of Carothers McCaslin's $1,000 patrimony to him.

While this willingness to give up power is Ike's highly commendable accomplishment, his wholesale repudiation of power, especially his refusal to involve himself in the day-to-day world of social interaction, is his downfall. In his self-denial, his eschewal of material comfort and the riches of his plantation inheritance, Ike fashions himself as a modern-day Christ, content to subsist on the merest necessities. It is critical to keep in mind that the training that Ike receives from Sam prepares him to *leave* the tumult and messiness of the world, or, rather, that is the use to which he puts it. While it conditions his mind for empathy, while it makes him open to experiencing moral outrage at what has been done to the blacks in his family, it does not show him a way to live *in* the world and act with this awareness and feeling.

The realization that he arrives at, as a result of his courageous confrontation of the unseemly actions of his grandfather, leads to his second empathetic act: to resolve to distance himself from the monetary gains of a system that permitted such desecrations of human dignity. He relinquishes his plantation patrimony and gives up his inheritance. This relinquishment is noteworthy on two fronts: that it occurs at all, and, second, that Faulkner couches Ike's decision within a lengthy, dense, and frustratingly convoluted dialogue between Ike and his cousin/surrogate father, McCaslin Edmonds.

That the relinquishment occurs is extraordinary. Ike gives up comfort and affluence for a life of Christ-like simplicity. The groundbreaking nature of the act demands a commensurate presentation. McCaslin Edmonds becomes the interrogating resisting presence and consciousness, testing Ike's resolve, as it were, on the one hand, and on the other tempting him to retract his renunciation and submit to the pleasures of the privileged world by pointing out to Ike that his renunciation will have limited and narrow impact, if that. In justifying his relinquishment, Ike turns to the language and rhetoric of epic and the symbolic import of the biblical landscape. The empathetic act is no longer one person's admirable imaginative bonding with another; rather, Ike invests it with significance that wrests it out of the realm of the personal into the allegorical.

Boltanski's (1999) comments, though drawn from the realm of suffering *observed*, are easily applicable to the realm of suffering rendered through discursive acts. According to him, the moral spectator of suffering may be seen as a composite of a reflecting self (whom he calls the *introspector*) and an observing self. When you have an "over-zealous introspector" who focuses on the observing self's interiority more than on the "suffering of the unfortunate," then "we know everything about the state into which the spectator is thrown by the spectacle of suffering but we no longer know anything about the person suffering"; in this situation, it becomes possible to criticize the spectator for "complacently being more interested in himself than in the person suffering" (45). In Faulkner's presentation of Ike, particularly within the context of his protracted dialogue with Cass Edmonds, we have an overzealous introspector. It is ironic that though his imaginative entry into the sparse fragmented text of the ledger entries illuminates the drama of Eunice's pain, this outward-directed imaginative and discursive empathetic engagement cannot sustain itself as such and quickly shifts inward as he makes sense of his relinquishment.

Ike's grand gesture of repudiation comes to a sterile conclusion. In removing himself from the world of social negotiation and emotional upheaval—all the tumult associated with asymmetries of power and human failings—Ike aborts the potential salutary consequences of his empathy. It is to others that he leaves the details of how to make reparations in the world. No one would deny that in relinquishing his inheritance and accepting a mere pittance for his survival, Ike signals his willingness to endure the long-term consequences of his empathetic act. But his removal of himself from the problematic exigencies of social interaction and embroilments of power effectively absolves him of ever having to make any hard decision involving the hearts and minds of individuals.

Thadious Davis's (2003) assessment of Ike's postrelinquishment life as a civic death (126) is astute. Ike may see this departure as his freedom ("Sam Fathers set me free" [Faulkner 1990, 286], he says), and it is freedom he gains, not just from the bonds of owning tainted property but also from the obligations and responsibilities of power. By redesigning for himself a life of minimal wants and equally minimal obligations, Ike has removed himself from the world in order not to have to worry about how to change it. Thus, one could argue that his second act of empathy, the relinquishment, while bold and magnanimous in its execution, is escapist in its consequences. So unusual, so atypical, is the gesture, that there appears to be no model for Ike to emulate other than a spiritual one of total abdication or as a manifestation of a predetermined allegorical Christian pattern. It is as if one must remove oneself from the world in order to convey the extent of one's empathy. But is this kind of empathy necessarily a meaningful one? Is the act of quitting the world a productive gesture of reparation, of making amends *in* the world?

Read against the backdrop of the politics of empathy presented in Alice Walker's short story, one could say that Ike's imaginative and empathetic leap in probing the commissary ledgers does not achieve its full potential. Walker's short story underscores the black recipient's unwillingness to accept unreservedly, without skepticism and resistance, the empathizer's gesture. In addition, I would argue that it is necessary not only to attend to the reasons for the black recipient's refusal to embrace the empathetic act without suspicion of its motivations but also, equally importantly, to recognize the near impossibility for the white well-wisher and empathizer to conceive fully the many interlocking variables that *already* sabotage the empathy, even before its visible manifestation, rendering it impure and partial.

However, and this is important to stress, the inadequacy and incompleteness of the empathetic act do *not* constitute an argument for withholding it. If anything, what Ike's courageous and extraordinary empathy reveals is the *distance*, the *chasm*, that must be crossed before a legacy of wrong can begin to be righted. Ike's "failure" of empathy, or his partially realized empathetic connection, dignifies the enormity of the black McCaslins' suffering and exploitation and confers upon the process of redress the necessary weight and density. The impulses that set in motion the original exploitation (slavery and the ownership of the black body as property) in the first place are so deeply rooted in the fallibility of humans, Faulkner seems to say, that, however well intentioned, a gesture such as Ike's can never achieve its intended impact. Perhaps the failure is Faulkner's as well—his inability to imagine and keep in play the full range of emotions and motivations in one's consciousness that would enable one to assess continuously and adjust one's response of empathy. Empathy, it would appear from a reading of "The Bear" and of *Go Down, Moses* more generally, cannot be dispensed in a single moment of intervention but rather requires constant interrogation and scrutiny and the willingness to refine one's responses. The ability to imagine the other's situation is not completed by a single instance of such a connection but rather through sustained and prolonged and continuous contact and appropriate corrections. This kind of empathy is harder to maintain than a momentary flash of imagination that leads one to consider the imperatives and concerns of an "Other."

War Games and Global Aggression: Whither Empathy?

Mark Twain's fierce anti-imperialist writings reveal his full engagement in the cause of global humanity. He had a deep disgust of hypocrisy, especially for

the expansionist agenda of the United States parading as a Christian civiliz-
ing mission. Writing at a time just following the imperial aggression of the
United States against the Philippines, after defeating the Pacific nation's erstwhile colonizer, Spain, Twain delivers a scathing critique in his 1901 essay "To
the Person Sitting in Darkness" of imperialism and of the tactics of American
soldiers whom he describes as little more than charlatans parading in the guise
of Christianity and causing the shedding of "blood and tears" and the "loss of
land and liberty" of people in other lands (1923a, 257). He cautions against the
allure of imperialist desire for territorial acquisition dressed up as missionary
zeal to civilize the savage and bring light to those persons "sitting in darkness"
(1923a, 250). Astutely, he discloses the dirty secret that this imperial and civi-
lizing mission is good business, because it allows us to acquire the resources
of those whom we wish to civilize (1923a, 255–256). Thus, his anti-imperial
rhetoric refuses to push to the sidelines the venal motives of the U.S. foray into
the Philippines and its subjugation of the islands' people.

In "The War Prayer" (dictated in 1904 but published after World War I),
Twain offers a remarkably empathetic perspective on the impact of war on
those who become the targets of U.S. military might. In this essay, his warning is dire, his attack on his readers doomsday-inflected. The setting of this
"prayer" is, not surprisingly, a church where the preacher praises God and
appeals to him to grant them success and victory in war. As the preacher delivers his sermon, a stranger enters the church, walks down the central aisle, and
ascends the platform to stand next to him. Then, he announces that he has
come from God Almighty and that it is his duty to inform the congregation
that along with every prayer they utter for God's blessing in war, there is also
an unspoken prayer. And he proceeds to tell them about this unspoken prayer.

Twain not only attacks the entire enterprise of war through the words of
this stranger with his "ghastly" visage; more importantly, he also assumes the
perspective of those who are unfortunate enough to be attacked by the machinery of war. The stranger cautions those who pray for victory in war that their
success comes at the expense of others' suffering. Military aggression inflicts
enormous suffering on people, and we should not pretend that there are no
consequences to our actions, the stranger implies. Twain delivers a satirical
thrust through this "insane" stranger. While we rejoice in the blessed quality
of our enterprise and pray to God to grant us glory, let us keep in mind that we
destroy lives. In a marvelously unrestrained catalog of the cruelties inherent in
war, Twain reminds his readers that when we pray for success in war, we are
simultaneously bringing down a curse on our enemies. This is the curse we do
not explicitly voice but which we implicitly hope will come to pass:

> O Lord our God, help us to tear their soldiers to bloody shreds with
> our shells; help us to cover their smiling fields with the pale forms of
> their patriot dead; help us to drown the thunder of the guns with the
> shrieks of their wounded, writhing in pain; help us to lay waste their

humble homes with a hurricane of fire; help us to wring the hearts of their unoffending widows with unavailing grief; help us to turn them out roofless with little children to wander unfriended. . . . [F]or our sakes who adore Thee, Lord, blast their hopes, blight their lives, protract their bitter pilgrimage, make heavy their steps, water their way with their tears, stain the white snow with the blood of their wounded feet! (1923b, 398)

Twain's capacity to stand back from a glorification of war and his refusal to embrace the nation's expansionist agenda is noteworthy.[7] At the same time, it is important to note that his empathetic identification does not erase the boundaries between him, Mark Twain, privileged American, and the people who will suffer the depredations of war. Every sentence of his prayer foregrounds in unmistakable terms the power of the United States relative to those who will become its targets. He does not assert that their suffering will become his because of his fine-tuned sense of empathy; rather, he notes with scathing honesty that he and his group will be the cause of their suffering. In so doing, he avoids the flaw of "egotistical drift," as described by Hoffman (2000) (see the Introduction), and the "fungibility of the slave's body," explained by Hartman (1997), wherein the white person feels acutely the pain of the slave's mistreatment because his imagination substitutes his own body for that of slave who is being physically abused (Hartman, 19). Twain, with characteristic and brutal honesty, is fully conscious of his privileged position as the American who will become the aggressor. His "hurricane of fire" is eerily prescient of the atomic bomb that the United States would drop on the Japanese city of Hiroshima on August 6, 1945. (John Hersey [1989] titles as "The Fire" his chapter on the impact of the bomb.)

In stark contrast to Twain's exhortation to denounce the rhetoric of glorious war is Gertrude Stein's intriguing indifference to the two atomic bombs that the United States dropped, the first on Hiroshima and the second, three days later, on Nagasaki. Stein's "Reflection on the Atomic Bomb," though written in 1946, was first published in 1947. There is something rather chilling in Stein's almost logical progression of ideas, beginning with the forthright declaration of disinterest:

They asked me what I thought of the atomic bomb. I said I had not been able to take any interest in it. . . . What is the use, if they are really as destructive as all that there is nothing left and if there is nothing there is nobody to be interested and nothing to be interested about. . . . [M]achines are only interesting in being invented or in what they do, so why be interested. . . . Sure it will destroy a lot and kill a lot, but it's the living that are interesting not the way of killing them, because if there were not a lot left living how could there be any interest in destruction. (Stein 1946)

Stein turns the question of the atomic bomb's impact on those who are directly affected by it into an exercise in logic and supposition. In her "reflection," the atomic bomb and its consequences become enmeshed in a clever weave of words and ideas where, like the modernist that she supremely was, she makes us attend more to the manner in which she crafts her response than to the import of the subject. The horrific reality eclipsed by her modernist play on syntax and phrasing is that the bomb's destructive power is so total that it obliterates people from the planet.

But let us for a moment assume that Stein is being ironic—and she is deliberately drawing our attention to the absurdity of her utterance: for example, the phrase that machines are only interested in being invented—as if it is not humans who invent machines of mass destruction. However, even if she means to be ironic and provide a satiric commentary on our ability to disconnect our emotions from the awful destructive power of something that we ourselves have invented, even so, her ultimate word on the bomb is that she is not interested in it because it kills, and she is much more interested in the living. The dead are dead, she seems to say. Once they are dead, they are not really the subject of art, because art concerns itself with the realm of the living.

However, people did survive the bombings. And they lived lives of unimaginable physical and psychic pain. Even if one were to grant the validity of Stein's interest in the living rather than the dead, then it is surprising that she does not once refer to the survivors as worthy of her attention. A full year after the bombings, it is inconceivable that Stein would not have known of the heroic struggle of the *hibakusha*, the survivors of the atomic bomb, to reintegrate themselves into society and life. One is left deeply puzzled by her ability to keep the response at the level of linguistic play and avoid a deeper ethical examination of the weapon as a monstrous human creation. As Christine Hong (2009) rightly says, "Whether sincere or ironic, Stein's indifference to the decision to use the bomb, let alone her breezy disregard for the bomb's profound human toll and enduring material consequences, speaks to Hiroshima's non-centrality within the US imagination" (125–126).[8]

A year after the bombs were dropped, John Hersey, a reporter for the *New Yorker*, was assigned to interview and write the memories of six *hibakusha*. His approximately thirty-thousand-word account was initially intended to be serialized in the magazine. At the last minute the editor, William Shawn, decided to run it in its entirety in a single issue. The *New Yorker* staff congratulated itself on this editorial decision, believing that it had helped to humanize the destruction and show the American public the faces under the mushroom cloud, which to the Americans had become the visual symbol of the bomb. Ben Yagoda (2001) writes of the stir that particular issue of the *New Yorker* created:

All newsstand copies sold out the day they appeared, and when Albert Einstein attempted to buy one thousand copies of the magazine, he was told none were available. . . . A reader wrote in to the *New Yorker* to say that "no one is talking about anything else but the Hersey article for the last two days, either in trains, restaurants, or in homes." Another commented, "I had never thought of the people in the bombed cities as individuals." In four half-hour installments, the evenings of September 9–12, the American Broadcasting Company presented a reading of the entire text of the article, with no commercial interruptions, and in England the BBC did the same. (192)

However, though copies sold rapidly and people read the article eagerly, no one actually went out and created a clamor about the decision to bomb civilians. Yagoda writes that when the congratulatory notes started coming in from all around the world to the editors at the *New Yorker* for their "bold experiment" in publishing the Hersey article in its entirety, one of the editors remarked, "I don't think I've ever got as much satisfaction out of anything else in my life" (2001, 193). Of course, there is every reason for the editors to take pride in their achievement; the Hersey article was the first narrative to appear in the United States that provided a different perspective than that of the overwhelming triumphalism of the government and military. The *New Yorker* is to be rightly commended for its intervention. But as intervention, it did not go anywhere; it did not appreciably change the conversation about the justification for the bombing.

Hersey's (2001) focus on the suffering on the ground paradoxically has the effect of keeping at a distance the cause of the devastation. The powerful and graphic images of "raw flesh" (26), people whose "backs and breasts were clammy," and a woman whose "skin slipped off in huge glovelike pieces" (45) invite us to look closely at the bomb's impact but not at the reasons for its deployment. Christine Hong's (2009) objection to Hersey's account is that "these humanized accounts have left unchallenged US atomic impunity. If American presence is everywhere implied in Hersey's report—indeed, is a precondition for the bombing—it is never overtly designated, much less historically identified, as perpetrator" (135). Phrases most commonly used to speak of the bomb's horrific appearance in Hiroshima and Nagasaki are "the bomb fell," "the bomb was dropped." About the U.S. bombing of Nagasaki, Hersey (2001) writes, "At two minutes after eleven o' clock on the morning of August 9, the second atomic bomb was dropped, on Nagasaki. It was several days before the survivors of Hiroshima knew they had company, because the Japanese radios and newspapers were being extremely cautious on the subject of the new weapon" (57). A reader in the United States could not be faulted for feeling that the Japanese radios and newspapers were wrong to withhold information; the focus is, therefore, not on the United States as the country responsible for the bombing of civilians, but rather on the deficiency of the Japanese media for not sufficiently keeping their citizens informed. When the

United States is mentioned, it is identified in language that is largely celebratory and intended to generate awe:

> The President of the United States . . . identified the new bomb as atomic. "That bomb had more power than 20,000 tons of TNT. It had more than two thousand times the blast power of the British Grand Slam, which is the largest bomb ever yet used in the history of warfare." . . . [It was] the first great experiment in the use of atomic power, which . . . no country, except the United States, with its industrial know-how, its willingness to throw two billion gold dollars into an important wartime gamble, could possibly have developed. (49–50)

The narrative of United States triumphalism, which was launched at the very moment that the bomb fell, includes as its principal component that the bomb helped to end the war by striking in the Japanese a fearful respect for the might of the U.S. military. The bomb demonstrated in unmistakable terms the magnificent capability of U.S. technology. It was touted as the weapon to end war, not as a weapon of unimaginable destruction.

To criticize the bombing is still unacceptable in public discourse. The unmistakable evidence of the ascendancy of the triumphalist narrative was the fierce controversy (1993–1995) over the Smithsonian's National Air and Space Museum's decision to exhibit the Enola Gay.[9] I will not go into the details of that controversy other than to say that the original curator of the exhibit came in for intense criticism because he was perceived as not sufficiently celebratory of and grateful for the achievement on the part of the United States and appeared to be biased in favor of the Japanese people.

The traditional and dominant narrative is that without the bomb, the atrocities of the Japanese Imperial Army would have continued unabated, requiring the United States to send in ground troops to invade Japan and overcome it militarily. A ground invasion would have killed hundreds of thousands of American soldiers; the bomb preempted such mass death (S. Walker 2005, 312). This narrative, of course, completely glosses over the fact that it was civilians who were killed at Hiroshima and Nagasaki—a total of two hundred thousand civilians, not soldiers of the Japanese Imperial Army. Of course, the justification for killing civilians is that the Japanese people had blindly supported their emperor's ambitions of conquest and so were to blame in part for the destruction that fell on them. Samuel Walker (2005) offers a valuable overview of the vast literature that addresses the reasons for the dropping of the atomic bombs. Whether, as Ronald Takaki believes, it was motivated by racism and hatred toward the Japanese people (S. Walker 2005, 313), or to impress the Soviets with U.S. military capability (312), or to hasten the end of the war and force Japan to surrender, it has been the only instance of the use of a nuclear weapon and, moreover, targeted at civilians.

John Whittier Treat's (1995) book *Writing Ground Zero* is a deep and thoughtful engagement with his subject-position as an American writing about Japanese literature that focuses on the bombings of Hiroshima and Nagasaki. His preface explores eloquently and poignantly his obligation to address the *human significance* of Hiroshima, an atrocity that created a "dumbfounded amazement over how the damage could have been so unexpected in its delivery, so brief in duration, so inexplicable in its power" (3). Yet despite the horror of those bombings, there has not been a world literature to match the enormity of the act. Treat notes, "there has never been a Japanese counterpart to Anne Frank's diary, a work disseminated among school children the world over, including Japan" (4). He further implies that there has been a systematic and deliberate attempt to see the bombing as strictly a Japanese affair and not a human-made catastrophe of global import. Treat is unequivocal in his condemnation of the bombings, calling them acts of "illegal violence" and "state-sponsored terrorism" (7) and "mass murder" (9), whose effects were not confined to those who were victimized by it at the time but to generations of Japanese who suffered the genetic mutations and other physiological poisonings from the radiation of the nuclear device. Treat will not let the United States ignore the fact that it shares with the Nazi perpetrators of the atrocities at Auschwitz and other concentration camps the awful distinction of having orchestrated the "mechanized dehumanization of civilization" (10). Most poignantly, he tries to understand how it is that the survivors of Hiroshima and Nagasaki harbor so little "of the rancor we might guiltily expect from them" (17), and he concludes that "assaulted by light and sound and heat that seemed to come out of nowhere, how could they focus on what and who produced, ordered, and executed such massive power in order to hate them" (17). *Hate*— he uses the word with no hesitation. That is the accusation he makes of the U.S. government; he equates Hiroshima to Auschwitz. "Wilful violence" (xi) he calls it, and that is the awful truth of the matter.

In 1995, when I was doing a story about Ram Uppuluri, a Japanese Indian American candidate from Tennessee running for the U.S. House of Representatives, I learned that his parents had been instrumental in launching a project to bring a traditional Japanese temple bell from Kyoto in Japan to Oak Ridge, Tennessee, the town where the lab was located that produced the uranium used in the atomic bomb. The Uppuluri family lived in Oak Ridge. Ram's mother is Japanese, and his father Indian (he is now deceased). Their effort to link the two cities through the physical presence of the International Friendship Bell encountered tremendous resistance from veterans' groups, who saw the Friendship Bell as an apology to the Japanese and an admission of wrongdoing by the United States. Ultimately, the Uppuluris prevailed, and the Friendship Bell is now a secular-sacred space within Oak Ridge.

However, as Isaac Weiner (2009) observes, the inscriptions on the bronze bell and the plaque that graces the pavilion in which the eight-thousand-pound bell is housed, say very little directly about the deliberate infliction of mass violence; instead, they refer to the atomic bomb's role in ending war and the resulting bonds of friendship between the two nations. The message is optimistic and hopeful for the future, with minimal evocations of national shame. Oak Ridge is itself not a site of violence but the site of the production of violence that occurred elsewhere. The city's contested feelings about its role in the Manhattan Project (as the nuclear initiative was called) is mirrored in the larger national context. The conflict involves, on the one hand, enormous pride in scientific research and the production of a technological weapon that literally stopped a global war, and, on the other, a sense of alarm at what this technology unleashed. But the deep divisions within Oak Ridge that the bell project provoked indicate that the nation is still unwilling to consider that its targeting of Japanese civilians was deeply problematic. Such acknowledgment does not require an eclipsing of the World War II atrocities of the Japanese Imperial Army.

The dominance of the "positive" American narrative of the bombing of Hiroshima is tied inextricably to postwar Japanese economic success. In this regard, Christine Hong (2009) is perceptively astute in her analysis: "Hiroshima, ideologically conjoined more to the future than the past, thus functions as an exceptional human rights story, a story not only of war crimes that appear to require neither redress nor reparations but also of the putative overcoming of historical trauma through US-sponsored post-war economic progress and democratic rehabilitation" (130). Further, Japan's own shame at its wartime atrocities has complicated its attitude toward the bombing.[10] In August 2010, the sixty-fifth anniversary of the bombing, John Roos, U.S. ambassador to Japan, attended the remembrance ceremonies. This was the first time that a delegate from the United States was present at the event. Roos's attendance was in no way meant as an apology, but more as a gesture of the comfort that now exists between the two countries and the erasure of that horrible linked history between them. That the United States helped get Japan on its feet and set it on the path of great economic success has removed any necessity for the Japanese to expect an apology. Their success and stature on the world stage appears to be compensation enough. Thus the American public and the U.S. government are permitted their indifference to the suffering perpetrated by the bombings, the Japanese are encouraged to focus on their postwar economic rise, and U.S. triumphalism prevails.

Yesterday, to End the War; Today, to Stop Terrorism

Today, the justification for arbitrary exercise of might is to prevent terrorism. The United States is engaged in a "global war on terror," and so the nation must be ever vigilant and clever. In H. M. Naqvi's novel *Home Boy* (2009), Pakistani protagonist and narrator Chuck leaves New York to return to Karachi because of the changed attitude toward Muslims that he experiences in New York. Chuck,

a young man who came to New York four years before 9/11 full of eager anticipation at the wonder of "America," finds that the city and country are no longer
hospitable to Muslims. He experiences firsthand the abuses of the Metropoli-
tan Detention Center (MDC) in Brooklyn, where he and his friends are held on
suspicion of terrorism. Though Chuck is released once it becomes clear that he
has no connections to anything nefarious, the experience leaves him saddened
and bitter about the *attitudes* of most Americans toward Muslims. In the pre-
MDC days, he "had no functional appreciation for prejudice," he says (153),
but in prison he has an awakening: "I understood that just like three black men
were gangbangers and three Jews a conspiracy, three Muslims had become a
sleeper cell" (153). What is particularly interesting about Naqvi's protagonists
is that they are hardly model persons. They are hedonistic, self-indulgent, and
somewhat immature and irresponsible young men who enjoy women, music,
and drink. Naqvi's challenge to us is to examine our own thresholds of acceptance of people and understand the limits of our capacity for empathy.

Chuck's prediction of the future is either blithely optimistic or deeply cynical, depending on how you read his sense that though today everyone is full of
antipathy toward Muslims, "later, much later, the pendulum would swing back,
and everybody would celebrate progress, the storied tradition of accommodation, on TV talk shows and posters in middle schools. There would be ceremonies, public apologies, cardboard displays" (Naqvi 2009, 153–154). But Chuck
and hundreds of other Muslim men who endure a harrowing time at MDC,
"America's Own Abu Ghraib" (133), surely could not be content with the
nation's self-congratulatory gestures of apology and institutionalized repackag-
ing of their pain for easy public consumption?[11]

So what will constitute a genuine reckoning of antipathy? In the final pages
of *Home Boy*, we read, along with Chuck, the newspaper obituary of Mohammed "Mo" Shah, an insurance agent from Hartford who had been attending a
conference at the World Trade Center when the planes struck. Mohammed
Shah is only one of many Muslims who died that day. Perhaps the first step
toward reversing antipathy is to acknowledge this simple fact—Muslims, too,
died on September 11—and to remind oneself of it continuously so as to avoid
the pernicious polarization of Muslims as terrorists and everyone else as victims and/or resistors of terrorism.

Chuck's experience at the MDC makes a skeptic of him and sharpens his
vigilance against the allure of the U.S. rhetoric of inclusion and diversity. Not
until he experiences firsthand the antipathy of the state apparatus of power
does he realize how naïve he has been. The posters and talk shows advertising
pluralism and diversity are, he comes to understand, commodified promises of
coexistence. Though his return to Pakistan is necessitated by the expiration of
his work visa, Chuck could have attempted to find an employer to sponsor him
for a new visa. Yet he chooses to leave the United States, and in his departure
we see the disillusionment that now dominates the consciousness of those who
once were eagerly enthusiastic about the United States.

No Illusions of Empathy

Deliberately resisting the allure of the United States sharpens vigilance and helps one guard against too comfortably nestling in the national embrace, which, after all, can quickly turn into a crushing and fatal stranglehold. An unfavorable turn of events can result in the state's metamorphosis into a malignant and hostile force affecting in adverse ways the on-the-ground realities of one's life: trust of neighbors, ease of movement, invitation to social gatherings, all the numerous minutiae of day-to-day living that become beset by barriers of exclusion and hostility. Therefore, a consciously adopted strategy of suspicion of the state is a rational response that many young Muslims may choose to adopt.

The Reluctant Fundamentalist (Hamid 2007) illustrates the journey toward suspicion and rejection of the seductions offered by the United States. The protagonist of this novel does not start out with such an attitude, however. Changez is, in fact, a very satisfied instrument of the American capitalist machine. The fundamentalism to which the title refers and which Changez eventually disavows is not religious fundamentalism but economic fundamentalism, à la free market enterprise. However, in the early stages of the narrative's plot, Changez is fully integrated into the allures and rewards of the capitalist doctrine. A graduate of Princeton, he lands an impressive job as a valuation consultant in Underwood Sampson, one of the top firms in midtown Manhattan. He is their star employee, and he gets sent around the world to assess the financial worth of businesses; he advises these business clients on how to improve their profit or whether they are too damaged to be repaired and must, rather, shut down. He executes his job with evident satisfaction, taking pride in implementing the fundamentals of a profit-driven way of life. "*Focus on the fundamentals*. . . . Underwood Samson's guiding principle . . . mandated a single-minded attention to financial detail, teasing out the true nature of those drivers that determine an asset's value" (98).

So immersed is he in the skills he has acquired and for which he is celebrated and rewarded in his place of employment that he is able to distance himself from the disruptions following the September 11 attacks on the World Trade Center buildings. The routine of his job and the class privilege of his position insulate him from the rapid disintegration of the lives of Pakistanis in New York who are not as fortunate as he. He observes:

> Pakistani cabdrivers were being beaten to within an inch of their lives; the FBI was raiding mosques, shops, and even people's houses; Muslim men were disappearing, perhaps into shadowy detention centers for questioning or worse. I reasoned that these stories were mostly untrue; . . . and besides, those rare cases of abuse that regrettably did transpire were unlikely ever to affect me because such things invariably happened, in America as in all countries, to the hapless poor, not

to Princeton graduates earning eighty thousand dollars a year. (Hamid 2007, 94–95)

Yet even Changez realizes that in the current climate of hostility, he cannot escape "the growing importance of *tribe*" (117), given that he automatically gets read as a "f—— Arab!" He clings doggedly to his job, immersing himself in its quantifiable tangibility: "I was . . . analyzing data as though my life depended on it. Our creed was one which valued above all else maximum productivity, and such a creed was for me doubly reassuring because it was quantifiable—and hence *knowable*—in a period of great uncertainty" (116).

But change comes to Changez, and it comes in places that far removed from Pakistan, in locations that have felt and resented the sway of U.S. capitalism. The first hint of Changez's unease with his allegiance to the American capitalist mantra comes when he is sitting in a cab in the Philippines, where he has gone to assess the value of a recorded-music business; he stares at the driver in the vehicle that has stopped alongside his cab in a traffic jam, feeling as he does so that he and this stranger share a "Third World sensibility" (Hamid 2007, 67), which accentuates for him the *foreignness* of the colleague who is seated next to him, this colleague with his "fair hair and light eyes [and] his oblivious immersion in the minutiae of our work" (67).

A more direct exposé of Changez's prostitution of himself to the dictates of the American money apparatus takes place in Chile. He has been sent to Valparaiso to analyze the financial viability of a publishing company. The chief of the publishing company, Juan-Bautista, loves books and knows something about poetry. He arouses in Changez a slow pride in the poets of Pakistan, one of whom is related to Changez. Juan-Bautista makes no secret of his disdain for Changez's job as he tells him that Changez has unthinkingly allowed himself to become an instrument of Western capitalist powers. In a fascinating comparison of Changez with the janissaries (warriors) of the Ottoman Empire, Juan-Bautista issues Changez an indirect challenge:

Have you heard of the janissaries? . . . They were Christian boys . . . captured by the Ottomans and trained to be soldiers in a Muslim army, at that time the greatest army in the world. They were ferocious and utterly loyal: they had fought to erase their own civilization, so they had nothing else to turn to. . . . The janissaries were always taken in childhood. It would have been far more difficult for them to devote themselves to their adopted empire, you see, if they had memories they could not forget. (Hamid 2007, 151)

Changez resigns his job at his Manhattan firm and returns to Pakistan where, as a professor of finance, he teaches his students to resist the pressures of American capitalism.

The novel begins with Changez in Pakistan, recounting to an unnamed interlocutor the sequence of events that has brought him back to his birth country. This interlocutor is most likely an American intelligence officer who has been sent to Pakistan to investigate the teachings of this "radical" professor. The entire novel unfolds as a monologue that Changez delivers. Hamid explains this narrative device as his attempt at countering the dominance of the U.S. voice on the global stage, particularly in matters related to terrorism (Gross 2007). What we have in *The Reluctant Fundamentalist* is the United States (through its agent) confined to the position of listener, forced to heed the discourse of other nations and to understand their urgencies. In Changez, we have an individual who moves voluntarily from being enthralled with the economic culture of the United States to adopting a position of deliberate dissatisfaction. Only when he assumes this perspective does he become aware of the seductions that have overcome him and prevented him from recognizing the depredations of the lives of others. His empathy is now channeled toward those countries that are caught in the web of the imperialist and capitalist ambitions of the United States. From the United States, he expects no empathy, no understanding.[12]

Changez's narrative voice is confident and self-assured. He gives his interlocutor no opportunity to speak. This is Changez's show, and he manages it superbly. The United States would do well to study Changez's change of heart carefully as it pursues relentlessly its indefinite "war on terror." Widespread antipathy and suspicion by the United States can produce only temporary and limited gains, at best. Worse, it alienates those who were once the country's acolytes and its enthusiastic champions.

2

Deserving Empathy?

Renouncing American Citizenship

I am prepared to fight until doomsday on these cases.

—WAYNE COLLINS, written response to a list of questions
from the Tule Lake renunciants

In the short period between December 18, 1944, and mid-January 1945, several thousand—5,589—U.S. citizens of Japanese descent renounced their citizenship. Most of them were among the internee population at the Tule Lake internment facility in Newell, California, which had by this time become generally known to Americans as the camp to which "disloyal" Japanese Americans were sent (those who had answered "No" to questions 27 and 28 of the loyalty questionnaire that all internees over age eighteen were required to complete in 1943).[1] Shortly after this act of giving up their U.S. citizenship, most of the renunciants regretted their action and wished to rescind their renunciation. The government, not surprisingly, would not accept their change of mind, observing that their initial act had been voluntary and therefore constitutional. To complicate the situation, when the war with Japan ended (in August 1945), the renunciants found themselves in danger of being deported as "alien enemies." The mass deportation would most likely have taken place had it not been for the intervention of a San Francisco attorney, Wayne Mortimer Collins, who first put a halt to the deportation proceedings (Christgau 2009, 167–168) and then went on to engage in a prolonged battle with the government to restore the citizenship of the renunciants. It took Wayne Collins twenty-three years, from 1945 until 1968, to resolve the cases of the Japanese American renunciants (he died in 1974, at age seventy-four). He was able to restore the citizenship of most of the petitioners (Muller [2006] writes that "of the 5,409 Japanese American renunciants who petitioned to restore their citizenship, 4,987—ninety-two percent—were successful").[2] During the nearly quarter-century legal battle with the government, he had little material support from any other organization; almost entirely on his own, he brought hope to thousands of renunciants and potential deportees who despaired that their lives would forever have no significance and who feared that they would have to live without purpose, excluded from full political membership in the United States and viewed with disdain in Japan. (The two individuals who provided Collins crucial help were Tule Lake internee (but not renunciant) Tetsujiro (Tex) Nakamura and attorney Theodore Tamba.) One grateful renunciant (who was among those whose cases had an early and a happy resolution in a restoration of citizenship) wrote to Collins in a letter dated February 7, 1946, "Today, my once troubled mind brims with boundless happiness—the surge of which comes from a greateful [sic] heart, for a work well done. Fortunately we have regained to some extent a new lease on life, a concession made possible by the ingenuity and invincible principle and a generous heart."[3]

In this chapter on Collins, I attempt to understand the circumstances influencing his empathetic perspective and his tenacious dedication to the cause of the renunciants through more than two decades of struggle. My discussion addresses itself to the question "What drives certain individuals to immerse themselves in the situation of others, even when the benefits to themselves are not obvious or immediate, even when they are made vulnerable by their pursuit of these causes, and even when they are displaced from positions of comfort?" Two authors have dedicated their books to Collins. Michi Weglyn's *Years of Infamy* (1976) honors Collins as the person "who did more to correct a democracy's mistake than any other one person." Donald E. Collins (no relation to the attorney) dedicates his book *Native American Aliens* (1985) to multiple people, among whom is Wayne Collins. In his preface, Donald Collins says of Wayne Collins, "without his dedication to civil liberties and perseverance in the face of government and American Civil Liberties Union opposition, many renunciants might never have remained in their native country, or regained their American citizenship" (4). Donald Collins's book focuses exclusively on the renunciation, reconstructing and explaining the circumstances that led to it. He gives us a glimpse into the strategy that Wayne Collins employed, first to prevent the deportation of the renunciants and then to rescind their renunciations and restore their citizenship. Weglyn's book is broader in scope and covers the entire internment period, with the renunciation occupying one chapter of a larger study. I use the work of Weglyn and Donald Collins and a host of other internment scholars (including Roger Daniels, Judy Kutulas, John Christgau, Eric Muller, and Peter Irons) to contextualize my reading of archival documents housed in the Wayne Collins Collection at the Bancroft Library at the University of California, Berkeley. His correspondence and legal briefs give us some insight into the nature of his empathy and help us understand his dedication to the cause of Japanese American renunciants and Issei internees.

Empathy, as I argue in the Introduction, is a complex emotion, whose emergence can be neither predicted nor formulaically enabled. In the case of Collins, it is impossible to ascertain precisely what predisposed him to become the kind of lawyer he was, a person whose contributions would be so gratefully recognized and textually memorialized. His pre-internment practice was not in any way extraordinary; perhaps one might characterize it as being rather insignificant. Peter Irons (1983) notes that when Collins first got involved in the legal challenges to the internment through being recruited to argue the Fred Korematsu case (see later in this chapter for a deeper discussion of Collins's involvement in *Korematsu*), he was a lawyer whose practice was "so marginal that he shared a secretary with the firm from which he rented a room" (117). Despite the "marginality" of his practice, however, Collins had a remarkably feisty spirit. He was a man of fierce principles, keenly committed to the ideals of equal justice and civil liberties. He was a member of the Northern California chapter of the American Civil Liberties Union (ACLU) and, as Nakamura remembers, often did pro bono work for the prisoners at Alcatraz.[4] Therefore, when Fred Korematsu was arrested and placed in prison for refusing to comply with the evacuation orders, Ernest Besig, director of the Northern California ACLU, approached Collins to take the case.[5] Perhaps through his work on the *Korematsu* case, Collins came to recognize something about what it means to be a person of Japanese descent in the United States, and to appreciate the difficulties of fully plumbing such notions as *loyalty* and *allegiance* and *culture*. At any rate, Collins's defense of the renunciants, which he began after his involvement in the *Korematsu* case ended (in December 1944), was grounded in a richly nuanced understanding of what the Issei (immigrant generation) and Nisei (U.S.-born Japanese Americans) endured through the official processes of pre-internment and internment orders. This deeply textured empathy was accompanied by a powerful belief that U.S. citizenship is a gift beyond measure and therefore worth fighting to repossess. This fierce faith in the value of U.S. citizenship (which I explore later in the chapter) may explain why he became so doggedly invested in helping the renunciants recover it. Perhaps he believed that the only way he could prove the intrinsic value of the prize was through the actions aimed at regaining it; in other words, to demonstrate the desirability of the object of pursuit in the unrelenting and unwavering dedication to the *process* of pursuit.

The length of Collins's commitment to the renunciants and the staggering number of cases that he took on are remarkable. The labor that he invested for the renunciants and the seemingly inexhaustible attention he gave to their cases did not diminish with time. Especially after 1951, when the government won a partial victory in its refusal to summarily rescind the renunciations, with Judge Denman of the Ninth Circuit Court of Appeals ruling that the renunciants would have to prove by individual affidavit that their renunciations had not been voluntary,[6] Collins (as Nakamura remembers it) must have written about ten thousand affidavits.[7] (Approximately 3,300 renunciants had to file individual affidavits; many of these affidavits went through three or four iterations, with Collins revising them to ensure that they addressed and refuted in proper fashion the government's arguments for upholding the renunciation.) He transformed himself into an affidavit-generating machine, and through his inexhaustible and obdurate confrontation with the government he "wore down" the structures of power. The magnitude of his contribution to the Japanese American community justifies, I would argue, this chapter's focus on Wayne Collins.

At least one other lawyer, A. L. Wirin, of the Southern California ACLU, worked on renunciant cases. But Wirin handled only three renunciant test cases (Kutulas 1998, 228–229). He did try to secure more cases, but the Tule Lake renunciants were suspicious of his full understanding of and commitment to their cause. Peter Irons (1983) observes that approximately forty lawyers were involved in cases having to do with the Japanese American community and the challenges to the evacuation and internment orders (347). Though Collins is celebrated for his work on the renunciant cases, it is important to remember that he was also centrally involved in the important Supreme Court case of Fred Korematsu. His experience on the *Korematsu* case may have taught him something about what it takes to do battle with the government.

I engage three broad themes: (1) Wayne Collins and his savage criticism of the government and people in power, and the relationship between his "rhetorical excesses" and the strategies of empathetic response; (2) the duress argument Collins employed as a legal maneuver, and the implications of this approach for the individual agency of Japanese Americans and for the value of citizenship; and (3) Collins's sensitivity to the feelings of his Japanese American clients, and his ability to understand something fundamental about the effects of arbitrary power on people's emotional and mental well-being.

Collins was outspoken in his criticism of the people in power who created the circumstances that, according to him, compelled so many thousands of internees to give up their American citizenship. The board of the national ACLU and the Japanese American Citizens League (JACL), organizations that one would expect to be sympathetic to the renunciants, were, in fact, hesitant to come to their defense. Collins's early support of the renunciants was, thus, noteworthy, given the reluctance of organizations that ought to have leaped to their defense. As I discuss later, the national ACLU and the JACL had different reasons for their unenergetic and lackluster response to the renunciants, but they both shared a wariness of appearing to be too vocal in their advocacy of individuals who had "voluntarily" given up the privilege of being U.S. citizens. Where the ACLU and JACL saw "disloyal" individuals, Collins saw circumstances and forces that left the individuals no choice other than to renounce. "Duress" was the argument that Collins would pursue in his fight to reinstate the citizenship of the renunciants. They were under pressure, and this pressure led to their act of renouncing. Collins emphasized that the duress was caused by the government; in this position, he differed from Wirin, who, though he too argued duress in the few cases that he took up, did not directly accuse the government of having created the conditions that led to duress. Wirin placed direct blame on the pro-Japanese groups within the camps and their strong-arm tactics of physical and psychological duress. But Collins saw these groups—their emergence and their escalating influence—as an indirect outgrowth of the government's failure to protect the internees. Nakamura remembers that Collins firmly believed that when the government evacuated and interned the Japanese Americans, it became responsible for ensuring the well-being of the internees.[8] Collins's view was that the government should have arrested and immediately curtailed the influence of the extremist groups in the camp, rather than letting them operate with impunity. But Collins's accusation of the government went far beyond the mismanagement of the camps themselves; he condemned the entire series of orders and events that stemmed from Executive Order 9066, and he was vocal in his view that governmental duress was cumulative and pervasive.

Duress may have been the legally pragmatic approach to follow, but it was also empathetically accurate. Though one may argue that Collins's emphasis on duress led to his envisioning the renunciants as helpless and fragile and therefore without individual agency, nonetheless he deserves credit for having fathomed the depth of the renunciants' confused state of mind and for his having the courage and perspicacity to lay the blame for their confusion on the government. Whether the reasons for advancing the duress argument were practical, self-serving, or altruistic, they undeniably reveal that Collins understood the psychological impact on people when they have been subjected to "arbitrary and capricious"[9] manifestations of power.

His was an empathy infused with anger, and he never let up on his critique of the government and did not ease the pressure on its representatives to acknowledge its culpability. In 1959, when the Justice Department had restored the citizenship of most of the renunciants and was taking credit for its ability to correct its mistakes, Collins was alone in his outrage of this misrepresentation of the true circumstances. Three hundred and fifty renunciants (all Kibei—i.e., U.S.-born Japanese Americans who were sent to Japan to be educated) were denied the restoration of their citizenship; Collins vowed not to give up. He was determined not to let the government persist either in its self-congratulation for the favorable resolutions or in its denigration of the reputation of the individuals whose cases had been unfavorably decided (Weglyn 1976, 263–264).

A cynic might say that Collins had grandiose notions of himself as the lone savior. He might have believed that without him, the renunciants would most likely have been deported and lost their citizenship irretrievably. Perhaps another reason for his involvement was that he wished to vindicate his loss in the *Korematsu* case (discussed later) or perhaps reestablish his legal credibility after the slight of his having been forced to share the Supreme Court spotlight with Charles Horsky, who was brought in to take the lead in *Korematsu* at the insistence of the national ACLU, which felt that Collins lacked the legal finesse to argue the case (Irons 1983, 259–262, 267–268). A third reason may have been his genuine faith in the integrity and value of the U.S. Constitution, which he wished to uphold. A fourth may have been his great distrust of arbitrary and unchecked power of all kinds and his refusal to accept the dictates of government without question; and, finally, one cannot ignore his absolute abhorrence of racism, evident in his biting attacks on General John DeWitt of the Western Defense Command, on whose authority and influence President Roosevelt proclaimed the order that led to the evacuation of people of Japanese descent from the West Coast and their subsequent internment in ten concentration camps.

Collins's commitment to the renunciants at first glance may seem to be contained within a problematic framework of exclusive attachment and loyalty to *one* nation. Especially when viewed from the present embrace of multicultural and postcolonial identities (with their incorporation of hybrid subjectivities and multiple cultural and national influences),[10] Collins's understanding of citizenship appears rigid and narrow. However, a closer examination of his ideas yields a more complex picture.

In September 1967, Collins received an invitation from Wesley Doi of the JACL to a banquet honoring the Issei for their contributions to the community. Collins was invited as a person who had helped the community immeasurably. Collins ignored the invitation and then, after the banquet had taken place, sent an explosive response that explained his position.[11]

The JACL, during the prewar and internment years, was most concerned about securing for the Japanese American community the goodwill and trust of the majority culture. Toward that end, they were overly cooperative with governmental authority and adopted a problematically "placating stance" (Bow 2001, 55) and "promoted Nisei assimilation and did not oppose the internment program" (Kutulas 1998, 212). The JACL urged the Japanese American community to demonstrate loyalty to the U.S. war effort (Hayashi 2004, 55, 69, 73) by obediently going to the camps and showing that they would do whatever it took to prove that they had the best interests of the United States at heart. The organization also did not support Nisei resisters of the war and was strong in its condemnation of them and the renunciants (Ngai 2004, 173, 197). Thus, when Collins received the invitation in 1967 to attend the JACL banquet to honor Issei and their contributions to the community, he erupted.

In his scathing reply to Doi, dated October 20, 1967, Collins writes: "There are no such entities as 'Japanese-Americans.' That hyphenated name consists of two names which are antithetical. One cannot be a Japanese and at the same time be an American. One cannot be an American and at the same time be a Japanese. Those who were born in this country are 'Americans.'" Clearly, Collins's sentiment strikes one as hopelessly outdated today. However, he was writing before the impact of the end of many colonial regimes could be felt, and the resulting diasporas and hybrid identities of many postcolonial subjects and the inherited memories of their American-born offspring would become evident.[12] His understanding of identity is centered in the single nation-state and also in the idealistic belief that the United States is the exceptional home for all those who seek new lives and new identities.

But his idealistic belief was wide in its embrace. Everyone who is born here is a full American, he insists, regardless of race. What is particularly interesting is that for him citizenship appears to be less a demonstration of performance or action (no act can strip one of citizenship, and there is nothing that one has to do to *prove* oneself worthy of citizenship) than a function of birth.[13] For Collins, the Kibei were every bit as American as the Nisei, and legally of course they are. But the Kibei were frequently distrusted because of their greater emotional connection (compared with the Nisei) to Japan, where they were sent to spend the formative years of their life, becoming educated in the ways of Japanese culture. To Collins, however, the Kibei were American, and his embrace of them was just as fervent as his embrace of the Nisei. In a 1959 communication to Michi Weglyn, in which he rages against the government's refusal to restore the citizenship of some renunciants, Collins voices his admiration for the Kibei and condemns the government for its rejection of them:

> The Justice Department sought to whitewash its own reputation by persisting in blackening those of young Americans *who had courage enough to stand up and fight for their rights*—Americans who would not brook insults forever. Practically all the young men denied their citizenship rights were Kibei. Their mistreatment is unprecedented in American history. (Qtd. in Weglyn 1976, 264; emphasis added)

Collins pays moving tribute to the Issei, as well, in his response to Doi's invitation. His deep understanding of what it means to be Japanese in the United States is cross-generational, and it reveals his capacity for envisioning the dreams of immigrants: "The pioneer Issei need no honor to be bestowed on them by the JACL for their contribution to the progress of their own children. . . . The arrival of the Issei in this country was a signal honor to our country and our people. . . . What they have done for this country is an honor to this country. This country owes them a debt it cannot repay."[14]

He is unrestrained in his criticism of the *people* of the United States for their indifference to the suffering of the Japanese American community and for having allowed so gross an injustice to be perpetrated on the community. "Had a representative portion of our people voiced immediate protest against the evacuation and, perhaps, had the JACL, as the pretended spokesman for the affected people, mustered sufficient courage to oppose the uprooting and imprisonment of these innocents in those concentration-camp-prisons the government would have halted its criminal action against them." With his characteristically hyperbolic invective, he declares that he does "not intend to forget or forgive the government oppressors for what was done to these innocent people under the guise of wartime military necessity." Nor will he forget that the "population at large was apathetic to the suffering it imposed on them" and that "the JACL was indifferent to what happened to them and that it did nothing to help them." He ends his letter by saying that the kindest thing that the JACL could do would be to "disband" and "disperse."[15]

Though his ethical and compassionate empathy for the Issei, Nisei, and Kibei is admirable, one could argue that Collins is insufficiently empathetic to the JACL. Their members, too, were victims, in a sense, of the racism of the times. Their overcompensation of loyal behavior could be seen as the result of the expectations placed on them to demonstrate their loyalty in unmistakable terms (see more in this regard in the discussion later in this chapter). Collins, however, saw them as having betrayed the Japanese American community and as having ill-understood the difficult position of the Issei. Perhaps it was the self-righteousness of the JACL members that he found objectionable—their strength in numbers should have led to their lending support for all members of their community. The JACL did write in support of Korematsu to repudiate the implications of the DeWitt report that Japanese Americans could never be trusted to be loyal to the United States, so it is perhaps unfair to condemn the organization unequivocally, the way that Collins does. But his outrage and invective in the response to Doi are typical of his quick temper.

Ability to "Out-Curse" Anyone

Shoshana Felman (2002) describes the function of law: "In its pragmatic role as guardian of society against irregularity, derangement, disorganization, unpredictability, or any form of irrational or uncontrollable disorder, the law, indeed, has no choice but to guard against equivocations, ambiguities, obscurities, confusions, and loose ends" (95). The law relies on "classifying logic" and on turning confusion and excess "into the technical, procedural coherence of the trial" (95). For law to be effective and to ensure the arrival at appropriate resolutions, questions of fairness and justice must be engaged dispassionately and with careful attention to reason and judgment. But, as Felman acknowledges, the decorum of law can frequently inhibit it from responding with sufficient alacrity and passion to the anguished call of human distress. The calculated and measured response of the law can come too late, be inadequate, and fail to rescue the individual or group from the numbing existence of a life lived in resignation. Joseph Slaughter (2007) makes a similar observation: the act of "legislating" is similar to the act of knowing in its "feeble ability to translate knowledge into outrage, action, or even acknowledgment" (11). This section focuses on Collins's outrage and his resulting inability (or perhaps conscious refusal, if we are to give him the benefit of the matter) to hew to the expectations of courtroom discourse in the *Korematsu* case. It is worth asking whether in his untempered articulation of rage against racism he was being productively empathetic to the Japanese American community or destructively ineffective in legal terms. A related question to ask is whether Collins could have produced any kind of positive outcome in the *Korematsu* Supreme Court case regardless of how he delivered his discourse.

Perhaps the point is less whether he should have tempered his rhetoric (even were he able to), and more that we should consider the possible functions his fierce critique against racism fulfilled. Might it have served as a valuable announcement to the Issei and Nisei that there were members of the legal profession who would not hide behind legalisms and who would demand that those in power be honest about their own attitudes and tendencies? Was his diatribe against General DeWitt a form of self-promotion, or was it an attempt to remind the court of the protections of the Fourteenth and Fifth Amendments? It is unlikely that Collins expected to gain points with his outbursts, because he knew that his style went against conventional discourse. Yet even if he persisted in his style because of his fierce belief that the court needed to be jolted out of its tendency to engage questions of law (and thereby ignore the complex terrain of human distress), his approach did not achieve the desired objective.

"Collins was a fiery, volatile lawyer with a quick temper, who was proud of his ability to 'out-curse anyone'" (D. Collins 1985, 4). Peter Irons (1983) says of Collins that he was something of a loose cannon and tended to employ a shotgun style of argument in court; he was a "lone wolf" (117). Daniel Tritter (2005) characterizes him as "an eloquent, if somewhat garrulous, solo practitioner" (271). He was irascible and tempestuous, opinionated and blunt, but he was dogged and obdurate and did not take kindly to being given orders by the national ACLU executive board. He was precisely the kind of fearless, supremely indomitable person the renunciants would need as their champion for the restoration of citizenship. When Tex Nakamura was asked as recently as September 2009 by interviewers Tom Ikeda and Barbara Takei why so many Japanese Americans would trust their lives and their futures to Wayne Collins, he replied, "One of the renunciants said he was half crazy, but perhaps we needed someone like him to fight the government."[16]

Many of Collins's professional colleagues considered his style abrasive and likely to jeopardize the chances for a favorable outcome in *Korematsu* at all levels of the judicial system (beginning with the district court and ending at the Supreme Court) if he were permitted to take the lead in the case (Irons 1983, 105–310, passim). Daniel Tritter's (2005) analysis of the Supreme Court dialogue gives us a good idea of the language that Collins chose to employ. Not entirely unfavorably disposed to Collins's style, Tritter speaks of "the strong medicine of Collins's rhetoric" (283) that invites "poetic analysis" (284). His diction, as the trial progressed, "mounted in ferocity," says Tritter (289), with his criticism of DeWitt escalating in intensity and concluding with "potent invective" (290), as he described DeWitt as a "military commander who cannot or will not endeavor to distinguish between a loyal citizen and a hostile alien" and who "lacks perception as well as judgment . . . [and] is a poor gardener who doesn't perceive the difference between a native plant and an alien weed" (qtd. in Tritter 2005, 290). "General DeWitt uprooted the whole garden," said Collins (qtd. in Tritter 2005, 291) and by doing so revealed the "constitutional infirmity of a few professional military minds" (qtd. in Tritter 2005, 291) who cannot see people as humans and think of them only as "targets."

Irons's account of the discussions preceding who should be lead defense in *Korematsu* reveals the nature of the misgivings that fellow lawyers had about Collins. His excessive and unmasked contempt for officials in power and his lack of restraint in his criticism of authority frequently worked against him professionally. His legal colleagues saw him as driven by unchecked passion rather than reason, and felt that he would be unable to operate within the framework of legal precedent and analysis. In the amicus brief he wrote on behalf of the Northern California ACLU for the *Hirabayashi* Supreme Court case, Collins gave Roger Baldwin of the national ACLU board plenty of cause for worry. "In language more suited to a soapbox diatribe than a legal brief, Collins excoriated General DeWitt and bullied the justices of the Supreme Court. Comparing DeWitt to Attila the Hun, Genghis Khan, and Hitler, in imposing 'brutish slavery' on the Japanese Americans, Collins painted the evacuation program as 'a cruelty that evokes horror and beggars description.' . . . Any member of the court who voted for 'this plot to wreck the lives of these innocent citizens,' Collins warned, 'will forever be enshrined in the hall of infamy as a symbol of bigotry, intolerance, and oppression'" (qtd. in Irons 1983, 194).

The national office of the ACLU did not want Collins as the lead attorney in the *Korematsu* case. The board felt that he lacked focus to address the judges' questions of law and might lose his train of thought. Collins could not maintain the necessary courtroom discourse of dispassionate logic and legal reasoning, and plunged instead into a cascade of verbal accusation and feverish attack. Tritter (2005) concludes that Justice Black, who wrote the majority opinion for the Supreme Court striking down the *Korematsu* challenge and acquiescing to the dictates of military necessity, was unmoved by Collins and may even have been negatively influenced by the tenor of Collins's language. Referring to Collins's linguistic passion as "an admixture of garbled mythology, mixed metaphor, and clichéd concluding diction" (291) and contrasting it to the government's argument, which was "merely a recitation of authority from Constitution, statute, executive order, military orders, and proclamations by DeWitt, all avowed to be valid" (291), Tritter notes that in his final decision for the court, Justice Black "turned a deaf ear to the passionate Collins rhetoric [and] rejected the accusations of racial prejudice as part of the process, instead holding that the convictions should stand on the basis of our being at war with Japan" (294).

Irons (1983) observes that in his ninety-eight-page brief to the Supreme Court, "Collins substituted excoriation of General DeWitt for a reasoned challenge to the legality of DeWitt's evacuation orders. . . . Collins equated him with Mussolini and Hitler in the 'barbarianism' with which citizens had been 'driven from their homes like cattle' and imprisoned in 'concentration camps'" (302). He concluded his brief by issuing an unusual and "impolitic" challenge to the Supreme Court: "General DeWitt let Terror out to plague these citizens but closed the lid on the Pandora box and left Hope to smother. It is your duty to raise the lid and revive Hope for these, our people, who have suffered at the hands of one of our servants. Do this speedily as the law commands you. History will not forget your opinion herein" (qtd. in Irons 1983, 303).

Perhaps Collins's extremely personal attack against General DeWitt was repugnant to the Supreme Court justices, and perhaps a tempered criticism of DeWitt's views on Japanese Americans might have been more effective in prompting the justices to question the validity of DeWitt's assertions about the inherent disloyalty and unassimilability of Japanese Americans. But such speculation may be worthless. Charles Horsky, who was the lead lawyer in *Korematsu* and who brought to the argument a more subdued tone, though no less pointed in its argumentative thrust, was not successful either in bringing the majority of justices to vote in favor of Korematsu to rule that his imprisonment for failing to report for evacuation was a betrayal of his equal protection and due process rights. DeWitt's report carried a great deal of sway with the justices, as Irons exhaustively documents, and any argument against it was seen as undermining the authority of the president and the military during a time of grave national danger.

The "suppression of evidence" (Irons 1983, 186–218) by the government lawyers on the trustworthiness and loyalty to the United States of most Japanese Americans resulted in the justices' being overly influenced by DeWitt's perspectives. Viewed in this light, Collins's obsession with discrediting DeWitt does not seem so irrational. He did shoot the ammunition where it deserved to be directed. The Supreme Court decisions in *Hirabayashi* and *Korematsu* were all predicated on believing the claims that DeWitt made and taking them as fact. So Collins, impolitic though he may have been, nonetheless was accurate in his accusations. Legal scholars Natsu Taylor Saito (2010) and Jerry Kang (2004) believe that the majority of the Supreme Court justices were themselves guilty of racism (though not of the overt and crass kind manifested by DeWitt), and this perspective may have prevented them from fully engaging Collins's loud and repeated accusations of DeWitt for his racism.

I do not mean to suggest that a change in Collins's style would have resulted in a different verdict in the *Korematsu* case. The Supreme Court justices chose to focus on extremely narrow aspects of all the signature cases and did not take up the broad question of the constitutionality of the executive order itself. Eric Muller (2006) and Jerry Kang (2004) both deplore the piecemeal nature of the government's "discriminatory and repressive program" (Muller 2006, 68). Muller (2006) makes the point that the Issei and Nisei felt the force of curfew, exclusion, and detention orders in quick succession, where the cumulative impact of these separate orders was a cruel truncation of their lives. "Yet the Supreme Court chose to test the lawfulness of the government's program in pieces—first the curfew in *Hirabayashi*, then exclusion in *Korematsu*, and finally detention in *Ex parte Endo*" (Muller 2006, 68). The Supreme Court justices ultimately based their decisions on a narrow feature of a complex series of official orders. They avoided having to discuss the constitutionality of Executive Order 9066 and the subsequent removal of people of Japanese descent (citizens and noncitizens) to the interior, away from the West Coast. Jerry Kang (2004) observes that "this segmentation technique . . . allowed the Court to obscure its own agency and thereby minimize responsibility for its choice" (955). Wayne Collins is notable for his scathing attack of the judiciary, refusal to capitulate to the authority of the Roosevelt presidency, and rejection of the narrative of military necessity.

The *Amistad* Detour

It is worth juxtaposing Collins's unrestrained and impolitic courtroom discourse against that of John Quincy Adams in the *Amistad* case,[17] so as to understand the paradoxical relationship between empathetic sentiment and empathetic action, particularly in the realm of law. Patricia Roberts-Miller (2002), in her analysis of the oblique and strategic approach that John Quincy Adams employed in his Supreme Court argument for the 1841 *Amistad* case, observes that Adams "succeeded in freeing the kidnapped Africans precisely because [he] did *not* make it a case about slavery" (22), and made the "case one of judicial, rather than African, independence." While conceding that his tactic was successful and beneficial to the imprisoned Africans, Roberts-Miller wonders what that kind of strategy teaches us about the value of "principled dissent and sincere outrage" (23). It is the phrase *principled dissent and sincere outrage* that I am most interested in as it applies to Collins, whose language in all his correspondence and arguments relating to the Japanese American cases—particularly *Korematsu* and the renunciants—is brimming with "sincere outrage" at the violation of principles that he considered sacrosanct.

Adams won the case for the Africans and saved them from certain death. The Spanish monarch claimed them as the property of Spain and demanded that they be returned to Spain, where they would certainly be executed for having killed their Spanish slaver-kidnappers. The case had been decided in favor of the Africans in the lower courts, but at each stage the Van Buren government had appealed the ruling in an attempt to placate the Spanish monarch and maintain good relations with her. Finally, the abolitionists approached Adams, now in retirement, to take up the argument for the Africans at the Supreme Court.

Roberts-Miller (2002) concedes that had Adams attacked the institution of slavery, he would likely have lost the case, and the Africans would have been turned over to the Spanish government. Some of the Supreme Court justices were slave owners themselves and others, though not slave owners, were not strictly antislavery either, because of their desire to keep the Union intact. Thus, paradoxically, Adams had to empathize with the Supreme Court justices' position—their "anti-anti-slavery" perspective (12) and their fierce desire for judicial independence from the executive—in order to achieve an outcome that gave to the Africans their freedom and personhood. Roberts-

Miller acknowledges the effectiveness of Adams's strategically employed rhetoric of conciliation and "decorum," but she articulates "a terrible dilemma in regard to rhetoric," namely, that in order to be effective, it is often necessary to "mute one's outrage and assuage and pacify unjust passions and outrageous prejudices" (22).

Roberts-Miller (2002) cites Adams as saying in his *Lectures* that "effective rhetoric depends on seeming to your audience to have their best interest to heart. It depends, hence, on decorum and sympathy, on remaining practical" (23). Adams rejects an unrestrained and nonstrategic show of passion: "When the ebullience of passion burst in peevish recrimination of the audience themselves, when a speaker sallies forth, armed with insult and outrage for his instruments of persuasion, . . . this Quixotism of rhetoric must eventually terminate like all other modern knight errantry and that the fury must always be succeeded by the impotence of the passions" (qtd. in Roberts-Miller 2002, 15). It is not that Adams attacks emotions per se, but it is emotion delivered in a particular way that he cautions against. "One can try to make one's audience feel outrage, but not by attacking them directly, and generally through appealing to their sympathy" (Roberts-Miller 2002, 15).

Adams operated from a perspective of empathy for the Supreme Court justices, some of whom were slave owners, by not taking up the abolitionists' perspective on the moral evil of slavery; rather he focused on the arbitrary exercise of executive power and the appearance that a capitulation to the dictates of the Spanish monarch would give about the independence of the U.S. judiciary. Roberts-Miller recognizes the utility of such an approach and realizes that it resulted in success for the Africans. But, she insists, the absence of a strong dissent delays the overthrow of unjust structures and practices, in this case slavery and the trafficking of the bodies of Africans. She observes, with no small frustration, that when there is no room for outrage in a setting where power is being deliberated, then what exactly is the value of a carefully delivered rhetorical strategy? Is outrage always injudicious in a court of law?

Collins was known for his "excessive" and flamboyant language, and it did not endear him to those he criticized or to individuals who felt that the tone of his criticism was actually counterproductive to those whom he wished to help. He gives free expression to his disdain and contempt for officials who, in his opinion, abused their power and acted on their racism. His is an utterance of excoriation, employed in the service of the Japanese American community. He was incensed by official positions and proclamations, and he made no secret of his view. The hyperbolic quality of the accusations he made of the government and its renunciation program, while essentially accurate in spirit, sometimes were factually untenable. For instance, in a nineteen-page letter to Attorney General Tom Clark on November 1, 1945, he observed, "These renunciants whom I represent have submitted to gross indignities and suffered greater loss of rights and liberties than any other group of persons during the entire history of the nation."[18] Though one must admire his bold championing of the renunciants, it is hardly accurate to say that their injustice is greater than, say, the injustice suffered by the slaves or the disenfranchised Native American populations. He was, however, not one to contain his anger.

Lone Champion

It is no exaggeration to say that Wayne Collins almost single-handedly labored for the renunciants. Though the San Francisco branch of the ACLU believed in the legitimacy of his efforts, and the director of the chapter, Ernest Besig, lent him emotional support, Collins worked independently so as to avoid having to heed the dictates of the national ACLU board. The national office did not take kindly to his maverick ways and his insubordinate character and, in fact, discouraged Besig from aiding Collins. Peter Irons and Judy Kutulas provide the fullest explanation for why the executive board of the national ACLU was reluctant to come to Collins's aid or even to express support for his efforts to restore the citizenship of the renunciants. Kutulas (2006) notes, "When national officers considered internment, they saw potentially thorny policy questions; when the West Coast affiliates considered the practice, they saw people in need, and their passion spilled over into their actions" (116). "Local people confronted what East Coasters almost deliberately tried to avoid seeing: the human costs of internment" (117).

Kutulas (1998) makes a strong case for the Northern California chapter's "quest of autonomy" (201), ascribing to its members an independence of spirit that was lacking in other chapters. Besig was director of the Northern California chapter of the ACLU, and he made no secret of his disdain for Roger Baldwin's capitulation to the Roosevelt administration. The argument the national office offered was that with friends in high places they could more easily ensure the humane treatment of the internees (202). Kutulas points out that to the members of the San Francisco ACLU, Japanese Americans were not abstractions who could be easily misrepresented and misconstrued as the enemy. They knew that the anti-Japanese sentiments of the West Coast "came from nativist and agricultural groups whose motives were hardly war-related" (212). Ernest Besig was Collins's staunch supporter in his refusal to capitulate to the dictates of the national ACLU, perhaps because like Collins he saw what was at stake in human pain and human dignity. Besig and Collins had little patience for the national ACLU board's appeasement of the Roosevelt administration (Kutulas 2006, 113–126).

In a March 9, 1946, letter to Miles E. Cary, principal of McKinley High School in Honolulu and an individual sympathetic to the renunciants, Collins voices his unequivocal contempt for the national ACLU and its Southern California branch:

The only American Civil Liberties Union that has exhibited any interest in the preservation of the rights of these mistreated renunciants is the American Civil Liberties Union of Northern California. . . . That office, from 1942 steadily has supported me wholeheartedly in the test suits brought to invalidate the vicious evacuation program and the subsequent detention of innocent persons. The American Civil Liberties Union of New York, a corporation of which Mr. Roger N. Baldwin is director, has steadily opposed these cases and, until recently, exhibited no interest whatsoever in the rights of these persons who renounced their United States nationality even though it knew the renunciations were the products of governmental duress and the duress of groups and gangs which were permitted to operate in Tule Lake under the eyes of the WRA [War Relocation Authority] officials.

. . . I assure that there is no genuine American Civil Liberties Union in the United States save and except the American Civil Liberties Union of Northern California.[19]

Kutulas (1998) writes that though a more supportive national ACLU would probably not have affected the outcome of the internment test cases, it would definitely have sent a "message of hope" to the internees (230) and perhaps helped them endure their internment with less despair. The Northern California ACLU, through Besig and Collins, was the internees' steadfast ally, and Collins the internees' and renunciants' unwavering partner. His commitment to them signaled the possibility of a return to pre-internment normalcy and the restoration of their damaged lives. His outrage became the vehicle of their outrage, the conduit through which they poured out their deep sense of betrayal. In a 1973 communication to Michi Weglyn, Collins voices in his characteristic fashion his fury at the indignities that the Japanese American community was made to suffer. His communication to her was written during the Watergate revelations, and he makes this comparison of the malpractices and abuse of power of the Nixon White House with what transpired during the Roosevelt years:

Compared to the past venality of scums, bums, and rascals who shamelessly destroyed reputations and exploited the misery of a people for personal notoriety and gain, and compared to the indecent and lawless connivance which then transpired between the executive and judiciary—when even judges wore epaulets under their robes—today's Watergate shenanigans are just fun and games. That the unconstitutionality of so many of the illegalities perpetrated were [sic] never conceded by the High Bench is scandalous—leaving us only a moment of passion removed from the destruction, once again, of our liberties. Given another manufactured hysteria over 'national security' or some such expediency to justify ends, citizens can again be carted off at the point of bayonets. This is America's evacuation legacy. (Qtd. in Weglyn 1976, 267–268)

The Uncertainty at Tule Lake: Misreadings
and Ambiguous Interpretations

Of the ten internment sites that were set up to segregate people of Japanese descent from the rest of the population during World War II, Tule Lake was identified as housing the most troublesome of the internees. They were, according to the War Relocation Authority (WRA), the most disruptive, the most resistant to the administration's dictates, and the most suspicious of any new proclamation by the government. Tule Lake housed the "no-no boys"— those internees who answered "No" to questions 27 and 28 of the loyalty questionnaire. People had refused to complete the questionnaire or to respond "Yes" to questions 27 and 28 for a variety of reasons. Many did so simply because they did not want to become separated from family members; others did so because they wished to register their anger and bitterness at the suspension of their constitutional rights; still others thought that they would automatically be drafted; and there were some who were clearly pro-Japanese. Among the "no-no" respondents were the obviously politicized internees; they were unwilling to accept the dictates of the government without challenge, and they used their actions (or non-actions) as symbolic protests. The "no-no boys" were deeply stigmatized by the JACL and the community at large (John Okada's eloquent 1957 novel *No-No Boy* portrays the anguish of one such rejected naysayer).

Tule Lake, once it was branded as holding the "disloyal," became a "deeply unhappy, even pathological, place" (Muller 2006, 45). Into this tense space, the government's pronouncements fell with greater ominous import and confused expectations than at other internment locations; because the Tule Lake population was already noteworthy for its radical residents (i.e., internees with a sense of betrayal and extreme bitterness against the United States), their reactions to orders and proclamation were unpredictable.

Amid these conditions, pro-Japanese groups began to assert themselves and exert influence at Tule Lake, unchecked by the WRA officials who ran the camp. The pro-Japanese internees, though in the decided minority, taunted the Nisei who were loyal to the United States with the worthlessness of their national belonging and impressed upon them that they would be better treated and accepted in Japan, provided they declared loyalty to the ancestral country. Over a period of two years, the camp increasingly became a place where pro-Japanese groups were given unfettered means to display their messages and flaunt their influence. Donald Collins (1985) writes that there was open goose-stepping, blowing of bugles, chanting of patriotic pledges to the emperor, and pressure to dress in ways appropriate to Japanese culture. A Japanese school was opened on the camp, and residents were encouraged to send their children to it (78).

Though the monolithic perception of Tule Lake was that it housed the most problematic internees, there was a diversity of sentiments among the camp members. Tule Lake had several categories of residents. There were the Issei, whose emotional connection was not unequivocally either to Japan or the United States but to their American-born children; they had succeeded in making a life for themselves in the United States and were ready to devote the rest of their years to the United States for the sake of their children; but the actions of the U.S. government following the bombing of Pearl Harbor had deeply disillusioned them about their adopted country, and in their disappointment and despair, they had turned to the old and the familiar—the home country of Japan—and saw themselves as returning there. Another group were the Kibei—American-born Japanese who had gone to Japan at a young age in order to be educated there and learn about their ancestral culture, and who had returned to the United States at age seventeen or eighteen to resume life in the land of their birth. A third group constituted the young minor children of Issei, and, finally, there were the adult Nisei, American-born Japanese. There were different degrees of disaffection with the U.S. government among these groups, with the Kibei perhaps the most resentful of their birth government's discriminatory treatment and the most likely to become radicalized against the United States. From this mix arose the political organizing groups who would then come to decree what constituted acceptable displays of loyalty and disloyalty relative to Japan and the United States.

Christgau (1985) explains that the government was eager to rid itself of the obviously pro-Japanese internees at Tule Lake who were causing trouble for the rest of the residents of the camp and performing their disloyalty in a manner that was evident to the nation. By the fall of 1944, these problematic internees "numbered nearly a thousand young men, and news of their pro-Japanese activities was being used as evidence that on the whole the evacuees were disloyal and should not be released" (4). By this time, the Justice Department was becoming less invested in the internment camps, realizing that there was no evidence to support the expected military threat from the Japanese American community and, further, the camps themselves were becoming an administrative nightmare. If the camps were to be closed, then the public on the outside would have to be reassured that the returning internees were trustworthy and loyal. Therefore, the government had to find a way to identify those who were undeniably disloyal and show that it was not releasing these individuals into communities on the West Coast. This imperative led Edward Ennis to come up with a list of reasons for amending the Nationality Act of 1940 so as to make it easy for persons to voluntarily renounce their citizenship if they wished to do so.

Though the amended act was originally intended to create the conditions that would make it possible for the militant pro-Japanese internees to be deported to Japan, in reality its consequences were wider and entirely unanticipated. When the amended act went into effect in July 1944, the expectation was that the extreme pro-Japanese Tule Lake internees would be most eager to renounce their allegiance to the United States, and so ease the way for them to return to Japan. But surprisingly, only 144 internees took up the renunciation offer. Though the pressure exerted by the pro-Japanese groups within the camp

continued to rise and there was much threat of violence against those who continued to express loyalty to the United States, not many camp residents took
the ultimate step of renunciation. However, as Wayne Collins rightly argued,
when once you set a bad thing going, it is extremely difficult to control the
consequences.

The renunciation act got out of hand after December 18, 1944, when word
reached Tule Lake that all the internment camps were scheduled to be closed
within a year and the internees would be forced to return to a hostile world
outside.[20] "Rumors spread that the government would either deport alien parents and separate them from their citizen children or force entire families out
to fend for themselves in hostile white communities. Pro-Japanese forces at
the camp capitalized on these anxieties, ratcheting up the already considerable pressure they were bringing to bear on camp residents to renounce their
citizenship" (Muller 2006, 47).

Contrary to all expectation, the announcement of the closing of the internment camps set off mass renunciations at Tule Lake. Between December 1944
and January 1945, approximately six thousand people at Tule Lake renounced
their citizenship. Donald Collins (1985) writes, "Tuleans, because of their fear
of the 'outside,' believed they had a safe haven in the concentration camp. . . .
As a result, their reaction to the news of the lifting of the exclusion of persons
of Japanese descent from the West Coast was a mixture of surprise, anxiety,
doubt, and shock" (88). They were afraid to return to hate-filled neighbors and
doubtful that they would ever be able to reconstruct their lives. The officials
from the Justice Department who came to Tule Lake to conduct the hearings
for voluntary renunciation complicated the situation greatly by asking, "Do you
want to go out, or do you want to renounce your citizenship?" (qtd. in Christgau
1985, 6). They gave the erroneous impression to the Tule Lake residents that
the only way they could remain within the protective space of the camp was
to renounce. Muller (2006) writes that "Justice Department officials, who had
been expecting a far smaller number of renunciants, were flummoxed by the
volume of requests. Camp administrators reported to a Justice Department
attorney that the atmosphere at Tule Lake was one of hysteria, and that the
camp might more properly be run 'as a species of mental institution'" (47).

When the initial "hysteria" subsided, and the renunciants had a chance to
consider what they had done, they realized the enormity of their action and
wished to undo it. Wayne Collins's initial appearance at Tule Lake had nothing
to do with the renunciants. He had gone there to look into the matter of the
stockade imprisonment of some of the internees; while he was at the camp, he
was approached by renunciants and the immigrant parents of renunciants who
wanted his help in rescinding the renunciations. Collins at first advised them
to contact other lawyers (D. Collins 1985, 113). The renunciants attempted to
enlist the help of other attorneys from all parts of the country, but they had no
success. The attorneys "objected to representing internees of Japanese ancestry
who had renounced their American citizenship, had been branded as disloyal

and subversive, and were being detained as alien enemies" (114). Only Collins agreed to represent them, though he continued to encourage them to find other lawyers. However, a democratically elected Tule Lake Defense Committee agreed that Collins would be their "sole attorney" (115).

The JACL wanted nothing to do with the renunciants. Concerned about further damage to their already fragile citizenship status, the vulnerability of which the internment was resounding proof, they refused to come to the aid of the renunciants, whom they saw as blemishing the image of the Japanese American community. Though as individuals they may have empathized with the confusion and anxiety of the renunciants, as JACL members they could not be seen as officially countenancing "disloyal" Americans who were not able to recognize the value of their citizenship. In their official capacity as representatives of Japanese Americans, they were obliged to perform a flawless citizenship.

A similar imperative guides the official actions and proclamations of the Council on American-Islamic Relations (CAIR) today; it has worked to build the image of a loyal, perfect American Muslim, one who is educated, heterosexual, hardworking, ready to serve in the armed forces, actively participative in time-honored American traditions such as the PTA and T-ball, and resolutely driven to achieve academic and economic success. Critiquing the narrow images of acceptable Muslim American–ness that the public service commercials produced by CAIR construct, Evelyn Alsultany (2007) urges us to resist an uncritical capitulation to the underlying expectations of "perfect Muslim"-ness (a phrase introduced by Mahmood Mamdani) to which Muslims in America are expected to hew.

One could argue that Wayne Collins's harsh criticism of the JACL's refusal to come to the aid of the renunciants was unempathetic to the difficult position in which the organization found itself and its sense of obligation to demonstrate the unassailable loyalty of the Japanese American community. Though he was rightly critical of the government's policies and the apathy or racism of the public that had stood by and done nothing to prevent the lives of Americans of Japanese descent from being needlessly dismantled, in his assault of the JACL he appears to have had scant understanding of the dynamics of power. One's own vulnerability does not necessarily lead to empathy for similarly placed vulnerable others. As Leti Volpp (2000) observes, for already vulnerable groups, the actions of individuals within that group get read as examples of cultural taint; therefore, there is enormous pressure on the members of that group to regulate the behavior of those who threaten to disrupt its image, and to present a public face that is deemed acceptable by the power structure of the dominant ethnic, racial, or religious group. The majority group, or the group in power, is the only group that has the luxury of having the illegal or questionable actions of its members read as individual aberrations and not as cultural identifiers. "The sophistication with which we understand hegemonic culture to be complicated and contradictory" is sadly lacking in our understanding of "outsider cultures," says Volpp (2000, 94–95).

"For communities of color, a specific individual act is assumed to be the product of a group identity and further, is used to define the group" (95). Therefore, Wayne Collins's hostility toward the JACL reveals his failure to understand the complex contextual forces at play. But his single-minded focus on the renunciants and his complete commitment to their cause was just what they needed to keep hope alive. It must have been deeply discouraging and hurtful to them that the representatives of their own community, members of the JACL, were unwilling to lend them support and were responsible for stigmatizing them. Collins's anger, though insufficiently nuanced and indiscriminate in its targeting, may have been extremely welcome to the renunciants and strengthened their resolve not to give up in the fight to have their citizenship restored.

Collins set out to prove that the seemingly voluntary renunciation of the Japanese Americans was in reality a carefully engineered act, the more pernicious and insidious for its voluntary façade. A typewritten record of the minutes of a meeting between Collins and the renunciants at Tule Lake has him saying to them:

> You sent for the application. That's one of the sad facts against you. The hearing officers said that they are here, if you want to renounce we are ready to help you renounce. But if you can show that you were nevertheless acting under compulsion, you have your point. For example, if you take a child and tell him to go over and jump across the 100 yard cliff. . . . Every step he takes is the result of compulsion. You are all children when you are under duress; It assumes that you are not able to think because you are under compulsion.

Collins impressed upon the renunciants that though the government might wish to make the case that the duress under which they operated was "community duress" (i.e., the pressure exerted by pro-Japanese members in the camp or Issei parents who wished to return to Japan), he was going to argue otherwise: "Here's the point: they have deported you from the West Coast; they put you into camps; and they have put you in here; they created the Hoshi-Dan [one of the pro-Japanese groups in camp] to intimidate the groups and did not prevent it. It was all governmental duress."[21]

In his eighteen-page communication to Attorney General Tom Clark in November 1945, Collins calls the renunciation hearings "farcical" and faults the government for not having informed the renunciant at the hearing "that a renunciation would result in his or her deportation to Japan." In his long list of litanies proving duress, Collins notifies Clark that the government's actions were arbitrary, unpredictable, inconsistent, and unreliable. Therefore, the internees' response was bound to be illogical and irrational:

> At the . . . time renunciation hearings were being held in said Center [Tule Lake] the government and its agents led the internees to believe

and since then has led them to believe, by word and conduct, that renunciations were not final but were subject to being withdrawn and cancelled, in like manner as requests for repatriation were subject to withdrawal and cancellation, and thereby lulled them into a false sense of security and also led them to believe that renunciation would not result in renunciant's involuntary deportation to Japan.[22]

Collins adjudged as duress not only acts of overt pressure but also the "capricious and arbitrary" rules and proclamations of the government that kept the internees unsettled and confused as to what would happen to them. The uncertainty of outcome was profoundly traumatic for many of the internees.

Collins's task was not easy. The renunciants had, by an act of volition, given up their U.S. citizenship. They were asked at the moment of their renunciation whether they were acting of their own free will and not in response to coercion, and only when and if they answered in the affirmative were their signatures accepted on the renunciation application. Collins had to argue the coerced nature of this seemingly volitional act. He had to demonstrate that despite the renunciants' sworn assertions of their free agency, they were trapped in a situation in which no act of theirs could be free. Secondly, Collins had to prove that the forces of coercion that contributed to the renunciants' action were generated and sustained by the U.S. government; therefore, the government was complicit in the renunciants' action, and, thus, the renunciations were invalid.

To pull off this strategy, Collins had to present the renunciants as confused, bewildered, unaware, psychologically vulnerable, and unable to make rational choices—he had to present them as powerless victims, helpless, and in need of a spokesperson. One could argue that such an approach infantilized the renunciants and so in a manner stripped them of their dignity, but Collins's view was that the greater indignity lay in the government's abuse of power—through a series of actions the government had rendered the Japanese Americans dependent on and subject to the dictates of officials in power.

Collins's ability to fathom the psychological complexity of the Tule Lake camp was remarkable. He was vehement in his opposition to the amended Nationality Act, declaring it to be unconstitutional, quite apart from the duress created by the government. In his notes for drafting the legal brief he would file, he writes:

The 14th Amendment makes "all persons born—in the United States—citizens of the United States and of the State wherein they reside." Obviously, citizenship, a substantive status granted and guaranteed by the Constitution, cannot be destroyed by Congress, the Executive or the Judiciary. . . . The grant creating national citizenship is of a constitutional dignity equal to that of the creation of the divisions of government and can no more be legislated away than Congress could legislate itself out of existence. Citizenship is the substance and fibre of the

Constitution. What Congress may not take away the Attorney General may not take away.[23]

The reasons that Edward Ennis (director of the Department of Justice's Alien Enemy Control Unit) offered for amending the Nationality Act so as to facilitate renunciations were, in Collins's view, measures that the government put into place in a sorry attempt to rectify a gross mistake—the original mistake of evacuation and internment; it was now presenting the amended act as something designed for the benefit of pro-Japanese internees, neglecting to consider the reasons that this pro-Japanese attitude had emerged in the first place.[24]

In a letter dated July 20, 1945, a female renunciant, Hide Takeoka, wrote to Ennis, pleading that he reconsider her request to rescind her renunciation of citizenship. She had recently received from his office a communication that there was little his office could do to revoke the renunciation of citizenship that she had voluntarily undertaken a few months ago. Takeoka is in despair, and she writes movingly to Ennis. Her language lays bare in compelling fashion the emotional state of the renunciants once they understood the implications of what they had given up:

> As you will see from my explanation of the circumstances which led me almost blindly, step by step, along that dark and dangerous path and into a pit-fall of renunciation, there was never even a speck of disloyalty towards the United States in my heart or mind. What may have looked to you and others as an act of disloyalty was merely the frantic behavior of a young girl who was desperately trying to find a path out of the confusion and darkness in which she found herself. I was very young, inexperienced, and very much afraid of being alone. I am sure that many more mature and braver people than I lost their way in this dark jungle and fell into the same pit or trap that I did. I wonder whether even you, with your great legal mind and with your abundant experience as a government official, if you had been in my place and confronted by my problems, could have avoided getting lost like I did and making the mistakes which I made.[25]

Though the dominant tone is one of abjection, there is also contained in the excerpt a definite challenge to the addressee, with Ennis being asked to imagine how he might have acted had he been in the same situation and subject to the same pressures. Takeoka's appeal for an act of empathetic imagination from Ennis is in effect what Collins was hoping to achieve from the government; the brief he filed in the mass suit to rescind the renunciations sought to explain to the attorney general how the circumstances under which the renunciants had executed their action were of a kind that would have compromised the rational thinking of any individual.

Paul Yamauchi, a medical doctor, himself an internee at Tule Lake and a renunciant, gives a chilling description in a letter to Attorney General Tom Clark of the impact of internment on a twenty-eight-year-old mother at Tule Lake and the extreme fragility of her mental state when, realizing the implications of her renunciation, she wished to rescind it, but did not get a positive response from the government:

> She was one of the many who renounced her American Nationality on the usual grounds of resentment due to evacuation. She had expressed a reconsideration of her case in order that she may remain in America to raise her family of two children. Because of the long period of uncertainty and worry as to the granting of her desire, she finally on December 5, 1945, went completely out of her mind and brutally murdered her three year old daughter, Sumiko, attacking the small child with a hammer in the most savage manner imaginable. Several large hammer blows were evident on the little girl's head, which resulted in a large hole in the left frontal area of her skull, showing macerated brain tissue exuding from the opening. . . . The sight of this pathetic incident has moved me greatly and has prompted my writing this letter to you. I personally acted as one of the attending physicians at Mrs. Fudetani's commitment to an institution. At the commitment, her own brother (a sergeant in the army from the Pacific front) testified in Mrs. Fudetani's behalf and informed the court that this long period of confinement plus the many periods of mental distress, worry, and uncertainty led to the insanity of his sister. . . . There have been instances of suicides and attempted suicides motivated by mental disorders due to abnormal living conditions in camp.[26]

The two judges who ruled on the renunciation cases, Judge Goodman of the San Francisco District Court and Judge Denman of the Ninth Circuit Court of Appeals, agreed resoundingly with Collins's duress argument, but Denman gave the government a crucial opening to mount a challenge. It was this opening that the government exploited to prolong for nearly twenty-five years a resolution of all the renunciant cases. Judge Goodman ruled that the renunciations were the result of "duress, menace, coercion, and intimidation" (Christgau 1985, 24); amazingly, he blamed, as well, the people of the United States, calling them "equally culpable" (24) for their refusal to hold their elected representatives to account. The government appealed his decision. At the level of the Ninth Circuit Court of Appeals, Judge Denman turned down the government's contention that it was not governmental duress that had caused the renunciations. In fact, he placed squarely upon the government the responsibility for the conditions at Tule Lake. However, he did not accept the mass nature of Wayne Collins's suit and would not summarily dismiss the renunciations of all five-thousand-plus people in the suit. He vacated the renunciations

of some thousand minors, but placed the burden of proof on 3,300 adult renunciants to show that their renunciations had not been voluntary (28).

Collins and his associate Tetsujiro (Tex) Nakamura filed more than ten
thousand affidavits over a period of ten years (described earlier). The narratives
in these affidavits are poignant, as the writers eloquently negotiate between
pride and pleading, resolve and doubt, assertiveness and apology (in the manner of the two renunciants whose letters I quote from earlier). Their strength of
character comes through in these affidavits even as the writers make the case
to the government that they had no choice in the matter of their renunciation.

Through the long years of filing these affidavits, Collins never gave up.
Perhaps there are two reasons for his tenacity: one was his unshakable belief
in the U.S. Constitution and the ideals he saw woven into it; the second was
his cynical attitude toward those in positions of official government power. In
2009, Tex Nakamura recalled a conversation he had had with Collins more
than forty years ago in which he asked Collins whom he voted for in the 1968
election, and Collins's reply was that he voted for Mahatma Gandhi. "He
wrote on the ballot, 'Mahatma Gandhi,'" Nakamura remembers. When the
interviewer presses Nakamura for details of how he responded to this assertion by Collins, Nakamura says, "'The guy must be crazy,' I thought. But you
know, come to think of it, . . . [h]e didn't believe none of these people, being
President, deserved that kind of job."[27] Unlike the national ACLU executive
committee of the 1940s, many of whom were unwilling to acknowledge that
President Franklin Delano Roosevelt would do anything to undermine civil
liberties, Collins saw clearly that power can lead people to make the wrong
decision.

The Value of Citizenship, Compromised or Whole

In preparing to file his brief for the renunciants, Collins makes the point in his
drafts that "dual citizenship is a myth." We have seen in his letter to Wesley
Doi of the JACL banquet committee that he was emphatic about the exclusive
American citizenship of the Nisei and Kibei. The scholars who have written in
praise of Collins (Weglyn, Donald Collins, and Christgau, for example) appear
to accept without question that the pursuit of an exclusive U.S. citizenship is
a laudable endeavor. Mae M. Ngai (2004) criticizes such a stance as a "valori-
zation of citizenship" (198), and she is uncomfortable that "the literature expresses incredulity that any American would renounce citizenship unless he
or she was in an abnormal state of mind" (198). She cautions that we cannot
discount "the influence of dual nationalism" (200) and would have us consider that "the renunciants were not exclusively patriotic citizens of the United
States who were but temporarily confused. Rather, they held complicated,
divided loyalties, a set of allegiances that sustained commitment to life in
America alongside affective and cultural ties, even patriotic sympathies, with
Japan" (200).

There are two points in Ngai's assertions that require response. Whether or not one places premium value on single-nation citizenship (versus dual citizenship), one cannot deny that rights and privileges technically inhere in national citizenship. Even the UN safeguards for individuals' human rights are bounded by the sovereignty of nation states. It is to the nation-state that the responsibility of protecting the human rights of those within its borders is given. Most states make clear distinctions between the privileges of citizenship and those of mere residency, so establishing or securing citizenship is a necessary protection. The protections of citizenship are especially important in times of national crisis, such as war. Though the citizenship of the Japanese Americans had been severely compromised during the Roosevelt administration, it was precisely the argument of citizenship that lawyers had available to challenge the government. I would submit that though many Japanese American renunciants may have desired the return of their citizenship for sentimental and idealistic reasons and faith in the privileges of U.S. citizenship, they were also undoubtedly clearheaded in realizing that without their citizenship, they would be further compromised in their efforts to reconstruct their lives. (At the time, the Alien Land Law was still in effect, for instance, and without citizenship, they could not own land.) Then as now, the absence of citizenship makes one vulnerable to deportation on the slightest of excuses. The laws are draconian, allowing for precious little hope.

My second response is to Ngai's (2004) point about "the influence of dual nationalism" (200) and the possibility that the Japanese Americans held "complicated, divided loyalties" (200). One is ready to accept the notion of dual citizenship today and to recognize that to have sympathies for the ancestral nation does not lead to a betrayal of allegiance to the current nation. The attachments may be layered and serve different ends—cultural and political; one may look to ancestral homelands for cultural fulfillment and yet be firmly anchored in political citizenship in the nation of one's birth, recognizing one's rights and privileges, obligations and duties. The case of Minoru Yasui, one of the four famous challengers to the curfew, evacuation, and detention orders, is precisely such an instance. He looked for a job after his graduation from law school and after he passed the bar exam in Oregon, and when he could not find one anywhere, he took a position with the Japanese consulate in Chicago. The minute that Japan declared war on the United States, he gave up his job there, in a clear understanding of where his political obligations lay and why it was necessary for him to demonstrate his political citizenship to the United States.[28]

A similar argument can be made for Arab Americans in the U.S. Army or Muslim Americans in the U.S. armed forces. The unfortunate case of Major Nidal Hassan notwithstanding, many of these soldiers are capable of simultaneously negotiating cultural citizenship and political citizenship.[29] In moments of political and national crisis, members of groups that are always considered to be not fully assimilable realize that their political citizenship has to be boldly and visibly performed so as to leave no doubt of their attachment to the

United States. The Kibei, who were the Japanese Americans most suspected of continuing loyalty to Japan because of their having been educated in the ancestral country, ironically were heavily used in the intelligence services during World War II to intercept and decode messages of the Japanese army.[30] So in this instance, the state deployed cultural citizenship in the service of political citizenship.

The more practical reason that Kibei and Nisei may have entertained notions of a continued emotional bond with Japan was that it was clear to them that their Issei parents were ineligible for citizenship. Citizenship is a coveted property—it confers on one a whole host of privileges and opportunities. Whatever the Issei had been able to acquire and accumulate despite their noncitizen status was stripped away through the processes of curfew, evacuation, and relocation. Not until the McCarran-Walter Act of 1952 were the Issei eligible to become naturalized citizens.[31] But as the fallout from the evacuation orders proved, economic vulnerability was not limited to the Issei. The Nisei, too, confronted in mistakable terms the fragility of their citizenship, as they hurriedly sold off property and assets to comply with the five days they were given to prepare themselves for evacuation. Judge Denman's report echoes the economic advantage that the majority community reaped when the Japanese American community was interned:

> The inevitable followed, after the meaning of the De Witt orders was understood. Unscrupulous secondhand dealers bought family possessions for a song. One can picture a widow bargaining for the family bedstead and kitchen stove while measuring the carrying capacity and load of her infants. Nor can one fail to apprehend the bitter sense of frustration of a doctor or lawyer at the loss of a long built up practice or that of the farmer trying to sell his partially matured crop, the result of years of soil improvement, to avid buyers who know the seller is but two or three days from his stockade.[32]

Under these circumstances, it made strategic sense for the Nisei and Kibei to maintain multiple loyalties and rely on Japan as a "backup" home. As Tex Nakamura remembers hearing from several Issei, they had sold off all their farm equipment, and so there was nothing for them to return to in order to begin a new life. At their age, they felt that going to Japan provided the best option.[33]

The renunciant Nisei and Kibei had to pursue all possible approaches to restore their American citizenship so that they did not forfeit permanently the privileges and opportunities that were rightfully theirs. Though their citizenship was compromised, it was legitimately theirs, and before they could challenge the government for the shoddy manner in which it had eviscerated the meaning of citizenship, they had to reclaim it. Collins's highlighting of the American-ness of the Nisei and Kibei was an extremely astute move. DeWitt had succeeded in casting suspicion on Japanese Americans as citizens more loyal to Japan than the United States. Collins's insistence on their American citizenship to the exclusion of all other loyalties was thus fully warranted, given the aspersions that DeWitt had cast on the community.

Saad Gul (2007) explains two contrasting tendencies in U.S. law: in one, judges and lawyers recognize the value of citizenship and work to preserve it for individuals in the face of formidable hurdles; in the other, lawyers and judges find ways to coerce citizens to renounce their citizenship as a "voluntary" act. The first tendency bears out the importance that Wayne Collins attributes to citizenship. The second proves his point that the government can create conditions under which the citizen is compelled to renounce voluntarily. An example of the first is the landmark case of Schneiderman, a Russian immigrant (who had come to the United States when he was three) who became a naturalized citizen but continued to profess Communist beliefs. He argued against the government that his support for communism should not deprive him of his citizenship. The case was so important as a test of "freedom of thought" (138) being an integral aspect of U.S. citizenship that former Republican presidential nominee Wendell Willkie took up his defense pro bono. The Supreme Court decided in favor of Schneiderman, and he retained his citizenship. So secure is the Fourteenth Amendment's protection of citizenship, whether by birth or by naturalization, that the government cannot take it away by force. Though one may find a citizen's beliefs and acts "repugnant," the Supreme Court affirmed that one cannot strip a citizen of this fundamental right of citizenship, says Gul (138). *Schneiderman* was making its way through the various levels of the judicial system precisely during the time that the Japanese Americans were interned. Writing for the majority, Justice Murphy delivered the opinion of the Supreme Court on June 21, 1943. The government had not established with sufficient certainty that Schneiderman did not or could not uphold the principles of the Constitution, the court said, and reminded the government of one of the fundamental values of the Constitution: "Here, they have hoped to achieve a political status as citizens in a free world in which men are privileged to think and act and speak according to their convictions, without fear of punishment or further exile so long as they keep the peace and obey the law."[34] Thus, regardless of Schneiderman's allegiance to the Communist Party, he could not have his citizenship revoked.

By contrast, argues Gul (2007), the recent (post-9/11) case of Yaser Hamdi illuminates a most deplorable disregard for the irrevocability of citizenship. Hamdi is a native-born (in Louisiana) U.S. citizen who was brought to the condition of "voluntarily" renouncing his citizenship, in much the same way that the Japanese American internees at Tule Lake were moved "voluntarily" to renounce theirs. Hamdi had been captured in Afghanistan in 2001, held in a prison there, moved to Guantánamo Bay, transferred to a navy brig in Charleston, South Carolina, and finally removed to Saudi Arabia, to join his family there. As part of the agreement for his release from the navy brig, Hamdi had to sign that he would, upon arriving in Saudi Arabia, report to a U.S. consular office and renounce his citizenship. Gul culls information from several sources that describe the conditions at both Guantánamo Bay and the navy brig to conclude that Hamdi's agreement to renounce was far from voluntary. He had endured extremely difficult conditions at Guantánamo Bay, perhaps even suffered torture there in addition to the uncertainty of detention, and the conditions had become so unbearable both there and in Charleston (where he was placed in solitary confinement) that he had agreed to anything just to get out. Gul states, "Since these detention facilities formed the mental and physical backdrop under which Hamdi made his decision, they are worth examining. The underlying reasoning, derived from the Tule Lake cases, is that an American citizen should not be put in a position where renunciation of citizenship appears to be the only reasonable option" (158). Gul claims that Hamdi was subjected to governmental duress in a manner similar to the internees at Tule Lake. "At the time of his plea agreement, Hamdi had been under arrest for almost three years, and the hopelessness of his situation must have impressed itself on him. . . . [O]ther detainees who have been subsequently released have talked about the powerful psychological and mental impact of prolonged and indefinite solitary confinement" (161). We have seen how the internees at Tule Lake were equally distraught because of the uncertainty of their future. Gul concludes:

> For Yaser Hamdi, the price of release from the "warehouse" [Guantánamo Bay] was his U.S. citizenship. To be effective, his renunciation must have been voluntary. . . . However, available accounts indicate that he acted under duress akin to that of the Tule Lake detainees sixty years ago. Ultimately, his statement that "I wanted to sign anything, everything, just to get out of there" drives home the conclusion that an independent observer would likely arrive at: his renunciation was probably not voluntary, and thus not valid. (163–164)

Individual Agency Amid Duress

If the duress argument Wayne Collins used risks stripping the renunciants of their individual agency, as Ngai (2004) argues, quite an opposite view of the renunciants' action emerges in Patrick Gudridge's (2005) reading of the situation. He argues provocatively that through the very act of renunciation, Japanese Americans were performing and displaying their political citizenship and asserting their full understanding of what citizenship really ought to be. Citizenship is a kind of contract between the state and the individual. The state gives protection; the individual gives allegiance. "Absent protection, allegiance is no longer obligatory. Absent protection, allegiance becomes, again, a matter of choice" (103). Gudridge makes the powerful assertion that

renunciation of citizenship at Tule Lake . . . marks one of the few occa-
sions (perhaps the only occasion) in which American citizens claim
and exercise (and are understood to possess and exercise) a freedom
to choose their government. In renouncing American citizenship, the
Tule Lake internees dramatized the fundamental premises of that citizenship. In renouncing citizenship, they proclaimed themselves constitutionally quintessentially "American." (107)

In the rescission letters they wrote or the affidavits they filled out after
1951, one need not see the language of the renunciants as unequivocally
rueful or apologetic. Rather, one could consider them as illuminating in their
specificity—as attempts at enlarging the cognitive capacity of the white
Americans who were assessing the validity of these narratives as proof of the
exigencies that confronted a group of people caught within the web of circumstances over which they had little control. Undeniably, the affidavits are an
instrument of state power, in that those desiring a reinstating of their citizenship were required to complete them and do so in a manner consistent with
the clarifications and assurances demanded by the state. But the affidavits
also served a purpose beneficial to the authors—not just as a means to regain
citizenship but also as a declaration of one's participation in a dialogue or inter-
change about the meaning of citizenship and national membership. Yes, they
were "carefully constructed representations of the renunciants' experiences and
sentiments" (Ngai 2004, 199), but they also provided, within the prescribed
structure, sufficient variability of specific details to convey the significant
uniqueness of each applicant's situation. Therefore, rather than confirming the
undifferentiated nature of the Japanese American renunciants, the affidavits
both firmly established the undeniability of duress and conveyed the diverse
portraits of thousands of renunciants. Through the relentless submission of
these affidavits, Collins, as Nakamura says, "wore down" the government.
That he did not give up underscores his refusal to capitulate to government
bureaucracy and to the power of the state apparatus.

In addition to the renunciants for whom he labored tirelessly for close to
twenty-five years, Collins also worked to restore the citizenship of two other
categories of individuals affected by wartime exigencies—"strandees" and
Japanese Peruvians. The "strandees" constituted two categories of individuals:
Japanese Americans who were in Japan at the outbreak of hostilities following the bombing of Pearl Harbor and who were therefore unable to return to
the United States while the war was still on, and renunciants who had moved
to Japan but desired to regain their U.S. citizenship and return to the United
States. Some strandees were deemed by the U.S. consulate in Japan to have
forfeited their U.S. citizenship because of certain actions they had taken, such
as serving in the Japanese army or voting in Japanese elections. Collins had to
make a convincing case that these strandees should also have their citizenship

restored. Collins assisted them in writing affidavits that sought to show that their acts of forfeiture were the result of coercion. His papers include testimonials from strandees who recount the circumstances under which they were conscripted into the Japanese Imperial Army or were forced to vote in elections in order not to be ostracized by family. So strong is Collins's belief in the notion of *jus soli* (place of birth) citizenship and so empathetic is his perspective on individuals caught in the conditions of war and unable to exercise their clear judgment (whether in the United States or Japan) that he invested a significant amount of energy in restoring the U.S. citizenship of these individuals.

A third category of individuals were the Japanese Peruvians. These individuals, who had lived in Peru for many years and had made successful lives there and raised children, were caught up in the racist hysteria following the bombing of Pearl Harbor. The Peruvian government took advantage of the hostility toward people of Japanese descent after Pearl Harbor to rid itself of Japanese Peruvians who were financially successful. A combination of racial distrust and animosity toward the Japanese led the Peruvian government to work with the U.S. government to have these Japanese Peruvians identified as potential traitors and to ship them to the internment camps in the United States. At the end of the war, the Peruvian government would not accept them back, and so these individuals were in danger of being deported to Japan. Collins was incensed at the unjust treatment of these individuals and the outrageous rules that were cited for their deportation—that they had entered the United States illegally and could show no proper documentation, when, in fact, their presence in the United States was the result of "abduction" and kidnapping by the Peruvian government, abetted by the U.S. government. Collins did not hold back his scathing criticism of the Peruvian and U.S. governments; with the help of the Northern California chapter of the ACLU, he brought attention to what he and the ACLU called "legalized kidnapping"—a program led by the State Department and endorsed by the attorney general (Weglyn 1976, 65); of the 365 Japanese Peruvians that Collins succeeded in "rescu[ing]" from the machinations of state power, 300 chose to remain in the United States, and, after 1952 when the citizenship laws were altered, many became citizens (66).

The misuse of state power was anathema to Wayne Collins, and he did not let governments assert questionable justifications for their actions. Collins did not live long enough to see the redress movement successfully culminate in an official apology from the U.S. government. Shortly before his death in 1974, he wrote eloquently and powerfully to Weglyn about the renunciants: "They were too young, and the adults too traumatized to fathom all that was happening to them when so damn much happened and only one side had the 'facts.' They were victims of a sham, a cruel deception. They were lied to from beginning to end. And if you go by our literary apologies and chauvinist court historians, they are still being lied to" (qtd. in Weglyn 1976, 268). He reveals in these words that his empathy for the renunciants and internees was ethical (he believed they had been wronged) and compassionate (he understood the mental suffering they experienced). "If they could do that to the Japanese they could do it to me," he declared to the renunciants in an October 1945 meeting at Tule Lake. Whether he made his pronouncement for effect or to generate confidence in his ability, one thing is undeniable: Collins fought for the renunciants with a ferocity that suggests he was fighting to restore his own faith in the integrity of the country, despite his deep disappointment in its leaders.

3

Hierarchies of Horror, Levels of Abuse

Empathy for the Internees

Emiko Omori, director of the documentary film *Rabbit in the Moon* (1999) on the internment experience of her family (her parents, herself, and her older sister), offers in voice-over narration one reason for the reluctance of the Japanese American community to talk about its wartime experience in the camps: "When we left the camps and found out what had happened in Germany, we felt we couldn't really speak about our own suffering. It was not that what we had suffered wasn't bad, but that it wasn't *bad enough*" (emphasis heard in Omori's voice). Considered alongside the Holocaust, the Japanese Americans' internment ordeal "seems" mild, hardly worth a mention; yet what Omori's comment suggests is that the silence that comes from consigning one's experience to the lower rungs of a hierarchy of horrors is precisely the kind of mindset that leads to ignoring or glossing over abuses of power that on the surface appear to be minor. There is no question that the Holocaust and the genocides in Rwanda and Darfur are outrages against humanity. Placing the Japanese American internment against these atrocities does not trivialize them; rather, through a conjoined consideration of the internment and these ethnic cleansings, we can recognize a *continuum* of abuse, in which it is easy to slide from a relatively innocuous position to one of real danger. Provoking anger for what happened to the Japanese Americans, generating empathy for their deprivations, their loss of freedom, their displacement, their betrayal—eliciting these sentiments ought not to be any more difficult than calling forth outrage at the ethnic cleansings of our century. Yet empathy for the Japanese Americans has not always been readily forthcoming. This chapter undertakes to examine the reasons.

One possible reason may be found in Kay Schaffer and Sidonie Smith's (2004) discussion of the paradigmatic place that Holocaust narratives occupy in the Western consciousness for understanding "the processes of victimization, remembering, witnessing, and recovery" (22). They claim that the "production, circulation, and reception of these stories have shaped modes of response to other events, histories, and contexts of suffering" (22). Given the centrality of the Holocaust to the West's understanding of unimaginable suffering and horrific human rights violations, it is not surprising that forms of suffering that do not carry the explosive charge of extermination camps and mass genocide tend not to receive sufficient attention. Further, Schaffer and Smith believe that the model of "witnessing" and "testimonial" from Holocaust survivors that gripped the world during the 1961 trial of Nazi officer Adolf Eichmann in Jerusalem established "individual suffering and psychic interiority [as] the ground of trauma" (22) and left no room for alternate modes of sharing and recovering from experiences of suffering.

Similarly, Mahmood Mamdani (1996), in critiquing South Africa's Truth and Reconciliation Commission (TRC), provides additional insight into the difficulty of eliciting outrage against abuses of power that on the surface do not appear to be horrific. His strongest objection to the TRC comes from feeling that the process excessively highlights only those injustices that occurred within the legal framework of apartheid—"detention, torture, murder" (5)—and glosses over the day-to-day injustices that people endured under the institutional oppression of the apartheid system—"forced removals, pass laws, broken families" (5). Moreover, argues Mamdani, the TRC zeros in on the perpetrators (the torturers, jailers, killers) and ignores the beneficiaries—individuals who, though they may not have wielded a club or pulled a trigger, nonetheless benefited from a sociopolitical system that privileged whiteness and reserved for its members all the resources and opportunities of the nation. The narratives or testimonies that receive most play and publicity in the TRC process are those that reveal flagrant violations of human rights or bring to light horrific acts of cruelty. Mamdani's point is that apartheid's heinousness lay not just in the "sensational" abuses of power but in the day-to-day trivial and banal indignities that every black, colored, and Indian person was made to suffer. These daily infringements may not have directly led to bodily injuries, but their indirect impact on the physical and psychological well-being of black, colored, and Indian South Africans was every bit as baleful as the more visibly and obviously brutal practices. South Africans, especially white South Africans, while they have been ready to condemn the horrors of apartheid as revealed in the testimonials heard through the TRC process, have not been as willing to examine and rectify the decades of institutional deprivations that black South Africans overwhelmingly suffered, the disadvantages that they must continue to live with for generations before the effects of segregation can be neutralized. "We arrive at a world in which reparations are . . . for those who suffered jail or exile, but not for those who suffered only forced labor and broken homes" (5).[1]

In her discussion of artistic exhibitions designed to heal the wounds of apartheid, Ingrid de Kok (1998) describes one installation that foregrounds the seemingly less harmful but more pervasive and entrenched instruments of oppression. This installation, by the architect Hilton Judin,

> investigated the relationship between spatial and social topographies, by interrogating the language of apartheid itself. Its attempt was to understand the relation of language to space, space to power, power to language, and thus to memory. . . . Entitled "Setting Apart," it consisted of a selection of archival documents, maps, and plans, tracing the imprint of power in the segregation of Cape Town. Judin's multipronged argument was mounted . . . against the language of planning and officialdom, and especially against the introjective power of that language. . . . [T]he installation used as witnesses the mass of paper that changed hands as apartheid orders and removals took place: all in the language of a bureaucracy that had total power to talk over the heads of its ciphers. (66–67)

Mamdani and De Kok remind us of the importance of documenting and revealing the extent to which the seemingly innocuous can in fact be deadly. They insist on our understanding that the language of "officialdom" can be as lethal as weapons of torture, rape, and annihilation. The TRC, because it principally highlights the sensational cruelties of apartheid, risks doing a grave disservice to the millions of South Africans who suffered the slow and steady burden of a lifetime of regulations, deprivations, and humiliations. One might say that the relative "mildness" of the injustice done to the Japanese American internees, in comparison to the "sensational" nature of the evil of the Holocaust's ethnic cleansing, has contributed to the former's invisibility as a contemptible exercise of state power motivated by racial prejudice. It is not surprising, therefore, that the task of stimulating empathy for the internees was slow and labor intensive and took many years to accomplish.

Empathy by Slow Degrees, Fragmentary and Piecemeal

However, there was definite opposition to the internment from many quarters (church groups and left-leaning newspapers, for example), an opposition that is comprehensively documented by Robert Shaffer's (1998) archival research. Though this criticism did not prevent the issuing of the executive order for internment, it nonetheless reveals that the country was by no means uniformly unconcerned about the abrogation of the constitutional rights of a segment of its population. Even in Arkansas, the state with the worst record of official hostility toward Japanese Americans, the Presbyterian minister Reverend John P. McConnell devoted an entire Sunday sermon in December 1943 to describe his recent visit to the Rohwer relocation center. "We need only to give ourselves a chance to know and understand them [the internees]," he exhorted his congregation, and reminded them of a parable in the Talmud: "'As

I walked in the mountain I saw in the distance—an animal. Nearer—I saw it was a man. Nearer still—I saw it was my brother.' That is the experience of the majority of visitors to these camps and of almost everyone of the 'Caucasians' working in them" (qtd. in Bearden 1999, 14). The voices of opposition were numerous but scattered, and they did not or could not coalesce into a roar of resistance. One wonders what a person like the children's librarian Clara Beard could have done. She was clearly sympathetic to the young Japanese American children who were frequent visitors to the San Diego Public Library where she worked. Before they left for the camp in Poston, Arizona, Beard distributed "handfuls of stamped self-addressed penny postcards to her young friends with an admonition to 'Please write to me, and I shall do the same'" (Estes and Estes 1999, 23). The letter writers, who were as young as seven and as old as twenty-two, sent her more than 250 responses. Should Clara Beard have translated her affection for the Japanese American youth into a politically vocal resistance to their removal? One might justifiably say that her postcard connection was complicit with the indignity of the forced evacuation and internment. Yet her gesture may have been supremely important to making the internees feel that not everyone on the outside hated them and that there was a fair chance of their being reaccepted into the communities that they had been made to leave.

Miné Okubo's (2004) testimony in 1981 to the Congressional Committee on Wartime Relocation and Internment speaks of the shame that editors of the New York–based magazine *Fortune* felt on learning of what had been done to the Japanese Americans on the West Coast. Originally, the editors had invited her to illustrate their special issue on Japan, but when they saw "the vast collection of drawings that [she] had on the evacuation, they were surprised and excited, and when they learned that American citizens were evacuated, they were ashamed, and they decided to look into the matter more, and they wrote an article called 'Issei, Nisei, Kibei'" (16). *Fortune*'s 1944 article was followed by the assistance its editors rendered Okubo in getting her sketches and accompanying commentary published by Columbia University Press in 1946 as *Citizen 13660*, one of the first memoirs on the internment.

These gestures by *Fortune* could be read in one of two ways—either as genuine reactions of shame that the country could so betray its own people or, as Jessica Knight (2006) scathingly observes, self-serving paternalistic celebrations of the nation's eventual sense of fairness. Knight lashes out:

> While the brief article ("Issei, Nisei, Kibei") is sympathetic to the mental, emotional, and financial toll suffered by the internees, ultimately editorializing strongly against internment, it is fractured into eight sections, spread over 110 pages—almost literally lost in a sea of anti-Japanese sentiment. . . . The article works strenuously to position the internment as anomalous, rather than as product of the same racist logic in which the magazine's own rhetoric is grounded. (4)

Knight's criticism, though accurate in the main, could be more attentive to the fluctuations of tone in the article that focuses specifically on the internees.

A reader who went no further than the opening page would assume that the article presents the internment or "protective custody" as necessary. However, there is a significant shift in tone toward the end of the first page, a shift that gets louder in its criticism of the internment as we progress through the article. One can only assume from this puzzling turn that the editors did not want at the outset to appear critical of the government or to risk alienating those among their readers whose anti-Japanese sentiments rendered them incapable of distinguishing between the wartime enemy Japan and people of Japanese descent living in the United States. So the editors appear to have resorted to a tactical move that would have the greatest likelihood of securing and holding the interest of their readers. The early lines of the article openly denigrate Japan:

> Too few . . . realize what persistent and effective use Japan has been able to make, throughout the Far East, of U.S. imprisonment of persons of Japanese descent. . . . By pointing out, again and again, that the U.S. put behind fences well over 100,000 people of Japanese blood, the majority of them citizens of the U.S., Japan describes to her Far Eastern radio audiences one more instance of American racial discrimination. To convince all Orientals that the war in the Pacific is a crusade against the white man's racial oppression, the enemy shrewdly notes every occurrence in the U.S. that suggests injustice to racial minorities, from the Negroes, to the Mexicans to the Japanese. ("Issei, Nisei, Kibei" 1944, 1)

Soon, however, the critical rhetoric is directed at the United States. The internment is said to present "an awkward problem for the U.S. if for no other reason than that the Constitution and the Bill of Rights were severely stretched if not breached when U.S. citizens were put in prison" (8). White Californians come in for especially harsh criticism: "It did not require a war to make the farmers, the [American] Legion, the Native Sons and Daughters of the Golden West, and the politicians resent and hate the Japanese Americans. . . . War turned the antagonism into fear and made possible what California had clearly wanted for decades—to get rid of its minority" (3). In addition to direct criticism of the white supremacists and the farmers who resented competition from the immigrant Japanese growers, the article displays a remarkable empathy for the suffering of the internees. Declaring as blatantly false the claim that internees were being indulged in the camps, the article observes, "No one who has visited a relocation center and seen the living space, eaten the food, or merely kept his eyes open, could honestly apply the word 'coddling' to the WRA's [War Relocation Authority's] administration of the camps" (6). That a paltry fifteen cents per meal was spent on each internee confirmed that the food, though adequate, was "close to the edge of decent nutrition" (6).

There is also deep understanding of the frustration and bitterness of Nisei who resisted the government and refused to sign the loyalty oath. The article does not identify these resistors by their commonly known label, "no-no boys"; it grants them a complexity of emotion that is unusual for the time. We learn about the "young Nisei who enlisted in California early in 1941 because he felt strongly about fascism"; this soldier was "abruptly thrown out of his country's army after Japan attacked the U.S. and put behind the fences along with all the other evacuees. In February, 1943, when he was handed a questionnaire on loyalty and his willingness to defend the U.S., he was too angry to prove his 'loyalty' that way; he had already amply demonstrated it" (13). The article recognizes that he is at Tule Lake [the camp where "disloyal" internees were held] "not because of his love for Japan, but as a protest to the government he honestly wanted to serve back in 1941" (13). The article ends with a forceful assertion of the deeply problematic nature of the internment or "protective custody" (17), as it was euphemistically called to suggest that the Japanese and Japanese Americans had to be confined for their own protection from the attacks of paranoid and hostile neighbors.

There can be no denying the position of the magazine's editors with regard to the Japanese American *citizen*; they are outraged that those who are citizens of the nation should be so unconscionably treated, and they predict grave consequences. Though their targeting of California as a particularly racist state is a tad too self-satisfied and smug (the implication being that the state of New York would never stoop to such racist acts), nonetheless, the power of their indignation is worth noting:

> The American custom in the past has been to lock up the citizen who commits violence, not the victim of his threats and blows. The doctrine of "protective custody" could prove altogether too convenient a weapon in many other situations. In California, a state with a long history of race hatred and vigilantism, antagonism is already building against the Negroes who have come in for war jobs. What is to prevent their removal to jails to "protect them" from riots? Or Negroes in Detroit, Jews in Boston, Mexicans in Texas? The possibilities of "protective custody" are endless, as the Nazis have amply proved. ("Issei, Nisei, Kibei" 1944, 20)

The *Fortune* article reserves its support principally for American-born Japanese. Though the Issei are by no means demonized, they are seen primarily in relation to the hope they invest in their American-born children. The appeal the *Fortune* article makes is an appeal grounded firmly in the notion that those born in the United States share a special bond, which the nation-state must recognize. What is shocking to the editors of *Fortune* is not that individuals of Japanese descent have been arbitrarily evacuated and imprisoned but that *American citizens* of Japanese descent have been so treated. Their empathy is an empathy born of the abstract notion of shared citizenship.

Eugene Rostow (1945), Yale University law professor, writing in *Harper's Magazine* in 1945, goes one step further. Though principally he, too, is profoundly disturbed at the government's violation of the constitutional rights of *citizens*, he does not relegate the Japanese "aliens" (the noncitizens) to a netherworld of horrors; to them too must apply the universal rights that every human, regardless of citizenship, is "entitled to [in] our general constitutional protections of individual liberty—to trial by jury, the writ of habeas corpus, and the other basic rights of the person" (201). In a frontal attack on the government, Rostow declares, "one hundred thousand persons were sent to concentration camps on a record which wouldn't support a conviction for stealing a dog" (199). He names the racial and regional discrimination inherent in the internment order: "Is it permissible to intern all Japanese who live on the West Coast, but to allow German and Italian aliens, and Japanese who live elsewhere [on the East Coast and in Hawai'i] general freedom? Surely the control and custody of enemy aliens in wartime should be reasonably equal and even-handed" (201). (It is tempting to read in the restraint of the East Coast and Hawai'i an enlightened attitude, but one should keep in mind that the motivation may have been more calculated than based on principles of justice: on the East Coast, there were too few Japanese to be considered a threat, and in Hawai'i the Japanese labor was so crucial to the plantation economy that to have interned them would have brought the business of the islands to a standstill.)

Elena Tajima Creef (2000) reminds us that many white spouses of Japanese and Japanese Americans chose to accompany their partners to the camps. She focuses on the artist Estelle Peck Ishigo, wife of Arthur Shigeharu Ishigo. Estelle, while interned for four years with her husband at the Heart Mountain camp in Wyoming, made "hundreds of sketches and watercolor paintings" (167) depicting the realities of the conditions in the camp; Estelle also wrote the commentary to accompany the drawings and paintings. The text and the visuals eventually became the book *Lone Heart Mountain* (1972).

Creef's description of Estelle Ishigo's narrative perspective offers important insights into the terrain of empathy.

> [Though in] the opening pages of *Lone Heart Mountain* Ishigo identifies herself as a white woman of European ancestry who sought official permission to remain with her Japanese American husband . . . the initial autobiographical account of her life in the camps quickly turns into a meticulous visual record of the physical and spiritual processes of uprooting, relocation, exile and degeneration of an entire ethnic community within which she quietly aligns herself yet all but disappears from view. (167)

Creef turns our attention to Ishigo's symbolic self-erasure as a white woman and her subsequent 'racial' transformation within this exiled community of color" (167). Within the narrative, Ishigo "renounce[s] 'whiteness' as a constructed category for race hatred, domination, and power, and steps symboli-cally into a 'Japanese American' subject position" (170–171). Ishigo makes a conscious decision to enter another subjectivity and experience a reality that she might never had access to had she chosen to remain in the comfort of her identity as a white woman. Ishigo's camp experience solidified her empathetic attachment to the Japanese American community, a connection that she initi-ated when she chose as a white woman to take the bold step of crossing the color line and marrying into a racial community that was clearly marked as marginal and alien.

Ishigo's submersion of her whiteness to her adopted Japanese subjectivity presents an interesting variation on the egotistical drift that Hoffman describes (see the Introduction). Her physical whiteness is perhaps a reminder to herself that she is different from the community with whom she has aligned herself. Yet, in speaking as an "insider," Estelle Ishigo does not seek to blur the bound-aries between herself and the interned Japanese and Japanese Americans and to redirect attention on to *her* suffering (which is what occurs in instances of egotistical drift, as we saw in Chapter 1 with Ike McCaslin). Rather, as Creef (2000) points out and as the text amply bears out, Ishigo turns the focus of the reader away from her and onto the other internees. She "all but disappears from view" (167), notes Creef, a disappearance that is redressed in Steven Oka-zaki's 1991 film on Estelle Ishigo, *Days of Waiting*, which restores her centrality to the internment narrative.

Creef's (2000) observations of the profound effect that *Days of Waiting* has on her students reveal the complex intersection of race and empathy: "many white students find themselves deeply touched by Ishigo's story and deeply troubled by their own symbolic shift from mere spectators of internment histo-ry to participants in it through the spectacle of this white woman in the camps" (172). This reaction, when considered with the reaction of Tina Chen's (2005) students to Julie Otsuka's (2002) novel *When the Emperor Was Divine* (which I discuss later), suggests that white students need a racial bridge to appreciate fully the suffering of people of color.

Lawrence Blum's (1999) analysis of antiracist pedagogical techniques pre-sents two terms—"ally" and "moral co-equal"—that are useful in understanding the obstructive influence of fear and privilege. An ally acknowledges privilege and keeps it in the foreground as though to remind oneself of one's obligation because of the advantage one enjoys; thus, an ally at one level *wills* himself or herself to imagine an alternate reality of vulnerability in order to *feel with* the suffering individual/group. A moral co-equal focuses on the shared cause that brings together him or her and the targeted individual/group; their differing racial or class or religious locations may have little significance in the context of the task at hand (136). Estelle Ishigo's (1972) decision to enter the camps may in the early stages be thought of as akin to the act of an ally. However, she does not persist in that position for long. If one continues with the bridge metaphor, then we may think of Estelle Ishigo as dismantling the bridge that others like her (i.e., white people) might hope to use to cross over to the other "shore" and learn the specific details of the internment experience. It is as though Ishigo has determined that the only way for the white community to responsibly engage the internment horror is to plunge into the chasm between the "free" white world and the internees and make their way through the experiential gap with the labor of their hearts and minds. She will not serve as their easy conduit. She invites them to become, like herself, moral co-equals in protesting this outrage upon their fellow human beings. The closing lines of her book are an eloquent statement of a shared humanity: "Human beings! Wandering over the mountains and across the seas you hear the music of all the earth and still you sleep in dreams. Mountains and seas still lie between you and yet, under the sky and over the whole Earth, The human race is only one!" (104).

One might be tempted to dismiss her urging as naïve and indifferent to the harsh realities of power differences; but Estelle Ishigo has earned her right to make this plea. She has, along with her fellow internees, endured the hardships of internment and the equally painful desperations of the postwar return of internees to hostile communities and barren employment opportunities. Some of the most moving passages of her book describe the bleak emptiness of the post-internment years, the paltry efforts of the administration to secure them safe and minimal housing, the lack of even unskilled jobs, and the mistrust of the general population. She writes, "Now after three years wherein wind, sand and snow had swept some minds and souls of all past held dreams, leaving them stark and bare with just enough to cover them and keep them deadly alive . . . [t]hey were filled with vague yearning and bewilderment; and when it was learned that they longed only for home, they were looked upon with disapproval and sometimes suspicion" (Ishigo 1972, 86). When they arrive in Los Angeles after a long train journey, they are "marched military-fashion under surveillance . . . down the roped arcade" (93). Ishigo recalls, "Tired and weary we marched quickly, embarrassed by our camp clothes and dusty shoes as the city people stood to stare at us" (93).

As a white woman who chose a life partner outside her racial group, Estelle Ishigo may have suffered a loss of prestige among members of her birth group. In a brilliant analysis of the 1997 Louise Woodward case (in which a white British nanny was tried for the murder of the infant of an Indian American man, Sunil Eappen, and his white wife, Deborah), Susan Koshy (2002) argues that the reason that Woodward ultimately received a virtual "acquittal" (the judge set aside the jury's verdict of guilty and found her culpable only of manslaughter, imposing a sentence of 279 days, time already served while awaiting and during the trial) is that Deborah Eappen's "racial transgression" was seen as unnatural and the Eappens, "as an interracial couple . . . mobilized no constituency" (45). That Ishigo suffered the same fate is borne out first by the neglect of her manuscript for almost thirty years before it could find a publisher, and second, by the neglect of her "body" itself, which was left to languish in abject poverty, as those who "discovered" her in 1983 saw (Creef 2000, 170). Estelle Ishigo's empathy for the Japanese and Japanese Americans cost her the empathy of the dominant group of which she was biologically a member.

Several other books written by white Americans appeared shortly after the internment. Among these are Karon Kehoe's *City in the Sun* (1946); Katharine Newman (1986) describes Kehoe as "a woman of good heart and compassion [who] went out as a teacher to the concentration camps" (141). Kay Vandergrift (1993) writes about the white Colorado resident Florence Crannell Means, who won the Child Study Association Award in 1945 and the Newbery award in 1946 for her book *The Moved-Outers* (1945): "Means met and talked with young California evacuees who were forced to live behind barbed wire fences in the Amache relocation camp near her Colorado home and wrote this story at a time when many Americans were unaware of, or unwilling to acknowledge, what was happening to U.S. citizens" (Vandergrift 1993, 365–366). Though the book won two literary awards, Vandergrift observes that many school and public libraries did not purchase it at the time of its publication because of their anti-Japanese and anti–Japanese American attitudes (366). James Edmiston's *Home Again* (1955) and Vanya Oakes's *Roy Sato: New Neighbor* (1955) focus on the difficulties that returning Japanese Americans experienced upon their release from the camps and in their efforts to restart their interrupted lives. The former is based on the true story of Tosh Mio, who immigrated to the United States in 1903.[2]

Ralph Lazo, a Mexican-Irish sixteen-year-old who had many Japanese American high school classmates, in a surprising decision for one as young as he, decided to follow his friends to camp. He remained with them in Manzanar for the duration of the internment. Yoshindo Shibuya, one of his friends and fellow internees, observed to the organization Nikkei for Civil Rights and Redress (NCRR), "He's a special guy, especially to do what he did. When you're kids you don't delve into something that heavy, but evidently he must have had some deep thoughts about this. That's probably the reason he said, 'I'm going.'"[3] Lazo, who died in 1992, had always been a strong advocate for justice, even as an adolescent, and in his life after internment he allied himself with many causes for racial justice and full participatory democracy. Lazo's desire at the time to be with his friends was a unique combination of empathy for the injustice they were undergoing and the need for a social network of friends he had come to rely upon. His courage and deep commitment to his friends are celebrated in the 2004 film *Stand Up for Justice* (also known as *Stand Up for Justice: The Ralph Lazo Story*). Even though his sister wrote to him repeatedly asking him to return home, he chose to stay interned. He willingly endured the hardships of camp life, so outraged was he by the internment and acutely conscious of the violation of his friends' basic rights.

Redress and Delayed Empathy

The activists in the Japanese American redress movement, which had its beginnings in the 1970s and culminated in 1988 with the Redress Bill that resulted in the official presidential apology and reparations to surviving internees, had the challenge of convincing senators and House representatives that the wrong done to people of Japanese descent was grave, unjustifiable under any circumstances, and deserving of restitution. Theirs was the task of underscoring the abuse of government power and seeking acknowledgment of loss of material property and constitutional rights. That the process was long and protracted indicates not only the predictable slow movement of bureaucratic structures but also the weight of testimonies that it took to demonstrate beyond a doubt that injustice had been done. The Redress Bill is best understood as a case of retrospective ethical empathy—an eventual acceptance of responsibility by the elected representatives of a people that their predecessors had violated an essential principle of democratic citizenship. That this retrospective ethical empathy is not universally felt by all Americans is evident in the words of Representative Howard Cable of North Carolina, who said in February 2003 that the Japanese American internment was justified and was a benevolent move.

During the protracted period of the redress campaign (beginning in the early 1970s and into the late 1980s), many non-Japanese Americans expressed their support for the internees and exhibited what one could call "retrospective empathy." Congressman Jim Wright (D-TX), House majority leader in 1980 and a member of the Commission on Wartime Relocation and Internment of Civilians (CWRIC), offered a moving testimony of his own feelings about the internment:

> With still remembered pain, I recall reading from the Southwest Reporter in 1944 the digest of the Supreme Court's ruling in this case. I had just returned from a tour of military duty in the Pacific where I had participated in combat missions against the armed forces of Japan. . . . Ingloriously and to our everlasting shame, the Court upheld as constitutional the act of our Government in rounding up the Japanese-American citizens, almost as though they were cattle, and herding them into corrals. . . . I swore then that whenever I had a chance to do so, I would speak out against it. For it was an unconstitutional and unconscionable undertaking, totally inconsistent with our most fundamental precepts. It deserves to be condemned today, just as it deserved to be condemned even then. (Qtd. in Maki, Kitano, and Berthold 1999, 95)

Both within and outside the community, there were conflicted feelings about the internment and the internees' response to it. One of the most prominent and visible Japanese Americans to oppose the redress movement was Senator Samuel Hayakawa (R-CA). He had lived in Chicago during the internment and had not personally experienced its effects. Maki and colleagues (1999) write that "he labeled the notion of redress a 'radical-chic fad'" (76) and testified to the CWRIC that for many of the older Japanese the internment was "a three-year vacation from long years of unremitting work on farms, in fishing boats, and in little shops" (104); he asserted that his "flesh crawls with shame and embarrassment" (104) at the demands for redress, because such pleading is below the dignity of Japanese Americans. The numerous historical reconstructions and literary representations of internment reveal the tensions within the Japanese American community about the appropriate response to the crisis, such as the advice of the Japanese American Citizens League (JACL) to cooperate with the government's demands and so demonstrate loyalty, and the dissenters' fierce opposition and resistance to any kind of obedience.

The extent to which the majority group's empathy was influenced by these disparate positions within the targeted community is unclear, but, as I argue later in discussing Guterson's *Snow Falling on Cedars* (1995), compliant internees—those who without protest acquiesced in their own internment because they saw it as a way to prove their allegiance, and who subsequently signed up to fight in the U.S. armed forces—were much more likely to elicit empathy than "no-no boys" and vocal critics of the internment order. Conditional empathy is a problematic phenomenon, especially when the violated group (or individual) has had its fundamental rights stripped away and is, despite that assault, expected not to react with bitterness and rage.

Recall the lady in San Francisco of Mitsuye Yamada's poem (in the Introduction). She blithely wonders why the Japanese Americans did not resist their evacuation and internment (and in so wondering absolved herself of any responsibility for their plight). Her passivity is a not uncommon response, as we see in Hisaye Yamamoto's short story "The Wilshire Bus" (1988b). The target of hostility is, in this instance, a Chinese American woman. She expresses her distaste for the boorish and drunken ranting of a white male fellow passenger on the bus, and as a result invites his xenophobic and racist diatribe: "Well, if you don't like it, . . . why don't you get off this bus, why don't you go back where you came from? . . . Why don't you go back to China where you can be coolies working in your bare feet out in the rice fields? You can let your pigtails grow and grow in China. Alla samee, mama, no tickee no shirtee. Ha, pretty good, no tickee no shirtee!" (1988b, 35–36). Two other passengers offer tentative gestures of empathy, but their reaching-out to the woman is too little and comes too late. One of the delayed and paltry offerings is that of a Japanese American woman, Esther Kuroiwa, whose first response is, not surprisingly, a sense of relief that because the man's curses are uttered with specific reference to the Chinese she is excluded from his hatred. She feels "quite detached. She found herself wondering whether the man meant her in his exclusion order or whether she was identifiably Japanese. . . . Then she was startled to realize that what she was actually doing was gloating over the fact that the drunken man had specified the Chinese as the unwanted" (36). Feeling a deep shame at her "moral shabbiness" (37), Esther draws upon a sense of ethical empathy and "turned towards the little woman and smiled at her . . . , shaking her head a little to get across her message (don't pay any attention to that stupid old drunk, he doesn't know what he's saying, let's take things like this in our stride)" (37). She has said nothing out loud when the man is hurling his words of hate. Instead, she offers a wordless empathy, though accompanied by a smile, as though the depth of her understanding should be apparent to her fellow Asian American traveler. However, she is not permitted any easy sense of solidarity and comfort. The Chinese American woman is not impressed, and looks at Esther with "a face so impassive yet cold, and eyes so expressionless yet hostile" (37).

Another passenger, a white male, makes a verbal declaration of empathy *after* the abusive passenger leaves the bus: "I want you to know . . . that we aren't all like that man. We don't all feel the way he does. We believe in an America that is a melting pot of all sorts of people. I'm originally Scotch and French myself" (1988b, 37). We are not told how his gesture was received, and the narrator's silence in this regard is significant. Earlier, we have seen that this same man "was smiling at the [Chinese American] woman and shaking his head mournfully in sympathy" (36) when the drunk is on his rant. That he speaks only when the drunken man has left the bus indicates that his words serve no purpose in undermining the drunk's assumption of shared (racist) power with the other non–Asian American passengers on the bus. In offering his words of comfort to the Chinese American woman and her husband, he is only congratulating himself on his own goodwill and making a relatively painless show of understanding. The narrator's silence suggests that his words ultimately have no value to the targeted individuals and that they function only to enhance his own self-image.

In "The Legend of Miss Sasagawara" (1988a), Yamamoto directly explores the complexities of empathy within the constraints of life in an internment camp in Arizona. With her signature understatement and delicacy, she focuses on the effects of internment on three different types of internees: a group of young women ("pushing twenty"), of whom the narrator is one; a thirty-nine-year-old woman who was a ballet dancer in her pre-internment life; and her father, a Buddhist minister. We are given a glimpse into Miss Sasagawara through the flippant rumor-laden descriptions and ridicule of the young narrator and her friends. Gossiping about Miss Sasagawara, Elsie says dramatically, "Oooh, that gal is really temperamental. I guess it's because she was a ballet dancer before she got stuck in camp. I hear people like that are temperamental. Anyway, the Sasakis, the new couple at the other end of the barracks, think she's crazy" (1988a, 20–21). Kiku and Elsie spend their days in camp dreaming of life beyond it—"first to finish college somewhere when and if the war ever ended and [they] were free again, and then to find good jobs and two nice, clean young men, preferably handsome, preferably rich" (21). Theirs is the hopeful perspective of youth; though bored at camp, they have not succumbed to despair, and they envision their future outside the confines of this bizarre imprisonment.

Against their optimism, Yamamoto sets Miss Sasagawara's despondency. Her troubled spirit manifests itself in strange irrational behavior—sudden explosions of temper, paranoid delusions of being spied on, and obsessive preoccupations with the young men of camp whose "joking and loud laughter" she watches transfixed, her head "bent to one side and . . . one finger in her mouth as she gaze[s], in the manner of a shy child confronted with a marvel" (1988a, 31). Her oddities eventually land her in a sanatorium, confirming the view of the youngsters that she is certifiably mad.

Her eccentricities serve an important function for the young internees who gossip about her to endure the monotony of their internment. Miss Sasagawara's father is also a subject of discussion, someone the youngsters can point to and speculate on. A Buddhist minister, he is, according to Kiku, "a slight and fragile-looking old man" (1988a, 21) who always "seemed to be wandering lostly . . . because he walked so slowly, with such negligible steps, or because he wore perpetually an air of bemusement, never talking directly to a person, as though . . . he could not stop for an instant his meditation on the higher life" (22).

Not surprisingly, Kiku and her friends have no empathy for Mari Sasagawara. She provides them with titillating tidbits of scandal of her purported descent into "madness." They take a kind of cruel pleasure in contemplating her odd behavior, specifically her sitting on an apple crate beside the bed of the young Joe Yoshinaga with "her long hair all undone and flowing about her . . . dressed in a white nightgown" (1988a, 31) and gazing lovingly at him as he sleeps. Miss Sasagawara affords an easy means to congratulate themselves on their own "normalcy" and their ability to triumph over the strangeness and unnaturalness of the internment experience. Through her, they can safely channel their frustrations and anger at being confined, letting her embody their collective sense of injury.

Kiku, who leaves camp to attend college in Philadelphia, where she has been allowed to go, gives upon her return to camp at the end of the semester an explanation for Miss Sasagawara's scandalous obsession with Joe Yoshinaga: she had "no doubt looked upon [him] as the image of either the lost lover or the lost son" (1988a, 32). Yet even as Kiku makes this observation, she feels a vague discomfort, a trace of an incipient empathy, as though her time away from the camp has made her more attentive to the complexities of human experience. She informs the reader that the glibness of her words troubles her, and she thinks seriously about Miss Sasagawara for the first time.

Later, while engaged in research back in college, Kiku stumbles on a poem by Miss Sasagawara in a literary magazine that had "suspended publication" some time during the war. When she reads the poem, Kiku finally enters into a meaningful empathetic understanding of what Miss Sasagawara had endured when Kiku and her friends knew her. The poem speaks of a man who saw the internment as a liberating opportunity to pursue "Nirvana, that saintly state of moral purity and universal wisdom" (1988a, 32). We realize that it is her father that Mari Sasagawara describes in the poem, and we, along with Kiku, begin to imagine how agonizing it must have been for her to live with a parent who had convinced himself (perhaps for his own psychic survival) that the internment was desirable because it allowed him "to extinguish within himself all unworthy desire and consequently all evil, to concentrate on that serene, eight-fold path of highest understanding, highest mindedness, highest speech, highest action, highest livelihood, highest recollectedness, highest endeavor, and highest meditation" (32–33). The poet asks movingly, in fact she begs to know, how this man could have been "deaf and blind to the human passions rising, subsiding, and again rising, perhaps in anguished silence, within the selfsame room?" (33).

Mari Sasagawara was an artist, a ballet dancer who in her pre-internment days had tasted the pleasures of performance and travel. Reading the poem strengthens Kiku's empathetic connection to Miss Sasagawara and allows her to fathom the depth of Miss Sasagawara's heart to understand the particular anguish she must have suffered. Mari Sasagawara not only had to give up everything that was meaningful to her; she also had to live with her suffering alone. She is betrayed not just by country, but also by her only surviving parent. Reading her poem enables Kiku to feel for her a retroactive empathy.

There can be no easy prediction of when empathy will emerge. Sometimes, a fear of becoming conflated with the victim can lead to one's withholding in public a display of empathy for the sufferer. Such restraint is especially likely to occur if the reason for the suffering is the hurtful action of the group or individual in power. In "A Fire in Fontana," an essay first published in 1985, Yamamoto revisits her own lack of sympathy for an African American man, Mr. Short, who was being threatened with death for choosing to live in an all-white town in California shortly after the end of World War II. Yamamoto was employed at the time (1945–1948) at the *Los Angeles Tribune*, which she characterizes "as the most creatively edited Negro newspaper in the country while it was alive" (Crow 1987, 77). The paper had hired her because, she says, it hoped to cultivate interracial friendship between blacks and Japanese Americans, the more so as blacks had moved into Japanese American areas during the internment and "Little Tokyo had become Bronzeville" (77). Yet despite the newspaper's own agenda of cross-racial friendship, Yamamoto did not cover Mr. Short's situation with the empathy it should have evoked in her.

Mr. Short arrived at the newspaper with details of the threats he had received, and he hoped to use the newspaper to mobilize support from the African American community for himself and his family. Yamamoto was assigned the story. Instead of reporting on Mr. Short's situation in a manner to convey the legitimacy of the danger he was facing, she chose to cast doubt on the seriousness of the threats confronting him. As a result, the support that Mr. Short hoped to receive from the black community did not materialize, and he and his family did indeed perish in the firebombing of his home by white racists.

There is no single explanation for Yamamoto's curious lack of empathy for Mr. Short. Only just released from the internment experience, she of all people ought to have empathized with his fear of being harmed. In an earlier essay, I observe, "Perhaps as a recent victim of the power of the state, Yamamoto wished to incorporate herself into the fabric of state institutions and so adopted the comfortable and complacent tone of 'impartial' journalism" (2006, 95). Here is a clear instance of proximate antipathy: Mr. Short's experience is too uncomfortably close a reminder of Yamamoto's recent trauma; the shame of being rejected by the country of her birth and the resulting sense of helplessness against the dictates of the state lead Yamamoto to retreat to the distancing device of reportage, stripped not just of bias but of emotion. Yamamoto does eventually return, several years later, to reflect upon her failure of empathy, as Grace Hong (1999) has shown.[4]

The Victims' Anger Inhibits the Evocation of Empathy

Elaine Kim (2000) records the vitriolic reaction that met her essay in *Newsweek* in which she expressed anger at the state's betrayal of Korean merchants and Korean Americans in general in the 1992 uprising in Los Angeles following the first not-guilty verdict in the Rodney King trial. As an Asian American, she learns that she is not permitted rage; melancholy, yes; sorrow, yes; but not anger.[5] Regardless of injustice suffered, oppressed groups are required to express their emotions in acceptable ways. In a similar vein, Mitsuye Yamada (1983) observes that when she was teaching *Aiiieeeee* (the anthology of Asian American literature of which Frank Chin is an editor), her white students were angry at the militant tone of the anthology's introduction. One student's response to the introduction is representative: "It made me angry. *Their* anger made *me* angry, because I didn't even know the Asian Americans felt oppressed. I didn't expect their anger" (35). Further discussion with her students revealed that they "'understood' the anger expressed by the Black and Chicanos and they 'empathized' with the frustration and sorrow expressed by the American Indian. But the Asian American??" (35). Yamada believes that the Asian Americans' reluctance to protest racism actively and to assert themselves aggressively in the face of obvious injustice has contributed in no small part to an inability on the part of the majority community to expect Asian American anger and to see it as evidence of deep pain. Frank Chin was among the first Asian American writers to reject containment of anger. The explosion of language that marks *Chickencoop Chinaman* (1981), for instance, announces in no uncertain terms that the Chinaman will not nod and bow, but he will rail. Chin's wielding of language transforms it from an instrument for imposing order (on emotions) to one of unleashing the chaos of affect. Expressions of anger as a mode of asserting cultural visibility are the focus of Tasha Oren's (2005) essay

"Secret Asian Man." She writes, "In my search for articulations of Asian American racial anger and grievance . . . , what I am in fact after are moments that rupture formulaic disregard and offer new ways of articulating Asian American experience" (341). When one gets angry, one "make[s] a spectacle of oneself and demand[s] attention. Thus the expression of anger . . . is simultaneously an act of agency and loss: loss of temper, composure, and self-control" (344), observes Oren, coming down squarely on the side of the "loss" of self control through anger in order to gain self-dignity and political visibility.

Mitsuye Yamada's poems on internment provide, as Anita Patterson (1998) observes, valuable insights into the poet's "profound ambivalence with respect to the creative practice of making and arranging images" (105). Even as she wields the aesthetic craft of poetry, Yamada refuses to allow it to discipline anger and pain. Referencing the poem "Evacuation," Patterson draws our attention to the lines in which the speaker (a young voice) records her obedience to the photographer's command to smile as she is boarding the bus that will take her to camp. "Yamada shows us that the acts of obedience on the part of the internees were neither voluntarily consented to nor precisely involuntary; that such acts stand as inadequate expressions of ties to the State, because they were simply performed as quickly, instinctively, and involuntarily as the child's smile" (111). And though the smiling faces of Japanese Americans were used by the propagandistic machinery of the government to establish the fiction that the state had only the best interests of the internees in mind, Yamada, says Patterson, "alerts us to the fact that for many internees, smiles afforded them a necessary, proud defense of privacy against an invasive and often hostile world" (120). Patterson concludes that Yamada would not allow her internment experience to fit into some neat "aesthetic that posited the necessity of the orderly and the arranged; of carefully screened memories that seamlessly fit together . . . ; of an always obedient, always smiling image of the self" (125). Yamada's poems, with their critique of carefully arranged responses, resist "the helplessly obedient endorsement of the internment on the part of Japanese-Americans" (124).

Discussing the poem "The Night before Good-Bye," in which the mother urges her daughter to "keep your underwear / in good repair / in case of accident / don't bring shame / on us," Patterson (1998) shows how the lyric voice rejects this "maternal admonition." Arguing that the mother's injunction is similar in its strictures to the "policing" of internment life, Patterson reads the poem as Yamada's refusal to allow her body to become compliant in its own imprisonment. "What the poem suggests is that the comprehensibility of the mother's admonition as a protection of privacy—her implicit, adamant belief that the best defense against racism is not to let anyone know that you suffer from its effects—does not in any way lessen the mandate for stalwart resistance to this admonition" (124–125).

Yamada's resistance to the aesthetic dictate of neatly arranging emotion takes on special significance when considered against the backdrop of the originary and intimate relationship between aesthetics and empathy (the word *empathy* itself coming from German roots and within the realm of aesthetics). The link between art object and "viewer" (or reader or listener) is the arena of aesthetics. K. E. Gilbert and H. Kuhn explain that empathy is a condition in which "we find things talking to us in our own language, and we are unaware that their voice is merely an echo of our own" (qtd. in Crozier and Greenhalgh 1992, 86). Thus, when we find ourselves responding positively to a work of art, be it a literary text or a painting or photograph, it is because that work mirrors the structure and discourse of our own expressive efforts. Simply put, we cannot empathize with that which arouses no aesthetic pleasure in us (i.e., unless the expressive form of the art work resonates for us, we are not moved by it). And because aesthetic pleasure is always determined by "the sociopolitical situation in which the viewer and object exist" (86)—in other words, is contextual—empathy too, is influenced by sociopolitical circumstances.

These influences are of particular significance in understanding the reception to Julie Otsuka's novel on the internment, *When the Emperor Was Divine* (2002). In an interview with Kelley Kawano (2002) of Random House, Otsuka says that she wanted her readers to see the characters as people first, not as Japanese Americans. She wanted readers to imagine themselves in the situation that confronted the characters in her spare novel—the situation of having to shut down your home, destroy your belongings, sell your property for next to nothing, and dismantle your life, all in preparation for being led away to be imprisoned and isolated from the rest of the country. Otsuka does not give her characters names, identifying them only with the generic labels of *woman, girl, boy, father*. Her narration works by suggestion and implication, hinting at what is felt but unable to be verbalized. Her characters hold in check the perceptions they register, the desires they feel. Some readers feel that her style is most appropriate for the effect she seeks to create of universalizing the emotions of the characters, of making them appear to be like everyone else, not alien, not different. But other readers fault her depersonalized telling, particularly her stripping the interned family of their names. If she wished to create empathy for her characters, then this device of their anonymity works counter to her goal, say her critics.

Tina Chen (2005), teaching the book at Vanderbilt University, speaks both to the value of universalizing the internment experience and to the limitations of such an approach. In the early sections of the book, says Chen, her students felt a kinship with the characters because they seemed to be like everyone else. "Students gravitated towards the ways in which they felt that the experiences delineated in the novel 'could have happened to anyone,' could even have happened to themselves. As part of celebrating the universalism of the story, students were clearly evacuating 'Japaneseness' to position themselves in empathetic identification with the characters" (168). Chen does not tell us who her students are—whether predominantly white, or from other ethnic and racial groups. Their empathy with the characters is a faux empathy, not dissimilar to the egotistical drift that Hoffman warns against (see the Introduction). The students relate to the suffering because Otsuka enables them to envision the family—the woman, the girl, and the boy—not as different in their Japanese-ness but as similar to any other family they know.

The book opens with the woman's perspective as she is getting ready to pack the family's belongings to leave for the transfer station en route to the internment camp. The father has been arrested several months ago, and there is no information about his whereabouts. These early pages suggest a sup-pressed but unarticulated empathy among at least some members of the domi-nant community. The woman enters the neighborhood hardware store to buy twine and tape, and the owner, Joe Lundy, engages her in casual conversation about the condition of her roof. She complains that it leaks and she has to use a bucket when it rains. "Nothing wrong with a bucket," Joe Lundy says, pushing back toward her the money that she has placed on the counter to pay him. "You can pay me later," he insists, and begins "to wipe the side of the register with a rag. There was a dark stain there that would not go away" (Otsuka 2002, 5). He does not look at her. One senses his desire to say something more meaning-ful, offer words of comfort perhaps, but one also gets the impression that he lacks the courage to vocalize his friendship. The woman is determined to pay him, and she does, even as he offers her "two caramel candies wrapped in gold foil" (6) for the children. As she leaves the store, he calls out, "That's a nice red dress" (6). She thanks him, calling him by his name, "Thank you, Joe" (6); she realizes that in all the years that she has known him, this is the first time that she has actually used his name. "It sounded strange to her. Wrong, almost. But she had said it. She had said it out loud. She wished she had said it earlier" (6).

It is significant that Otsuka focuses on the *woman's* regret at not having made any earlier attempt to establish an easy camaraderie with Joe. It is as though she blames herself for having kept apart from a full and rich integra-tion into the social give-and-take of the neighborhood. One wonders why the author has not probed further *Lundy's* inability to voice the embryonic empa-thy he is experiencing. His limitations remain unexplained. Nor do we know what the woman feels about his sputtered utterances. Does she recognize them as woefully inadequate, ultimately ineffectual, and requiring no sacrifice of power on his part, no interrogation of his privilege? Or is she grateful for and comforted by his attempt? The barrenness of their interaction underscores the distance between her and him and the tragic separation of their worlds.

In the second section, delivered through the girl's perspective, we find almost no trace of empathy. There is obvious antipathy—as evidenced by the brick that someone from the outside throws into the lighted train (revealing its cargo of "Japanese" faces) as it passes by in the dark through the expanse of the country's interior. The lights are on, the shades are up, and they become easy targets. After that, the soldier commands them to keep the shades down. We learn from the girl's observations that there is a world outside that seems to be intact, with people whose lives unfold with no care in the world, with no major crises. The girl imagines, "A man walking alongside the tracks would just see a train with black windows passing by in the middle of the day. He would think, There goes the train, and then he would not think about the train again. He would think about other things. What was for supper, maybe, or who was winning the war" (Otsuka 2002, 28–29).

Several reviewers have remarked on the attention to detail in Otsuka's writing, the smallest gestures and specifics of landscape that she recreates in her language, the minutiae of trivialities that she describes. Michael Upchurch (2002) describes the novel as "muted . . . terse but eloquent" (14), praising Otsuka's "gift for compression" (14). Anne Stephenson (2002) applauds Otsuka's "deliberate restraint" and describes the novel as "slender and visually elegant" (8D). Gretchen Gurujal (2002) writes, "It is almost as if Otsuka decided that to conscientiously delve into the intricacies of this shameful period in America's history would be too difficult, perhaps impossible, for the type of story she wanted to write. So she created a parallel allegory of sorts hovering just above the surface of history, creating an effect that is especially eerie in such a brief story." Jessie Thorpe (2003) is equally enthusiastic: "This slim volume possesses a unique voice, truly the author's own. Every scene, every moment is carved with precision. This is an exquisite novel, in the sense that a tastefully small diamond, brilliantly faceted, is polished to a solid, sparkling essence."

These enthusiastic responses to Otsuka's aesthetic chiseling, to her obvious attention to craft, appear to reward Otsuka for sublimating her anger/ distress into careful and precise observation. The manner in which she communicates pain and rage allows for the easy consumption of her internment narrative, because it presents itself primarily as work of description—an artistic recording of the physical details of the experience rather than a highlighting of the emotional complexities of the characters (with the exception of the father). I am reminded of W. H. Auden's "praise" of Adrienne Rich's first and award-winning collection of poetry: he notes that she has "good manners," and her poems "are neatly and modestly dressed, speak quietly and do not mumble, respect their elders . . . and do not tell fibs" (qtd. in Langdell 2004, 13). Later, Rich rejects the allure of this praise for good artistic behavior, breaking free and allowing herself to be "dragged by the roots of her own will / into another scene of choices" (Rich 1986, 23). She refuses to be the obedient child complying with aesthetic rules and coveting awards. I do not mean to suggest that Otsuka is intentionally obedient to any articulated expectation placed on her to exercise restraint in the display of anger and pain. But the core of her chosen aesthetics and the mode in which she is most comfortable expressing herself is to focus on representation of visual detail, the particularity of what her characters see, and what they look at and record in their consciousness. In college, Otsuka first took up painting, and then, when she thought that she was not a very good painter, turned to writing. Her prose reflects the attention to detail that marks a visual artist. There are meticulously drawn descriptions of setting and action, and every word is made to count, to build mood, tone, or character.

The effect is one of a gradual accretion of suggestions, the accumulation of bits and pieces that slowly coalesce.

In the final section of the book, the language splinters into shards (to use a phrase of Meena Alexander) and the emotional rage and distress of the father break through. He rejects the role he is expected to play in a voice edged with sarcasm: "*Such a delightful little people! Everything so small and pretty!*" (Otsuka 2002, 142), shattering the container in which he has locked in his feelings. The words hammer, unrelenting: "I'm the slant-eyed sniper in the trees. / I'm the saboteur in the shrubs. / I'm the stranger at the gate. / I'm the traitor in your own backyard. . . . So go ahead and lock me up. Take my children. Take my wife. Freeze my assets. Seize my crops. . . . Assign me a number. Inform me of my crime" (143). This outburst, vastly different in tone from the rest of the novel, invites the harsh criticism of *New York Times Book Review* critic Michiko Kakutani (2002), who sees it as "ill-conceived" and "a shrill diatribe" (E6), the one false note in an otherwise flawlessly executed literary performance. In this section, all the suppressed emotion of the preceding chapters breaks through, and we get a full blast of the anger, pain, and despair of the man suspected of treason and wrenched away from his family and life. Kakutani is not impressed by its style: "Such enraged declarations, however understandable, do not possess the subtle, emotional power of the previous portions of 'When the Emperor Was Divine,' and they distract attention from the resonant and beautifully nuanced achievement to be found in those foregoing pages" (E6). Tina Chen (2005) offers a different perspective, and one, I would submit, that restores to the father the dignity of his personhood. She sees this last section, with its drastically different narrative style, as forcing upon the reader an ethics of caring, insisting on the reader's engagement with the father in his uniqueness as a person of Japanese descent. In this section, Otsuka jettisons the universalism of the previous chapters and demands that the reader attend to these people not as universalized tropes of dispossessed and displaced beings but very particularly as individuals of Japanese origin who have been unfairly targeted at a certain historical moment.

As Chen (2005) points out, the second-person address of the father's outburst, where he refers to the reader as *you*, stands as an accusation of the reader's complicity in perpetuating the conditions that made possible the treatment he endured:

> The father's direct address to the reader thus suggests that the audience to whom he addresses his "confession" is not just the government authorities who took him away from his family in the middle of the night wearing only his bathrobe and his slippers, but also the reader, someone who might also believe that "I'm the one you don't see at all—we all look alike. I'm the one you see everywhere—we're taking over your neighborhood." (168)

Chen (2005) reads this final chapter as Otsuka's refusal to allow easy empathetic identification. Arguing for an ethics of knowledge in the reading of literature, a stance that is wary of an easy embrace of the pleasures of empathy, Chen observes that the "confrontational tone" of the last chapter "restructure[s]" (168) the relationship between reader and characters from one of easy empathetic identification with the universality of the characters to a reckoning with their difference and the author's challenge to readers to connect to the characters *despite* their difference. In her analysis, Chen recommends, as I have elsewhere, a reading posture that does not always seek complete knowledge or the control of mastery:

> In illuminating both the pleasures of empathy and its problematic consequences, Otsuka delineates a position with great pedagogical potential, one in which readerly empathy as an unexamined site of feeling and response can be transmuted into an engaged accountable critical sympathy that acknowledges alterity not through an impulse towards mastery but through an ethical component to reorienting the self in relation to Otherness. (Chen 2005, 169)[6]

The Misuse of Empathy

The restraint evident in the bulk of Otsuka's (2002) text, though it may, on the one hand, enable a shallow identification with and empathy for her characters, is, on the other hand, supremely important for what it reveals about the value of deferred interpretation. In the final section, the character of the father articulates the danger of drawing hasty conclusions by challenging his interlocutors: "Who am I? You know who I am. Or you think you do" (142). *You think you see "me" in all my guises*, he says to them: *the waiter, the store owner, the shoeshine boy, the priest, the judo teacher, the gardener, the chicken sexer, and the numerous figures that populate your everyday reality. But what do you really know?* This is the question he exhorts them to probe. Seeing does not mean knowing, and collecting impressive quantities of observed data does not automatically lead to meaningful understanding. He mocks them for their quickly constructed conclusions about Japanese Americans: "Put it down in writing—*is nervous in conversation, always laughs loudly at the wrong time, never laughs at all*—and I'll sign on the dotted line. *Is treacherous and cunning, is ruthless, is cruel*" (143–144).

Otsuka's text, in its refusal to move from seeing to understanding/knowing, stands in contrast to the overly interpreted data of the social scientists and anthropologists who were assigned to study the internees in the 1940s for the War Relocation Authority. These researchers drew hasty but confidently asserted conclusions from their ethnographic observations of life in the ten internment camps to which 120,000 Japanese Americans were confined. Orin Starn (1986) notes:

The underlying assumption throughout was that the anthropologists could formulate scientific laws about individual and social behavior in the camps, enabling them to anticipate the outcome of different administrative policies. Some ethnographers were even more ambitious, believing that observation of the relocation centers could provide general laws of human interaction. Leighton's . . . *The Governing of Men*, for example, describes 17 administrative principles thought to have "validity which is independent of any political theory or design for living." All 17 were based on Leighton's research at Poston. (704)

Starn (1986) does not mince words about how the anthropologists "broke disciplinary taboos about mixing science and politics" and that "instead of confronting power with truth, anthropology was to supply information to power" (705). Because in gathering their information and making their observations, the ethnographers were principally concerned with proving to themselves their capacity to read the internees and predict their behavior, the wealth of data that could have been used in the service of the internees' physical and emotional needs ended up serving the exact antithetical end:

The reports, articles, and books that anthropologists produced describing the camps as communities helped justify relocation to the international community and to a domestic community eager to find that Executive Order 9066 was not inconsistent with the American way. In their published writings, WRA ethnographers told Americans what they wanted to hear—that far from being an ugly irrational racist enterprise, relocation was fair and democratic. (Starn 1986, 708)

Caroline Chung Simpson (2001) offers a similar thoughtful analysis of the numerous studies, showing that on the one hand the anthropologists largely empathized with the internees in their feeling betrayed by the government, while on the other the social science researchers believed that the internment experience, despite its unfortunate similarity to imprisonment and its egregious abrogation of civil liberties, offered an efficient means of socializing those of Japanese descent into American culture and weaning them from the authority of family patriarchs. Simpson's thoughtful critique of the camp analysts' reports points to the volatility of the interpretive process. She argues convincingly that the process of gathering information about a person or group, however comprehensive in its scope, does not necessarily protect against facile inferences. In the false confidence of acquired knowledge, one is likely to arrive at the wrong conclusions. She writes:

Although it is . . . true that most camp analysts sympathized with and tried to assist the evacuees in getting hearings for their political objections to the ordeal of internment, the efforts of the analysts

often merely effaced Japanese Americans' claims to rights and justice by simultaneously embracing them within and then distancing
them from the national agenda. The problem of Japanese American
internment was thus effectively turned away from questions of camp
conditions . . . to proving that Japanese Americans could somehow
merge their Japanese behaviors with American traditions and thereby
foster the flowering of a new generation or type of Japanese American.
But this vision depended on Japanese Americans' submission to the
paternalism of the state and its institutions in a manner that banished
them from full participation in the political discourse vital to their
agency as citizens. (70)

Misplaced Empathy?

Tasha Oren's (2005) assessment of the Hollywood film version of David Guterson's enormously popular novel *Snow Falling on Cedars* (1995) is provocative:
"moral *alignment* with the long-suffering Asian Americans is maintained, while
allegiance is strictly reserved for the white male through whom the audience
experiences the narrative. To put it bluntly, we are urged to *understand* the
Asian American . . . but to *feel* white" (355). In this section, I examine Guterson's novel to see whether and how its structure prefigures the Hollywood
treatment that leads ultimately to the viewer's feeling *for* the white man though
intellectually condemning the injustice to the Japanese Americans.

Guterson's text features the snowy and foggy landscape of the northwest
United States, the island of San Piedro off the coast of Washington state, where
salmon fishing and strawberry farming constitute the means of livelihood. The
climate is challenging, the work hard, the snow and fog unrelenting. Like the
desert of Israeli writer Amos Oz's books, the physical landscape of this novel is
an external reflection of the protagonist's inner disquiet. Ishmael Chambers is
both the self-constructed outsider and the exact opposite of the articulate and
thoughtful narrator of *Moby-Dick*. He is not really an outsider, not really cast
out in the manner of the biblical Ishmael. He sets himself apart, as the disaffected and disillusioned newspaper reporter, but he does not use this voluntary
marginal status to gain insight either into the Japanese American internment
or the circumstances that have brought Kabuo Miyamoto to trial for murder
in the post–World War II world. Ishmael has become cynical for two reasons:
because of his participation in and loss of his arm in World War II, fighting the
Japanese in the Pacific, and because of Hatsue Imada's rejection of him—her
declaration that her love for him can never be total because she has realized
that she can only be with someone of Japanese descent.

Guterson makes Ishmael a victim of love to enlist our empathy for him.
One wonders whether this reliance on love springs from a notion that love is
the ultimate boundary-crossing phenomenon in a society comprising peoples
of diverse races, ethnicities, and religions. Love, however, is an individualized

experience located in a single person and his or her partner, but its ability to effect change at the collective level is minimal. If anything, Ishmael's unfulfilled love for Hatsue leads to his self-imposed psychic isolation. Laura Kang (2002), Renee Tajima (1989), and David Mura (2005), among others, have commented on the prevalence in Western literary texts and cinema of the theme of interracial love between the white Western male and the Asian female, where the latter's body becomes the territory upon which several oppositions and desires get played out: the enlightened Western male versus the authoritarian and patriarchal Asian male (or, the Asian male as undesirable and effeminate); the mysterious East endlessly available for the Westerner's delectation; the compliant and submissive Asian female versus the white woman who challenges Western patriarchy. Guterson's text does not participate fully in any of these reductive oppositions, but it is worth asking whether he is guilty of Mura's (2005) accusation (not made in connection with Guterson's novel, admittedly) that "for white Americans to think of themselves as innocent and good, the internment camps cannot be remembered. Or, if they are brought up, they are remembered only in a truncated and safe form" (611). While Guterson does not minimize the injustice of the internment (showing, through the responses of various members of the San Piedro community, the utter outrage of it), it nonetheless is presented as the reason for Hatsue's return to her Japaneseness and her rejection of Ishmael. The internment cost Ishmael his love, and because it cost him his love he has become a hollow human being. While this linking of aborted interracial love with the internment does not necessarily constitute a trivializing of the internment experience, one cannot help but wonder why Western treatments that engage the internment critically (not eclipsing its injustice) feel compelled to couple it with love (as in Alan Parker's 1990 film *Come See the Paradise*). Mura (2005) attributes this linking to a desire on the part of Westerners to redeem the white male (615) from complicity in the internment.

Guterson does not use the internment in service of Ishmael's redemption but as the reason for Ishmael's psychic dysfunction. Even more than his participation in the war, even more than the cruelty of battle, the loss of Hatsue because of the interruption in their romance caused by the internment is the deep wound that festers in Ishmael. Moreover, it is in the internment camp at Manzanar that Hatsue replaces Ishmael with Kabuo Miyamoto, the Japanese American man she marries. Thus, it is not just Hatsue and the Japanese American community who suffer grievously as a result of the internment, it is also Ishmael Chambers, who is a walking dead man as a result of it. While I would not go so far as to say that Guterson, too, is guilty of treating the internment in "a truncated and safe form," I would say that the interracial romance acts as a veil, a thin veil but a veil nonetheless, that diffuses the harsh glare of the internment's blinding injustice.

As a result of his psychic wounding, Ishmael Chambers is but a shadow of the fearless newspaper editor that his father was and that had earned him the respect and deep affection of the Japanese American residents of the community. Ishmael owns the newspaper that he inherited from his father, who had the integrity and vision to remind his community of the trust and support they should give the Japanese-descended residents among their midst. Arthur Chambers's articles during the hysteria and paranoia following the bombing of Pearl Harbor by the Japanese Army highlight the contributions of the Japanese residents of San Piedro. For his courage, Arthur Chambers receives death threats from and cancellations of subscriptions by the more xenophobic members of San Piedro. By contrast, Ishmael withholds information; he does the opposite of what someone in his situation and position ought to do. He silences himself. Hatsue commands Ishmael to claim his editorial authority by writing about the injustice of Kabuo's trial in his newspaper.

Snow Falling on Cedars was first published in 1994, a few years after the success of the redress and reparation movement for Japanese Americans who suffered internment. Therefore, it seems to have come to the attention of the reading public at a particularly appropriate moment in the nation's reevaluation of its reprehensible wartime conduct. The questions one might ask are: What if Kabuo Miyamoto had *not* been a decorated member of the U.S. armed forces? What if, as an internee, he had refused to serve, had been one of the 'no-no boys' who answered no to questions 27 and 28 of the loyalty questionnaire that all adult internees had to complete?[7] The "no-no boys" refused to serve in the U.S. armed forces because they felt that the country had forfeited its right to require their military service by its betrayal of them in stripping them of their fundamental rights as citizens. In asking how Kabuo might have been perceived by the jurors or his own defense lawyer had he been a "no-no boy," I am not posing an idle speculative or rhetorical question, one that asks us to comment not on the narrative that Guterson has written but on one that he could have written. I am asking us to consider the scenario of Kabuo as a "no-no boy" as a means to test the limits of empathy.

Would it have been possible to evoke or generate readerly sympathy for Kabuo if he had not said to Hatsue that "he *had* to go to the war? It was necessary to demonstrate his bravery. It was necessary to demonstrate his loyalty to the United States: his country" (Guterson 1995, 92). What if he had said instead, "I will not fight because my country has betrayed me by mistrusting and imprisoning me in this internment camp, by thinking of me as a potential traitor"? Might it not have complicated the readers' (and by implication the jurors') stance toward Kabuo? If he had been a person unwilling to enlist, would the jurors have been able to see themselves as capable of making a similar refusal to serve in the military? Under the same circumstances as his, could they have imagined the depth of hurt, anger, and rejection that Kabuo could have felt and which could just as easily and understandably have led to his refusing to serve as to his eagerly enlisting? The defense lawyer Nels Gudmundsson's closing statement for the defense appeals to the jurors' empathy for a fellow patriot. He uses the fact of Kabuo's heroism and external evidence of loyalty to his country as the basis of appeal to the jurors' sense of fair play. He names the prejudice that is implicit in the state's case against Kabuo, but the reason he advances for their needing to resist this prejudice is predicated on a questionable argument—goodwill toward one who has conducted himself according to expectations. "He has returned to find himself the victim of prejudice—make no mistake about it, this trial is about prejudice—in the country he fought to defend" (417). "He is counting on you to remember this war and to see Kabuo Miyamoto as somehow connected with it. And, ladies and gentlemen, . . . let us recall that Kabuo Miyamoto is connected with it. He is a much-decorated first lieutenant of the United States Army who fought for his country—the United States—in the European theater" (417).

Perhaps this is the ultimate lesson that one must derive from Guterson's (1995) portrayal of Kabuo and his father, Zenhichi: their "perfection" is necessary for their survival within the community and their acceptance as characters worthy of our empathy. The only reason that they are accorded a measure of acceptance in the community is that they are self-effacing, supremely hardworking, and extremely attentive about not causing any trouble.[8] David Mura (2005) writes movingly of the efforts by Japanese Americans in their post-internment lives to seek to minimize attention to themselves by becoming as "white" as possible in their behavior; theirs was an act of psychic self-denial, necessary for survival in a skeptical and hostile world (613). Would Arthur Chambers have been as willing to speak in behalf of his Japanese American neighbors if they had not been "model" citizens and "model" neighbors? Were they worthy of protection only because they strove to cause no trouble? Is their difference overlooked only because they have totally capitulated to the behavioral expectations placed on them? These questions help us see past the idealized portrait of the San Piedro Japanese American community to imagine the complexities that could be investigated within the context of white empathy. Mrs. Chambers's (Ishmael's mother's) empathy, too, is related to the wartime heroism of Kabuo. When Ishmael is recounting to her Kabuo's "inscrutable" expression and demeanor and apparent lack of remorse, judging from the immovability of his face while in the courtroom (Ishmael is reminded of the propaganda films that he saw while training as a soldier during World War II and stationed in the Pacific that emphasized the treachery of the Japanese soldier and his disregard for life—"It's characteristic of the Jap to be sly and treacherous. He won't show what he's thinking on his face" [Guterson 1995, 344]), Mrs. Chambers reminds him, "Like you, Ishmael, he served in the war. Have you forgotten that—that he fought in the war? That he risked his life for this country?" (345).

Ultimately, one must remember, the Japanese Americans' model behavior served them not at all. Their "white neighbors looked on, people who had risen early to stand in the cold and watch this exorcising of the Japanese from their midst" (Guterson 1995, 79). Empathy, where it did exist, was fleeting and paltry. Carl Heine, Sr., laments that eight days is not enough for a family to wind up and get ready to leave, to shut down a life (125–126); one wonders whether he would have found eighty days more acceptable. Or whether the emphasis on the short period of time is his way of indirectly demonstrating empathy because he knows he cannot more directly do so in the presence of his wife, Etta, whose hostility for the Japanese Americans is virulent. Perhaps it is Guterson's skill that he leaves us to see the gaps between the two communities, the chasm so wide that where bridges of empathy begin to be erected, they are at best flimsy structures likely to fall apart easily.

That the relationship between the two groups is tenuous and fragile is made evident in the words *human sacrifice* to describe the Japanese American maiden who is crowned as the Strawberry Princess at the annual festival. Guterson shows us that the bonhomie and goodwill are superficial—a recognition that the bonds are based on economic necessity alone, the white farmers needing the Japanese American community solely for the labor of the pickers. That the connection is lubricated by the selection of the Strawberry Princess from the Japanese American community underscores the role of the woman as the conciliator and bridge between two communities suspicious of one another. She receives "her crown with a bowed head from [the] mayor . . . an unwitting intermediary between two communities, a human sacrifice who allowed the festivities to go forward with no uttered ill will" (Guterson 1995, 78).

The cheer and camaraderie of the Strawberry Festival notwithstanding, Guterson (1995) writes that when the Japanese army bombed Pearl Harbor and the administration issued Executive Order 9066 calling for the evacuation of all persons of Japanese descent, the white community of San Piedro stood by silently. There were those who objected, but their objections carried little weight because there were not sufficient numbers of them. We hear of Kaspars Hinkle, the coach of the high school baseball team, who is outraged that his "starting catcher, second baseman, and two outfielders, . . . not to mention his two best pitchers—were going to miss the whole season" (210). He protests, "None of these kids were spies!" As in the case of Arthur Chambers's editorials highlighting the loyalty and contributions of San Piedro's Japanese Americans, one is tempted to wonder whether Hinkle's gesture of solidarity and empathy would have been forthcoming had the young Japanese American ballplayers not been assets to the team. These scattered instances of the white community's resistance to the racial targeting of their Japanese American neighbors underscore the inexorability of state power. The machine of governmental authority, once set in motion, can feed off the fear of the citizenry and proceed relatively unimpeded in the execution of its wartime agenda. Thus, while those like Carl Heine, Sr., and Coach Hinkle may find the government's actions objectionable and irrational, they have little power to effect change. In fact, and this is the area of empathy that Guterson does not explore, is there *anything* that Heine and the coach *could* have done to delay and perhaps prevent what happened to the Japanese Americans among their midst? Thus, what Guterson shows in his narrative is that while one can feel latent empathy for an individual or group, that inner goodwill may have little influence on the crisis confronting the targeted individual or group. Singular instances of empathy are just that—isolated flashes of understanding and connectedness. They do not cohere into a force sufficiently strong to resist the onslaught of a decree of power by the state.

Related to the structure and influence of state power is the framework of the legal system. Much of the time-present of Guterson's novel unfolds in the courtroom where Kabuo is being tried for the murder of Carl Heine, Jr. Guterson is careful to present a cast of characters that is as balanced as possible: while the sheriff and coroner are, along with the witnesses for the prosecution, quick to settle on Kabuo's guilt, in no small part because of his Japanese heritage, the judge is scrupulously fair—in his cautions against needlessly prejudicial testimony that has no bearing on the circumstances of the case—and the court-appointed defending attorney is wholly committed to making a strong case for reasonable doubt. The physical evidence, however, appears to point strongly toward Kabuo's guilt, and the prosecutor focuses on this evidence, buttressing it with the testimony of witnesses such as Sergeant Maples. The jurors, about whom we know little until almost the end of the novel when we see them in the jury room deliberating on the evidence, essentially are, with the exception of one individual, presented as unimaginatively faithful to the literal and narrow interpretation of the available evidence. The one juror, Alexander Van Ness, who holds up the verdict is an important player, but this person's lone stance comes as something of a surprise because we are given no indication of the jurors' thinking before this moment. In fact, his refusal to go along with the rest of his peers is critical to the ultimate outcome of the case. His holding up a quick verdict is what makes possible the judge's quick move to dismiss the case in light of the new evidence presented to him.

Kabuo's freedom is held in the hands of two individuals: the lone resistant juror and Ishmael Chambers. Quite by accident, when Ishmael is going through the coast guard's reports, he stumbles on a log that reveals that on the night that Kabuo is alleged to have murdered Carl Heine, Jr., a large freighter had strayed off the main channel as a result of fog. The wake of this large vessel, Ishmael realizes when he sees the time against the coast guard's log, could have resulted in all the circumstances that led to Carl Heine's being tossed against a hard surface and coming to his death. The physical evidence that at the moment is being interpreted as sure evidence of Kabuo's guilt could just as easily be explained as resulting from the freighter's wake. Meanwhile, the resistant juror is presented as meticulous in his interpretation of the abstract ideals of accuracy and justice. He is a man of complex thinking, unwilling to jump to hasty conclusions, resistant to specious analogies and correspondences, and determined to weigh carefully the weight of evidence against Kabuo. He insists on a continuum of wrongdoing, pointing out that because one is a liar does not automatically follow that one is a murderer. His "obstinacy," his refusal to be railroaded in following his peers' deductions, provides Ishmael's belated sense of justice the opportunity to bear fruit.

The difference between Ishmael and Alexander is also a difference between recklessness and meticulousness. Ishmael recognizes that his knowledge of the coast guard's notes about the large freighter gives him the power to affect a person's life, his future. That knowledge, coming to him in his condition of wounded rejection and sense of betrayal, creates within him a turmoil that he cannot adequately process or translate into responsible action. We learn from the narrator that "the truth now lay in Ishmael's own pocket and he did not know what to do with it. He did not know how to conduct himself and the recklessness he felt about everything was as foreign to him as the sea foam breaking over the snowy boats and over the pilings" (Guterson 1995, 428). This recklessness, though new to him, nevertheless grants him, if only temporarily, a feeling of newness, an opening up of a dimension of himself that he has not known about, not encountered. He can dwell on its effects on him, taste and experiment with its impact. The luxury of playing with this emotion of recklessness and also of the power contained within it is both pleasurable and disturbing. It is a flirtation with a new emotion that could cost the defendant his life and freedom. Such power is precisely what the narrator of Alice Walker's (1981) story "Advancing Luna and Ida B. Wells" rails against (see the Introduction). True, Guterson presents Ishmael as a man caught up in a moral dilemma faced with deciding what he will do with the power in his pocket, and true that Ishmael ultimately does the right thing, but one cannot forget that Ishmael has the potential of using that power recklessly to deprive a man of his freedom and life, and that he comes to this state of reckless power as a result of his privileged access to information, such as the coast guard's report.

It is further ironic that he comes by this information in the process of researching archived reports of previous storms. This is the story—the chaos of this prolonged snowstorm—that he *chooses* to write over the story that he is entreated to write, which is the story of the unfairness of Kabuo's trial. Just a short while ago, Hatsue has criticized him for his silence as a newspaper editor:

> Kabuo's trial is unfair. . . . You should talk about that in your newspaper. . . . Kabuo didn't kill anyone. It isn't in his heart to kill anyone. They brought in that sergeant to say he's a killer—that was just prejudice. Did you hear the things that man was saying? How Kabuo had it in his heart to kill? How horrible he is, a killer? Put it in your paper, about that man's testimony, how all of it was unfair. How the whole trial is unfair. (Guterson 1995, 325)

Ishmael's response is to take refuge in a platitude about the universal unfairness of things: "I'm bothered, too, when things are unfair, . . . [b]ut sometimes I wonder if unfairness isn't . . . [ellipsis in original] part of things. I wonder if we should even expect fairness, if we should assume we have some right to it" (Guterson 1995, 325). Hatsue's impatient rejoinder dismisses Ishmael's attempt to characterize unfairness as a naturally occurring phenomenon, as a force that persists as a kind of free-floating condition of the universe over which human beings have little control. Instead, she returns unfairness to the realm of power, to the active and deliberate choices of action *people* make: "I'm not talking about the whole universe. . . . I'm talking about people—the sheriff, that prosecutor, the judge, you. People who can do things because they run newspapers or arrest people or convict them or decide about their lives. People don't have to be unfair, do they? That isn't just *part of things*, when people are unfair to somebody" (326). Ishmael, by equating the unfairness of society's power-wielders to whom Hatsue refers with her unfairness at rejecting him as a life companion, exhibits an inability to look beyond the individual realm—to see the larger forces at play that ring not just his relationship with Hatsue but the condition of being from a minority nondominant group in a sociopolitical context. However, he does ultimately do the right thing by going to the sheriff with the evidence about the freighter and therefore becomes an important player in Kabuo Miyamoto's release.

The closing paragraph of the novel offers a brief meditation on the relationship between accident and human will. We are invited to celebrate a universe in which, despite the unpredictability and randomness of events, the capacity of the individual to make choices of action reigns supreme. Speaking from Ishmael's perspective, the narrator declares, "The heart of any other, because it had a will, would remain forever mysterious. . . . [A]ccident ruled every corner of the universe except the chambers of the human heart" (Guterson 1995, 460). Ishmael can bask in self-satisfaction that he has finally shaken off his spiritual malaise and reentered the world of humanity, and it would be uncharitable to deny him his moment of gratification. Yet the problem with ending on this celebratory note of individual resolve is that it obscures the overwhelming obstacles posed by institutional structures. For instance, if Kabuo had been convicted as guilty *before* Ishmael's decision to act on his knowledge of the freighter, the process of securing his release and exonerating him could conceivably have been long drawn out and extremely complicated (as the film *After Innocence* [Sanders 2005] makes abundantly clear). True, institutions are set up by individuals and so, theoretically, individuals have the power to circumvent institutional processes. But not all individuals have such power, and frequently even those with the appropriate power take refuge in the structures of institutions rather than engage the difficult ethical questions or invest the empathetic energy that would enable them to justify, to themselves, bypassing institutional hurdles. And yet ultimately we must rely on individuals and on the capacity of each person's humanity to imagine and to empathize. One shudders to think of this awesome power that rests within each person, and the terrifying consequences that can result from misapplications of this power.

4

Guantánamo

Where Lawyers Connect with
the "Worst of the Worst"

But do you hear me, oh Judge, do you hear me at all?
—Detainee OSAMA ABU KABIR, "Is It True?"

The location is Guantánamo Bay. The detainee, lawyer, paralegal, and translator form a quartet. This meeting, inside an interview/interrogation room, is unusual, because it results in the announcement of happy news. The detainee Adel, a former Saudi Arabian police officer who was traveling to Pakistan for eye surgery when he was captured, is finally being sent home. Adel hugs the lawyer, attorney Anant Raut, and thanks him. "I put my faith in Allah, . . . and Allah sent you" (qtd. in Raut 2008, 14). Adel was in Guantánamo Bay for five years. Anant Raut, formerly of the law firm of Weil, Gotshal & Manges, is one of approximately three hundred lawyers who have been engaged in detainee defense work since 2002. This chapter spotlights the lawyers' pro bono work on behalf of the detainees. But it is not an uncritical paean to the Guantánamo Bay lawyers. Rather, I use the lawyers' involvement in detainee defense work as a springboard to explore the complex conditions under which engaged citizenship emerges. I examine the public's complex and conflicted responses to the lawyers' detainee work (ranging from admiration to downright hostility), probe the seductive promise of legal discourse, and analyze the emergence and manifestation of empathy in lawyers at this fraught moment in the nation's history.

It is important to acknowledge Lauren Berlant's (2002) scathing criticism of "a politics of feeling" and heed her suspicion of sentimentality. Her challenge—"What does it mean for the theory and practice of social transformation when feeling *good* becomes evidence of justice's triumph?" (112)—draws attention to the limitations of *affect* in the context of ethics and cautions us against a simple altruistic interpretation of the lawyers' detainee defense work. What Berlant finds problematic about "the centrality of interpersonal identification and empathy to the vitality and viability of collective life" is that it "gives citizens something to do in response to overwhelming structural violence" and, in effect, assuages the citizens' anxiety concerning the fairness of the state (108).

Berlant rejects an individualized politics of "feeling bad" (for others) as a precursor of necessary action to restore a sense of feeling good. Her rejection provides a necessary corrective to self-congratulatory attitudes of empathy and forces us to go beyond mere sentiment. Examining the pro bono lawyers' detainee defense work against the backdrop of Berlant's critique is at once useful and distracting. Why do the lawyers get involved in the first place? They are not paid for their work, and, as will become evident later, their participation entails considerable inconvenience and psychological distress. So their legal representation of the detainees does not immediately result in feeling good. Yet one could argue that they enlist themselves in this work in order to feel that they are not sitting idly by while the legal edifice that organizes their professions is systematically eviscerated. They have "something to do," to use Berlant's words, and this refusal to be passive in the face of arbitrary executive power may in fact lead to their feeling good.

Where Berlant's argument ceases to be useful, however, is when we try applying it to the complex relationships that develop between the lawyers and their detainee clients. The construction of the detainees as "the worst of the worst" and as incapable of suffering (i.e., their suicides are not really evidence of deep pain but rather are publicity stunts in asymmetric warfare) has precluded the emergence of a publicly embraced politics of feeling with regard to their captivity. The detainees are denied subjecthood of any kind—being consigned to the category of potentially lethal weapons. Therefore, the lawyers' gradual awakening to the suffering of the detainees is a necessary first step in the reconstruction of their personhood. There is no question that these personal connections between lawyer and client are ultimately insufficient as challenges to the exercise of state power or to the assumptions undergirding the "war on terror." Thus, by no means should this presentation of the lawyers' detainee defense work be taken as an uncritical accolade. At the same time, however, it would be unproductive to see their participation as guided principally by self-enhancing and self-preserving motives or as contributing, in the final analysis, to the reification of legal discourse. Jean Stefancic and Richard Delgado (2005) explain that lawyers can "lose their way" when they rely too heavily on legal structures and precedent rather than on the urgencies and realities of the specific case at hand. The detainee lawyers' journey to Guantánamo Bay may be seen as a particularly bracing education in how *not* to lose their way. Whether the lessons from that education are likely to affect the nature of their involvement in nondetainee contexts remains to be seen.

Though critical legal theorists have long pressed for an ironic perspective on the law (pointing out that law is formulated by and favors groups in power), even those who interrogate the law admit that it provides the surest way of codifying desired attitudes and behaviors and ensuring their application, especially when we are tempted to withhold these attitudes and behaviors from those we find incomprehensible or repugnant. Elaine Scarry (1996) observes, for instance, that "the work accomplished by a structure of laws cannot be accomplished by a structure of sentiment" (110). She argues that laws give permanence to and call into play the two desired practices of "imagining others" (where the group in power formulating the laws envisions the reality of others unlike itself) and "unimagining oneself" (i.e., downplaying the urgencies of one's own reality so as to make room for the urgencies of others' realities) (107). The pro bono lawyers, I would argue, initially are not motivated by either consideration. They enter the field of detainee defense work primarily in response to what they perceive to be a desecration of the law.

Though Guantánamo Bay is the most "visible" flouting of all the declared ideals of the U.S. Constitution, it is also, as some experts have indicated, a more benign place of horror than other "black sites" of which the public is entirely unaware.[1] In this sense, one must agree with lawyer Clive Stafford Smith (of the anti–death penalty and antitorture advocacy organization Reprieve) that Guantánamo Bay is "a massive diversion" (qtd. in Brittain and Slovo 2003, 33). This distraction, this diversion on an international scale, draws attention away from the terrible nightmares of other prisons in other parts of the world, whose violations, at the behest of the U.S. government, went undetected.

Equally absent from the public consciousness are the many detention centers within the United States. Shubh Mathur's (2006) work as a translator for detainees in the Passaic and Bergen County jails in New Jersey offers a record of the rampant violations suffered by thousands of South Asian, Muslim, and Middle Eastern men in the months after September 11. "Most of the arrests took place between 2 and 6am and the 'midnight knock' came to be dreaded. Men were taken away from their homes in handcuffs, while their wives and children were held off at gunpoint" (34). Irum Shiekh's study of six detainees, *Detained without Cause* (2011), provides detailed oral history testimony of the practices in detention centers and at rendition sites elsewhere in the world that destroy individuals physically and psychologically.

It is tempting, therefore, to consider the Guantánamo lawyers' work as complicit in the government's efforts to focus the public's attention on Guantánamo Bay through intermittent engagement with questions about the legality and ethics of its existence, and in doing so divert the public from attending to human rights violations in detention facilities *within* the United States. However, it would be wrong to see the lawyers' intervention as having no value. Through their relentless challenges to the Bush administration, they have succeeded in reducing the numbers of detainees at Guantánamo Bay from seven hundred to less than two hundred. They continue to press for the release of other unlawfully held detainees who remain under the Obama administration. One lawyer tells the story that when President Bush was reelected for his second term in 2004, her client lost all faith in the American people. "They hate me," he said, seeing in Bush's reelection the people's endorsement of his indefinite captivity at Guantánamo Bay.[2] The detainee lawyers thus can be seen as the relatively benign face of the United States, and their efforts in behalf of the detainees may have purchased for the nation some admittedly small measure of goodwill from the hundreds of men imprisoned at Guantánamo Bay and from their families and communities in the many different countries from which they come.

I focus on civilian lawyers, many of whom are from the private bar, rather than military officers in the Judge Advocate General's (JAG) corps, because the former voluntarily offer their services and do not come to detainee defense work in response to dictates from commanding officers, as do the latter. Though the JAG lawyers provide spirited defense of their clients (see the many newspaper articles on Michael Mori, who became a hero in Australia for his representation of Australian national David Hicks, who was held in Guantánamo Bay for five years,[3] and Mahler's *The Challenge* [2008], for an in-depth study of former JAG lawyer Charles Swift, in this regard), I am primarily interested in the reasons that civilian lawyers *choose* to participate in this work and to invest thousands of pro bono hours in getting their detainee clients released from Guantánamo Bay. We may rightly view with cynicism the lawyers' declared motives. Lawyers have spoken of their respect for the Constitution, outrage at the excess of executive power, and belief in the fundamental right to a fair trial. Even if we question the sincerity of these assertions, it is impossible to deny that for most detainees, the lawyers were their only reason to hope that they would ever be freed from the state of living death that was or continues to be their existence in Guantánamo Bay.

Attorney Anant Raut gained national visibility in 2007 when he responded, in a letter published in *Salon* magazine, to the accusation by Clive (Cully) Stimson, then undersecretary of defense for detainee affairs, that law firms that were engaged in detainee defense work were receiving monetary compensation from questionable sources. Stimson recommended that the firms' corporate clients should do their patriotic duty and cease doing business with these law firms. Specifically, Stimson said, "I think, quite honestly, when corporate C.E.O.'s [sic] see that those firms are representing the very terrorists who hit their bottom line back in 2001, those C.E.O.'s [sic] are going to make those law firms choose between representing terrorists or representing reputable firms, and I think that is going to have major play in the next few weeks. And we want to watch that play out."[4] Stimson ultimately had to resign for his unfortunate and ill-advised remarks, which drew swift and vociferous outrage from prominent judges and the American Bar Association.

Raut's rebuke to Stimson is titled "Why I Defend Terrorists." Writing with unabashed idealism, Raut invokes the sanctity of the U.S. Constitution and presents his involvement in detainee defense work as the epitome of patriotism. Raut concludes that it is Stimson who lacks patriotism for his suggestion that law firms should ignore their duty to uphold the Constitution. In an eloquent response to Stimson's comments, Raut asserts, "Mr. Stimson, I don't defend 'terrorists.' I'm representing five guys who were held or are being held in Guantanamo without ever being charged with a crime, some of them for nearly five years. . . . The people I'm defending were caught up in the adrenaline and paranoia of our nation's darkest hour. All we're asking for is a fair hearing. Why does this frighten you so?" (Raut 2007, B3).

Elsewhere, Raut critiques the deeply problematic practices of the Bush administration in the aftermath of the September 11, 2001 attacks, observing:

> There's a thin veneer of civility that allows us to coexist in civilized society. Periodically, it gets punctured, and barbarity erupts in controlled bursts, whether between Serbs and Bosnians, Sunnis and Shias, or Luos and Kikuyus. But it's laws that force us to resolve our disputes through reliable and fair procedures, that accord the weak the same rights as the strong, and provide each man his due process. And when you remove that last layer of moral recognizance, there is no bottom to stop our fall. (Raut 2008, 13)

Raut's characterization of the law as "that last layer of moral recognizance" reveals his fundamental and unshakable faith in this body of discourse.

Likewise, Mahvish Khan (2008), an Afghan American law student who came forward to offer her services as a Pashto translator, writes that she was compelled to involve herself in this work because "as a law student and a daughter of immigrants, I thought the prison camp's very existence was a blatant affront to what America stands for" (1). It is significant that she needs to reassure herself of and justify her faith in the country's professed ideals of evidence and justice: "I was young and idealistic. But so were the framers of our constitution when they tried to establish the rights and responsibilities of a young nation. All my life, I'd been taught that the United States guarantees everyone certain inalienable rights" (2). Though she may have felt a human connection to the Afghani detainees because of her shared ancestral heritage with them, her principal reason had less to do with the detainees themselves and more to do with her own compulsion to ascertain the legitimacy of her nation's rhetoric.

Stephen Oleskey, of the Boston law firm Wilmer Hale, who was the lead attorney representing six Algerian detainees, voices a similar sentiment. He took up the detainee cases when the firm was invited to do so in 2004 because he wanted to actively challenge the executive branch's disregard of law. "I was very tired of merely whining to friends and family about how upset I was about the absence of the rule of law in the establishment and operation of Guantánamo Bay prison. The precedent being set of a new kind of U.S. prison deliberately established outside the reach of U.S. domestic law and not subject to the Geneva Conventions was very disturbing to me. I had spent 35 years practicing law at all levels of state and federal courts and deeply believed in the well-established due process protections and general fairness of the American justice system. Yet I had done little to protest or counteract what was happening at Guantánamo. I saw this as an opportunity to do something concrete that could have some impact and move me from passive observer to advocate in the justice system in which I had spent my entire professional life."[5]

The aspect of detainee work that has most surprised Oleskey is how it changed his own perspective. "While the incoming Bush administration had certainly made it clear that many of its policies would be very different than those of the outgoing Clinton administration, few had foreseen that the new administration would take the country into two wars or announce and carry out what it called a worldwide war on terror following 9/11, utilizing 'extraordinary renditions' featuring torture, 'Black Hole prisons' around the world and the indefinite detention at a permanent U.S. military base in the Caribbean of hundreds of men seized in many countries. What had been done by the time of the Supreme Court decisions in June 2004 in *Rasul* [see below] and *Hamdi* [see Chapter 2] was to decide as a matter of formal United States government policy to confine men for life without trial or even formal charges. Guantánamo itself was made possible by interpretations of U.S. and international law by highly trained and highly credentialed lawyers in the Justice Department's Office of Legal Counsel who provided the Bush administration with secret opinions justifying torture and indefinite detention that could be carried out without even a fig leaf of due process. I realized the time had come for me and others to advocate for the form of justice system in which we had spent our lives and in which we had such pride. I was also amazed at how completely Congress had abdicated its role in failing to legislate necessary checks and balances to control the executive's actions at Guantánamo, leaving it entirely to the courts to determine what other process there ought to be."

Sabin Willett of the law firm Bingham McCutchen, also located in Boston, explains why he became interested in representing the detainees.[6] "It was in 2004, when I couldn't stand to read my newspaper anymore; the Abu Ghraib photos had hit the press. I was restless during the second half of 2004, feeling that things were going badly, things were terribly wrong, but wondering as a private citizen, what can one do? Late in '04, early '05, a partner of mine who had an international law interest invited me to a seminar on Guantánamo organized by the Boston Bar Association. The panelists were a couple of academics, somebody from the Naval War College, an army captain. What they were saying was that the process of detention and interrogation at Guantánamo was illegal under our own law."

Willett channeled his restlessness and sense of something being amiss, and he began to familiarize himself with the legal questions associated with the detainees. "I started doing research, studied the *Rasul v. Bush* decision, and eventually found myself directed to the Center for Constitutional Rights [CCR; the nonprofit civil rights legal advocacy organization in New York City that became the nerve center coordinating the hundreds of lawyers engaged in detainee defense work]. They needed someone to take up the Uighur [ethnic

Chinese Muslim separatists] cases, so in March '05, we filed our first case on behalf of two Uighur detainees, Abu Bakker Qassim and A'del Abdu Al-Hakim. I didn't know the first thing about Chinese Muslims, but we took up the case and filed in their behalf. I knew next to nothing about them; I hadn't met them. And you don't even know if your client knows that you exist. I met them for the first time on July 14 and 15, 2005."

Wells Dixon is a young lawyer who took a leave of absence from the New York law firm of Kramer Levin Naftalis & Frankel (where he focused principally on white-collar criminal defense but started representing detainees in mid-2005) and began working for the Center for Constitutional Rights in July 2006. He is now an attorney for CCR. Dixon believes fervently in the sanctity of the U.S. Constitution. "The reason why habeas counsel [lawyers fighting for the detainees' right to challenge their detention in court] have become involved varies from lawyer to lawyer, from firm to firm. For me, federal power is something that I was always interested in, and its abuse was something that always troubled me, so it was really a natural extension of the criminal defense work that I was doing. Having said that, for me and for most other habeas counsel [from the private bar], what we observed specifically with respect to Guantánamo was an erosion of the rule of law in our country. The notion that the United States would seek to create an enclave outside the reach of any law, in which it could detain and interrogate—essentially do whatever it wanted to do with respect to these detainees, without any oversight by the courts, without the power of judicial review—was something that really was unprecedented in our legal system. It was very deeply troubling to me, and I think it's deeply troubling to many of the lawyers who have been involved in these cases. So, at least initially, it was for me and for many habeas counsel a matter of principle. The way I've described it to people at other times is to say that this was a response by the private bar to what was perceived as real erosion of the rule of law. I'm not talking just about the Constitution and laws of the United States, but the rule of law in general and our commitment as a nation to the rule of law. I think there was also an element to this, that this was a great legal challenge, and that cases that were litigated and are still being litigated are in many respects the most important cases concerning the power of the federal government, the president in particular, under the Constitution. These are seen as extremely important legal cases."[7]

One could view with deep skepticism and cynicism the lawyers' declared faith in the legal system and the United States Constitution. It is possible that their entry into detainee defense work has far less to do with idealistic belief in the legal structure and more to do with their calculated and strategic assessment that taking on this challenge would likely bring them high professional visibility. In fact, one detainee directly accuses his lawyer of such a motivation: "You're really here because you want people to see you as a big lawyer who represented the famous Guantánamo detainees, right? . . . Is this going to help your business when you tell people you freed a man from Guantánamo?"

(Khan 2008, 70). Another ironic view of the Guantánamo lawyers' participation is that they take pride in "going to 'Gitmo'" (or GTMO, the widely used term for Guantánamo) as a kind of rite of passage into an exclusive club. Veena Dubal of the Asian Law Caucus observed (at a November 18, 2010, roundtable discussion at the American Studies Association conference in San Antonio) that Guantánamo lawyers enjoy a degree of both national and international visibility that are denied lawyers who assist with the cases of domestic detainees. These latter lawyers labor in obscurity and with minimal resources (office support staff and other kinds of infrastructure). The counterargument to such a view is that many Guantánamo lawyers prefer to remain anonymous because of the hostility they encounter for their defense of detainees. They become involved, in the words of one lawyer, "at great sacrifice to themselves and their careers, because they see it as the right thing to do."

Other skeptics of the Guantánamo lawyers' idealistic and altruistic motives have remarked that the practice of law is principally an adversarial enterprise in the United States, a battle in which the strength of the players is calculated on the basis of their aggressive ability to best their opponents. The lawyers, the skeptics say, see themselves in the most exciting, because it is the most demanding, fight against a most formidable opponent: the executive branch of the U.S. government. Entering this arena of conflict enhances their battle-worthiness, so to speak, because they are then seen as tested in the hardest circumstances of all.[8] A variant of this view is that because lawyers are trained to be adversarial, they cannot but respond to what they perceive to be the executive branch's flouting of the rules of the game. Finally, as Jeremy Robbins of Wilmer Hale points out, "There are some people who say that the pro bono work we do is just a way for us to feel better about the large amounts of money we make on our other cases."[9] Wilmer Hale's pro bono detainee work has cost the firm, in terms of unremunerated hours, close to $40 million.

Thus, empathizing with the detainees for their wrongful detention is typically not the foremost of the lawyers' initial motivations. Sabin Willett made clear that he "did not want to be defending any 9/11 murderers" when he first approached the Center for Constitutional Rights. Oleskey reminded me that empathy cannot emerge unless one goes down to Guantánamo Bay and establishes a relationship with the detainees. In an e-mail I received on March 2, 2011, Willett made an additional and telling point: "the more interesting thing about this is that it reflects the mythology that exists around GTMO to those who don't meet and understand (or haven't yet met) the actual detainees. There are few alleged 9/11 murderers there; and most of the people who have been there, including many people still there have nothing to do with terrorism."

Holding the Legal Line until the Politics Kicks In

Alan Ray, legal theorist and expert on issues of Native American law, characterizes as "attenuated theater" the secrecy attending the detainees' military hearings during the years of the Bush administration. Normally, says Ray, a courtroom is a forum for performance. The adversarial nature of the courtroom proceedings is the perfect stage on which both defense and prosecuting attorneys can perform their respective roles and, in the process, exhibit both the power of the law (in the figure of the prosecution) and its inherent fairness (in the figure of the defense counsel). But in the case of the detainees, the secrecy of the military commissions—with so few outside viewers being permitted and no recordings ever being made available for public consumption—is odd and intriguing.[10]

The work of the lawyers proceeds for the most part outside the frame of public discussion. But Oleskey emphasizes that the lawyers' intervention was critical: "The [Bush] administration used fear as its trump card. It's our job as lawyers to bring some distance between the public and that fear." He says, forcefully and eloquently, "We're holding the line for the rest of you, we're giving the rest of you time to let that deep wound [of the September 11, 2001, attacks] heal that was so terrible. We are making it possible for the rest of you to remember what we stand for. . . . Look, the administration began with a theory that all these men are terrorists and that it would therefore lock them up and make up the rules to keep them locked up. We said, 'Not so fast. There's the Constitution, so you can't make up the rules,' and we also said, 'Not so fast, they're not all terrorists.' So the administration tried to come up with less-than-desirable processes to show that they are all terrorists, and we challenged them on those." Oleskey believes that the lawyers, through their objections to the arbitrary exercise of executive power, are fulfilling the democratic obligations that ought to be the general public's responsibility. One may wish to fault him for what could be considered hubris, but there is also no denying that the public and its elected representatives in Congress voiced little outrage to what was and is continuing to take place at Guantánamo Bay.

Shortly after he assumed office, President Obama pledged to suspend the questionable trial procedures of the Guantánamo Bay facility and shut down the notorious prison within a year. Neither has happened. The issue of what to do with the 171 detainees still lingers, and President Obama has abandoned his initial plan to try Khalid Sheikh Mohammed, the detainee who masterminded the 9/11 plot, in civilian court and opted to go instead with a military commission at Guantánamo Bay. His reversal of the promise he made in 2009 to shut down Guantánamo Bay feels to many of his strongest supporters like a betrayal. He has been thwarted at every step by the Republicans in Congress, but the president has not used their obstructions as an opportunity to initiate national conversation on what the presence of Guantánamo Bay says about the ideals of the nation. Admittedly, the country is more preoccupied with the economic survival of millions of unemployed Americans than with the fate of the Guantánamo Bay detainees or detainees in domestic holding centers. It is, therefore, easy to consign to some dim part of our memory the assiduous effort of lawyers (from many different spheres, including the academic world, public defender system, and private law firms) who steadfastly kept the pressure on the Bush administration and challenged its detainee policies and practices.

One lawyer has become famous. Neal Katyal, the Georgetown University law professor who won the Supreme Court case challenging the detention of Salim Hamdan, Osama bin Laden's driver, and the process by which the Bush administration intended to try him, is one of the protagonists of Jonathan Mahler's book *The Challenge* and was deputy solicitor general in the Obama administration.[11] But there are hundreds of other lawyers whose work, though less visible, served the equally critical function, in Oleskey's words, of "holding the legal line until the politics kick[ed] in." These lawyers prove the truth of Giorgio Agamben's (2005) contention that the transformation of the "constitutional order . . . underway to varying degrees in all the Western democracies" (18), particularly after September 11, 2001, is known to politicians and jurists, though "unnoticed by citizens" (18). One might say that they understand the truth of Agamben's critique that "at the very moment it would like to give lessons in democracy to different traditions and cultures, the political culture of the West does not realize that it has entirely lost its canon" (18).

The lawyers exhibit a remarkable faith in their capacity to intervene and force the state to recognize the laws it has flouted. Theirs is not the helplessness of citizens confronted by an overwhelmingly complex state apparatus; in their refusal to give way to despondency, they are similar to the lawyers of post-apartheid South Africa who challenged the Mbeki government to live up to its constitutional obligations and provide HIV-positive pregnant women with the necessary medications to prevent mother-to-child transmission of HIV. However, there is one significant difference between the lawyers at every level of the legal infrastructure in South Africa and the lawyers, even those working for the detainees, in the United States: the former proudly declare their "activist" credentials, whereas most of the U.S. lawyers, by contrast, are hesitant to do so. Though the effect of their actions may be no less revolutionary than the intervention by the South African lawyers, the U.S. attorneys involved in detainee defense work are, for the most part, reluctant radicalists.[12]

The Problematic Allure of Legal Discourse

The lawyers have absorbed heavy criticism for their representation of the detainees. The negative reactions span the gamut from branding the lawyers as misguided, unpatriotic, or naïve (from those on the political right) to self-aggrandizing or complicit in the Bush administration's practice of seeking refuge in legalities (from the political left). In February 2006, Gitanjali Gutierrez, one of the attorneys at the Center for Constitutional Rights, was a guest speaker in the course Introduction to Human Rights being taught at the University of Massachusetts Boston. She made a powerful and moving presentation on her work with her detainee clients at Guantánamo Bay. Most of the hundred-plus students who attended seemed inspired by her efforts and awed by her determination not to succumb to despair. However, one student, a self-declared left-leaning thinker, was not entirely impressed. Her question refocused the audience's attention to abuses within the U.S. prison system and the seemingly unstoppable growth of the prison-industrial complex fed by a punitive culture of criminalizing minor offenses. Guantánamo Bay is horrific, no doubt, was her implication, but Guantánamo Bay does not necessarily warrant more outrage than the egregious violations of our domestic prison infrastructure. In response, Gutierrez acknowledged the many abuses of the prison system, and she noted that quite a few of the guards at Guantánamo Bay had "cut their teeth" in U.S. prisons and were bringing to the detainee facility all the worst practices of that environment. But, she argued, she had far greater hope of eventual justice for prisoners in mainland facilities than those at Guantánamo Bay, because the American prison system falls squarely within the ambit of Constitutional law, in contrast to Guantánamo Bay, whose relationship to the Constitution and to international law on prisoners of war was constantly being tested and challenged by the Bush administration.

A similar criticism infused the question that Gutierrez and two other lawyers, Anant Raut and Marc Falkoff, faced in April 2008 at the conference of the Association for Asian American Studies (AAAS). This time the question came from the reputed historian Gary Okihiro. The title of the panel was "Guantánamo Bay and the Conscience of Asian American Studies," and the three panelists were Gutierrez, Raut, and Falkoff. Okihiro asked, "You are doing very important work, but some people would argue that what we have now is a democracy of the elite, where ordinary citizens have little input into how the country runs, and decisions that affect everyone are made by a handful of people in places of power." Okihiro appeared to suggest that the legal battleground in which the panelists were expending their energy was an esoteric and abstract space that had little to do with urgent questions of justice and humanity. His frustration, and that of the large part of the audience, seemed to be directed at the legalisms that intellectualized suffering and enmeshed the detainees' horrific experience at Guantánamo Bay in intricate maneuvers of rulings, appeals, stays, injunctions, and counterrulings. In a subsequent e-mail communication to me dated February 2, 2009, Okihiro added that what he objected to "besides the esoterics of lawyering, was this almost blind faith in democracy and its institutions held by the attorneys. [T]hat is, Guantanamo appeared an aberration within that mindset, when in reality, it might reflect accurately US (imperial) democracy and its institutions!"

An uninterrogated and naïve subscription to the institution or rhetoric of law can be deeply problematic. The law can be fetishized, as Mahmood Mamdani (2002) has compellingly argued in his analysis of the apartheid (South African) state's reliance on carefully promulgated and implemented laws to maintain its segregationist policies, and as the torture-legalizing formulations of John Yoo and others of the Office of Legal Counsel under the Bush administration demonstrate. Mamdani observes that the apartheid government "both fetishized and brandished legality" (49), and he asks, "If a crime against humanity was perpetrated under the cloak of a rule of law, then how are we to understand the very notion of a rule of law?" (49).

In a similar vein, Wendy Brown and Janet Halley warn that

> politics conceived and practiced legalistically bears a certain hostility to discursively open-ended, multigenre, and polyvocal political conversations about how we should live, what we should value, and what we should prohibit, and what is possible in collective life. The presumptive conversion of political questions into legal questions can displace open-ended discursive contestation: adversarial and yes/no structures can quash exploration; expert and specialized languages can preclude democratic participation. (2002, 19)

Samera Esmeir (2006) delivers a more pointed critique of law, questioning its fundamental formulations. Referring in particular to human rights law, she observes: "it is difficult to conceive of the dehumanization of an oppressed person unless we first accept the idea that humanity can be taken away or given back. In our time the law, and human rights law more specifically, claims jurisdiction over the declaration of this status" (1544–1545). The problem with linking the human "with the logic of legal status" (1547) is that one's humanity becomes fragile. A juridical concept of the human, Esmeir argues, rests on the assumption "that humanity can be taken away" (1549). Such an attitude privileges "law's ambition to transform humanity into a juridical status, which precedes, rather than follows and describes, all humanity" (1544). Esmeir cautions that such dependence on juridical conceptions of humanity risks casting those who are "abandoned" by the law or constituted by rogue laws (such as those articulated by South Africa's apartheid regime or the Bush administration's Office of Legal Counsel) as passive victims awaiting help. Provocatively, she calls for an extrajuridical way of relating to our fellow humans, unmediated by the structures of law: "What is needed is the forging of concrete alliances with human beings who await not our recognition but our participation in their struggles" (1545).

Esmeir's critique is particularly relevant in light of the gross asymmetry of power in the relationship between lawyer and detainee. The detainee is unequivocally vulnerable, without any control over the use of his body. The lawyer's position relative to the detainee is one of immense power and mastery. Without the lawyer, the detainee could become nonexistent or exist only as a number. The lawyer's empathy may stem from altruistic motives, but it is almost impossible for the lawyer to evacuate all sense of power from the display of empathy. One might ask, in the manner of Lauren Berlant, whether empathy emerges precisely because the lawyer is in a position of total power. Is the lawyer's empathy predicated on the detainee's passivity and helplessness? Consider, for example, this telling interaction between a lawyer and his detainee client, recounted in Mahvish Khan's (2008) memoir: The lawyer has been persuading the client to sign a form. The client refuses to do it, perhaps because he does not trust the lawyer specifically, or perhaps because he is generally suspicious of the system at Guantánamo Bay. Despite the attorney's repeated efforts, the client does not succumb. As a result, in a fit of pique, the attorney "abruptly" rises, "pick[s] up the wall phone, and call[s] the guard to end the meeting" (205). When Khan registers her surprise and asks why the attorney has been so brusque, he answers that it is "a tactic to gain control of the meeting. By walking out, he may have given the detainee the sense that his lawyers weren't coming back" (205). It would appear from this attorney's desire for control that his investment in the detainee-defense process is prompted by his expectation that the detainee will fulfill the role of abandoned victim awaiting help. This lawyer, one presumes, wishes to fulfill his part in the pre-determined script and play the role of powerful dispenser of aid. Here, what-ever initial empathy the lawyer may have had reveals itself to be inextricably enmeshed in dimensions of power. The detainee, by refusing to sign the forms, exhibits an autonomous sense of self-dignity and choice, a response that the lawyer cannot accept because it disrupts the power structure in which he is the privileged player. His final action is an attempt to restore the power balance in his favor. In this instance, the lawyer becomes the metonymic emblem of the state, the very entity that has consigned the detainee to the status of abject humanity. The form that the lawyer wishes the detainee to sign is ironically the visual proof of the constricted ways in which the state seeks to regulate the interaction between two human beings. The form highlights, as Berlant (2002) puts it, "the problem of trying juridically and culturally to administer society as a place . . . void of struggle and ambivalence" (112). The detainee, for his part, has thwarted the lawyer's desire to "feel good" and has challenged the lawyer by refusing to be the obedient and grateful supplicant.

Daniel Kanstroom's (2007) riveting history of the laws surrounding exclu-sion, removal, and deportation provides ample proof that legal structures and language have always served the purposes of groups in power to oppress and dispossess those whom they see as obstacles in or undesirable to their ultimate goals. Of the Fugitive Slave Act of 1850, he observes that "it was analogous to a modern deportation law, with no discretionary or mercy com-ponent. People with families, jobs, and various types of roots in new commu-nities to which they had fled faced forced legal removal back to places where they feared the most inhuman treatment" (83). Of the Indian Removal Act of 1830 he notes that several justifications were offered: "How does one justify the forced removal of . . . a people? One might, as Justice Field did in the *Chinese Exclusion Case,* describe the threat posed by the group as 'a menace to our civilization.' One might seek goals of 'public peace and stability.' And one might also paternalistically describe forced removal as a benefit for the affected group" (67). Kanstroom's study is invaluable for its careful disclo-sure of how the nation's leaders have systematically used the language of law to endorse the most inhumane treatment of peoples they view as inferior or the enemy. "By the late nineteenth century, *legal* Indian removal was a well-accepted and well-understood conceptual model. It involved forced movement, by the federal government, of non-European people" (Kanstroom 2007, 64; emphasis added). The law was constructed entirely to favor the European settlers, and the Indians' "structural constitutional, treaty-based, and individual rights claims all faced insurmountable doctrinal hurdles grounded in a plenary power doctrine" (64) or "sovereign, constitutionally unrestrained" (16) power. By the turn of the nineteenth century and into the twentieth century, "congressional power over Indians . . . faced no constitutional limitations and no judicial oversight at all" (74).

Given that Congress is the legislative body, what this meant is that laws were crafted wholly to the benefit of the white settlers, in much the same way that apartheid laws were crafted by the National Party government in South Africa from 1960 until the 1980s. The law is a mask that allows those in power to believe that they act with discretion, rationality, and caution. Furthermore, the law stands as an external force that allows those in power to distance themselves from the ethical questions embedded in their own actions. "It is not we who render these cruel decisions," they seem to say. "We have no option but to follow the law." Kanstroom (2007) makes this point with particular force when discussing the application of deportation laws in the post-9/11 era (225–249).[13]

The lawyers' experiences with the Guantánamo Bay detainees both reveal the dogmatism of law (and so confirm Gilles Deleuze's skepticism of law) and, at the same time, provide the initial impetus for contact that can lead to the uncharted waters of a deep and meaningful relationship. The rigidity of law, as Gilles Deleuze critiques it, precludes an encounter between individuals that is open to surprise and spontaneity. According to him, "The encounter alone accounts for the conditions of real thought and experience. . . . [O]nly an unanticipated and violent encounter can stimulate thought past the purview of recognition and force it to think" (Lefebvre 2008, 72). Law, as he reads it, functions in the manner of a script that predetermines both the style and the substance of the connection between individuals and groups. In contrast to such a scripted relationship, Deleuze calls for a more spontaneous interaction between human beings. He claims that "an encounter occurs whenever clichés, habits, categories, and propositional certitudes are no longer sufficient to account for, think, and react within a situation. . . . It is with force and necessity that encounters cause us to break from dogmatic thought and the recognizable form that dogmatism assigns to the outside" (Lefebvre 2008, 73). Deleuze's call for attending to the unfigured possibilities of an encounter parallels Jacques Derrida's mediations on the "ideal of the just decision" as necessarily haunted by the "'ghost of the undecidable' . . . inasmuch as the rule which is supposed to be applied necessarily falls short of the concrete case in its singularity" (Gehring 2008, 62). Both Deleuze and Derrida, then, resist the ways in which the discourse and application of law allow no room for the singularity of specific experiences. The law, as they see it, leaves little openness for the truly open and infinite encounter.

From the Script of Law into the Unscripted Terrain of Human Discovery

Deleuze's and Derrida's objections to the limitations of the language of law are compelling and undeniable. Nonetheless, I would argue that within the context of the Guantánamo Bay detainees, the law in fact functions as the protective tether with which detainee lawyers venture into the open waters of humanity and participate in an experience that might otherwise never have occurred. Through this encounter, the old frames of reference and action are slowly dismantled and new ones reconfigured. Thus, while the law itself is not a radical articulation, it facilitates entry into relatively amorphous spaces where there is no fixity and all relationships are in flux. Simply put, the law enables lawyers to journey to Guantánamo Bay and to begin the "familiar" and "comfortable" attorney-client dialogue. However, once the initial contact has been made, as a result of and through law, then an entirely different type of unscripted discourse comes into play

Mahvish Khan (2008) records the many remarkable relationships between detainees and lawyers that develop at Guantánamo Bay. Some of the attorneys "were greeted with bear hugs and ongoing gratitude. A few formed such a rapport with the prisoners that once the legal issues were dealt with, they spent the rest of the time talking about cricket or sharing photos of their wives and children. Some attorneys and clients told jokes, played cards, or took turns quizzing each other about their respective cultures" (86). In another example Khan provides, the lawyer willingly submits to a redrawing of the usual pattern of relationship, in an effort to achieve some kind of meaningful connection to his client. "One lawyer told me that he often felt like a glorified waiter and social worker. Some of the Arab clients gave their attorneys grocery lists. One of the Kuwaitis once asked his lawyers to bring him two large pizzas, three McDonald's fish filet sandwiches, ice cream, ten Hershey's chocolate bars, eight KitKat bars, a package of Oreo cookies, and a half-gallon of chocolate milk" (91). Portland lawyer Chris Schatz even wrote a poem to his client Chaman Gul, in which, through an act of empathy, he imagines himself in Gul's position and tries to understand what he must feel like to be in Guantánamo Bay: *"day after day my captors try me with their questions, / insisting that I be other than what I am, / when I answer, the voice I hear is no longer my own, / my soul has become a wisp of smoke, my heart—a stone"* (90). Khan herself brings roses for Gul.

Stephen Oleskey observes how remarkable it is that the men he represents preserve their sense of humor and their humanity despite the horror of their situation. "They smile and joke and laugh with me that someday we will have a feast together. We have to wonder at the failures of our legal system to accomplish their release." Oleskey recalls that one client, whose blindfold was removed when he was transferred from one location in the camp to another, saw the Caribbean Sea for the first time in six years. He did not know that he was imprisoned near an ocean. The clients have not spoken with their families since they've been at Guantánamo Bay. One client's child died of a congenital heart disease during his term of imprisonment. "Telling him about his child's death was one of the most challenging things I've had to do," Oleskey remarks. "His wife couldn't write to him about it, because she isn't allowed to communicate any personal news." Oleskey and his associates see the Algerian men three times a year. They talk to their wives before and after each visit.

One of the Algerian detainees, Lakhdar Boumediene, was on a hunger strike at the time of my conversation with Oleskey. He is the person whose name the recent Supreme Court case (*Boumediene et al. v. Bush*) bears that resulted in the 5-to-4 decision reinstituting habeas rights to detainees. He was being force-fed to ensure that he did not die of starvation. Oleskey says, rather cynically, that he is being kept alive only to forestall enraged protests in Karachi that another Muslim man has died at the hands of the United States. It is clear that Oleskey has come to know and admire the detainees' fortitude. One of his clients was held in solitary confinement for more than a year (from June 2006 until the fall of 2007) because he would not impress upon the other detainees that committing suicide is forbidden by the Qur'an (several detainees have made repeated attempts to take their own lives, an act stemming from sheer desperation, but one that has been characterized by military officials as a public relations stunt and a weapon of asymmetrical warfare). Oleskey marvels at how this man endured and survived that year of isolation with a single bulb in his cell shining on him all the time. "He had nothing else to read but the Qur'an. Maybe he found his courage and strength there," Oleskey speculates. "I wonder whether the Bible could have given me such strength. Thankfully, I haven't had to find out." Boumediene was released from Guantánamo Bay on May 15, 2009, to France after seven years in captivity.

Sabin Willett and his colleagues from Bingham McCutchen are representing the Uighur detainees at Guantánamo Bay (more on the Uighurs later). I ask Willett, "What has most surprised you about or been the most unexpected aspect of your work with the detainees?" He answers immediately, "What has most affected me is that these people become human when you meet them. They are no longer just a theoretical concept within the context of what's legal and what isn't; they're not an unfamiliar, strange, remote name. You realize that he's a person—someone who tells jokes; he's a guy who has two daughters and has a father with a heart condition."

Willett remembers something that has affected him profoundly. "On our . . . visit, on August 31, 2006, I met with a guy that we had never seen before: Abdulnasir. He had been trying to meet us for a year. He has been in prison for more than four years. Remember, no one ever explains to these people why no lawyer has come to see them, why no one has tried to contact them. So when we finally show up, he doesn't know if we're lawyers. For all he knows, we could be interrogators trying to trick him. We had just had some very tough meetings with other clients, detainees who had lost hope, had become frustrated—they were tough meetings.

"Abdulnasir is soft spoken, smart; he has learned a lot of English, because he answers us before the translator has finished translating what we've said. He accepts the tea we've brought. It's coming up toward noon, towards the end of the meeting, we have fifteen minutes to go, and he says, 'I want you to tell me the downside of the lawsuit.' We tell him that there's no downside. He then lets us know that the conditions in camp have gotten much worse in the last six months, and his bed sheet has been taken away. He wants to know if that's because of the lawsuit. I assure him that it's not, but he's not convinced. 'It's tough without the bed sheet.' Trying to sleep on the steel bulkhead is really difficult, you have to imagine.

"Suddenly the translator's face falls. And he [Abdulnasir] speaks sternly to her, the first time that he has been anything but polite, but she's silent. It looks like he's insisting that she tell us what he's saying. 'You must translate that,' he says to her roughly. Outside, after the meeting, she tells us that he wants to drop the suit. It occurred to me that he had drawn the best inference that he could, given what he had gone through and given the realities of what he endured. He had come to a rational conclusion that the American justice system is truly meaningless. But that it might have cost him his bed sheet. It really shook me, it really made me think, 'I'm part of this totally ridiculous worthless system that isn't even worth a bed sheet.'"

I'm impressed with the force of Willett's narration; even over a cell phone connection, the impact that this recounting has on him is clear. He continues, "We're going to focus on the nine clients we have, until we can get them all out or until we're fired." I assume mistakenly that he means fired by the military. He corrects me: "No, until the clients fire us." I express surprise that the clients could fire them, that the detainees could jeopardize their already slim chances at ending their imprisonment. Willett helps me understand: "You can't imagine the paranoia, the hopelessness, the despair, the utter depression cut off from any kind of human contact. You can't put someone in a cage for years [many of these detainees were apprehended in early 2002] and say, 'Have a nice conversation with me.' It took us six months to get a four-hour meeting with someone who has been brutalized for close to six years." In an opinion piece in the *Boston Globe*, Willett (2006) writes, "The other day [then] Senate majority leader Bill Frist spoke of being within 'ten yards of vicious terrorists at Guantanamo.' He almost snarled as he said it. I don't know who he saw, but I wish he'd joined me in Camp Echo with Abdulnasir and formed his judgment of this gentle man at the closer quarters from which physicians usually observe patients" (A11).

Wells Dixon also represents Uighur detainees, as well as detainees from across North Africa and the Middle East. "I'll tell you that when we came back from Guantánamo one time, we were particularly depressed by what we had witnessed. I remember that three people we met with during our visit were men who had been declared by our government to be *non*–enemy combatants [i.e., they did not pose any danger to the United States and had no connection to terrorist activities]. Each of them responded in various ways to his experiences in Guantánamo. Each was equally moving. One of them was very practical about it, very pragmatic. He wanted to know about his legal case, about legal strategy. One of them was very philosophical. He asked questions like 'What does it mean to be innocent in the United States?' For him in many ways it was the existential horror that was as bad [as] if not worse than the actual horror of being in Guantánamo. Then the third was a young detainee who had been captured when he was a teenager, and he reacted as you might expect a typical teenager to react. Each of these men reacted differently to their surroundings, but the bottom line was it created a real sense of urgency on our part. It was not just a matter of principle anymore. These men were factually innocent of any wrongdoing, had been captured and brought to Guantanamo by mistake, and they were really suffering terribly as a result of their indefinite detention."

Marc Falkoff's empathy took the form of gathering the poems written by detainees (an arduous task, given all the scrutiny to which the detainees' and his actions were subjected by the military) and then publishing the collection. Falkoff is a faculty member at Northern Illinois University School of Law and a former attorney at Covington and Burling; he represented seventeen Yemeni detainees. The idea of poetry as the perfect form through which to spark a connection with the detainees came to Falkoff when he read the poem "In the Leupold Scope" by Iraq veteran Brian Turner (see the Introduction for my detailed analysis of this poem). Falkoff saw the poem as an empathetic outreach from a soldier to an Iraqi woman, and it occurred to him that a similar outreach through poetry might evoke in the American public a sense of shared feeling with the detainees. That the poems survived and made it into the collection *Poems from Guantánamo: The Detainees Speak* (2007) is miraculous. Initially, the detainees had no writing tools, so many of them scratched their poems on foam cups, "inscrib[ing] their words with pebbles or trac[ing] out letters with small dabs of toothpaste" (3). Many of the poems were destroyed or confiscated before they came into the hands of the lawyers. Falkoff writes that the Pentagon was fearful of poetry's insurgent value, because of its perceived ability to serve as a vehicle for transmitting coded information (4). The existence of the collection thus represents a vindictive triumph for Falkoff and the other lawyers who supplied him with their clients' poems. It is a slim collection, no more than twenty-two poems (by seventeen detainees), but Ariel Dorfman (2007), in his afterword to Falkoff's collection, exhorts us to read them thinking of the prisoners "breathing in and out those words, close by an ocean they can hear nearby but never see and never touch. Think of them, now represented to their faraway foes by words of fire and sorrow, asking us to listen, to acknowledge the buried flame of their existence" (71–72).

The pro bono attorneys function as witnesses of this remote and difficult-to-access space, bringing back to the public glimpses of its terrain, its "residents" (detainees, guards, and military personnel) and its surreal codes of behavior. I would argue that Guantánamo Bay is the site where lawyers can become radicalized into their own humanity, where they untether themselves from legal definitions of who is a "lawful enemy combatant" and who an "unlawful enemy combatant," and turn instead to the surprise and unpredictability of face-to-face encounters. The lawyers find themselves uneasy with legal terminologies for describing the detainees and, instead, embrace the opportunity simply to come into awareness of the complexity and depth of the individuals before them. One could describe their shift of perspective as a gradual realization of the limitations of legal discourse in determining a person's status as worthy (or unworthy) of the term *humanity*; what transpires in the rooms where lawyer, paralegal, translator, and detainee come together is nothing short of a restructuring of consciousness.

Initially Cautious, Slowly Enlisted

In the early days of the Bush administration's argument for Guantánamo Bay as a location for holding suspected terrorists indefinitely and without charge, there was little domestic legal challenge to the government's position. Initially, the challenges came principally from outside the United States, from international bodies such as Amnesty International and Human Rights Watch, and foreign governments (Britain and Australia, for instance). There was practically no opposition from within the country. There is a kind of mythology of trust about our government that we labor under, that is both advantageous and a detriment to the functioning of a democracy. Oleskey observes perceptively that "Mythologizing means we don't have to reflect on who we are. A myth lets us avoid introspection." In the United States, there is, despite the history of Watergate, a reluctance to doubt the president. Watergate is seen as an aberration. Or, as has become commonplace to say about the American public, we have no sense of history and we believe that we can constantly reinvent ourselves.[14] If not for our capacity to forget history or disregard it, how could we repeat a hundredfold in Guantánamo Bay what we have since apologized for in the Japanese American internment—that our unconstitutional rounding up and sequestering of 120,000 Japanese and Japanese Americans (most of those interned were U.S. citizens) was an act of racism? There is incredible hope and innocent idealism in the idealized and mythologized perception of government, which is both the strength and weakness of the American democracy. Therefore, most of the legal establishment sat aside and watched the Office of Legal Counsel articulate the legal justifications for creating a prison at Guantánamo Bay for suspected terrorists.

The Bush administration invoked the "state of exception" as a legal instrument with which to institute new modes of imprisoning and interrogating those considered to be enemies of the state. His Office of Legal Counsel dedicated itself to articulating the legal justifications for declaring Guantánamo Bay outside the jurisdiction of the United States and deeming the captives who were to be sent there from the "battlefields" of Afghanistan ineligible for prisoner-of-war (POW) treatment under the Geneva Conventions and the Uniform Code of Military Justice. Through the language of law, the Bush administration's Office of Legal Counsel justified setting up a zone beyond the reach of law, declaring that the law gives the executive branch the power to circumvent the law during a "state of exception."[15] Agamben (2005) describes this paradoxical condition: "if exceptional measures are the result of periods of political crisis and, as such, must be understood on political and not juridico-constitutional grounds, . . . then they find themselves in the paradoxical position of being juridical measures that cannot be understood in legal terms, and *the state of exception appears as a legal form of what cannot have legal form*" (1; emphasis added).

The first significant challenge to the administration came from the Center for Constitutional Rights (CCR), which became the hub of the legal activity in behalf of the detainees at Guantánamo Bay through its Guantánamo Global Justice Initiative. The CCR coordinates the activities of several hundred lawyers (a handful of whom are staff attorneys at CCR; the rest are from private law firms), organizing the myriad activities that constitute the complicated task of representing the detainees. CCR was founded in 1966 as "a non-profit legal and educational organization . . . dedicated to advancing and protecting the rights guaranteed by the United States Constitution and the Universal Declaration of Human Rights" (Center for Constitutional Rights, n.d.). The offices of CCR are extremely basic, painfully Spartan even, belying the earthshaking work that its attorneys do. The organization took on the Bush administration with a ferocity that was all the more noticeable in the near absence of checks and balances exerted by Congress on the executive. The center has also published the book *Articles of Impeachment against George W. Bush* (Melville House, 2006) and mounted a vigorous campaign to initiate public discussion on the need to challenge and (at the time) unseat President Bush for his flouting of the Constitution.

Michael Ratner, the lead attorney from CCR who filed the first challenge in the case that has since gained fame as *Rasul v. Bush*, says that most people, including those who were part of civil rights organizations, were worried about being seen as unpatriotic and believed the government's propaganda that the men being held in Guantánamo Bay were, indeed, hardened and dangerous terrorists who would blow up the country at the first opportunity.[16] Ratner was already suspicious of Guantánamo Bay because of his prior challenge to the Clinton administration's use of it to hold Haitian refugees who were HIV-positive.[17] It may have been Ratner's earlier engagement with the Cuban location and his position at an organization that has a history of scrutinizing violations of human rights and due process that led him before others to see that something was seriously amiss at Guantánamo Bay, with the Bush administration's use of it as a prison for hundreds of men deemed to be terrorists.

When the Center for Constitutional Rights filed the case in 2002, they had very little legal or public support. In fact, as the Web site declares, they received a great deal of hate mail and threatening phone calls. Over a period of several months, as the case made its way through the escalating levels of the judicial infrastructure, and each ruling confirmed the Bush administration's contention that Guantánamo Bay was outside the reach of U.S. law and so gave no habeas protections to the detainees, the CCR attorneys kept doggedly appealing the negative decisions and pursuing their cause, moving the case up to the next level of the infrastructure. (Habeas corpus, a core principle of the Western democratic judicial system, grants the prisoner the right to be physically present in court and demand to be informed of the basis for the imprisonment.) When the case finally arrived at the Supreme Court, several amicus curiae briefs were filed along with *Rasul*, the most famous of these being that by Fred Korematsu, the Japanese American who challenged his internment in 1942.[18] In June 2004, the Center for Constitutional Rights won a historic victory in *Rasul v. Bush*, and the detainees were declared to have full habeas rights (i.e., the right to challenge the legality of their detention) and the right to counsel.

The "opening up" of Guantánamo Bay by the Rasul decision made it possible for lawyers to consider involving themselves in detainee defense work with the secure knowledge that they were operating within a legally endorsed framework. Guantánamo Bay was now a legitimate battleground, one they could enter without being deemed unpatriotic. The question that hovers around Rasul and Guantánamo Bay is, "What would have happened or how would the lawyers have responded if the Supreme Court had ruled Guantánamo Bay beyond the reach of habeas protections and outside the jurisdiction of the United States?" Would the lawyers have taken to the streets in outrage? Would there have been a public outcry? Would constituents have written to their elected representatives demanding an inquiry? Or would there have been a resigned acceptance of the Supreme Court's ruling, particularly because it concerned, in the words of Stephen Oleskey, "brown men with long beards"?

The Supreme Court ruling in favor of detainees' habeas protections at Guantánamo Bay presented the image of a United States where respect for the rule of law still holds sway, where basic humanity is still intact and justice cannot be thwarted. However, behind these rulings, or under cover of these rulings, the Bush administration simply delayed its legal obligations. These delays received minimal media coverage, and there was little public criticism of the failure to implement the ruling. The Supreme Court decisions thus served the purposes of the Bush administration in communicating the image of a president accountable to the law of the land even as it enabled his administration to resist implementing the specific details of the rulings.

Lawyers who initially rejoiced in the Supreme Court's *Rasul v. Bush* ruling and believed that it would finally allow them access to the detainees held at Guantánamo Bay instead found their every move for meaningful communication with their clients thwarted or severely constrained. Everything, right down to the notes they took of their conversations with the detainees, was scrutinized by the military. Carolyn Kolker (2005) describes the bizarre process: "Before boarding the plane back to Fort Lauderdale, lawyers must surrender client notes—that sacrosanct symbol of the attorney-client privilege—to a gunnery sergeant who passes them to Defense Department lawyers for classification review" (98). The numerous pages of notes are counted and then "put in classified envelopes with classified stamps" sometimes taking as long as "35 days to mail the notes back to the U.S." (98). These restrictions are the endpoint of an arduous clearance procedure and rigorous stipulations as to how often lawyers are allowed to visit their detainee clients and how many individuals are permitted to be present in the cell at any given time.

Guantánamo Bay is a zone of shifting meanings where language and law are protean and malleable—"solitary confinement" morphs into "single-occupancy cells" (Glaberson 2008, A27), and "suicide attempts" are disguised as "manipulative self-injurious behaviors" (Brittain and Slovo 2003, 40). Amy Kaplan (2003) suggests that Guantánamo Bay is an "uncanny space . . . , a kind of ground zero, a new foundation on which the American homeland is being rebuilt" (92). It is the kind of space where, in the words of Agamben (1995), "human beings could be so completely deprived of their rights and prerogatives that no act committed against them could appear any longer as a crime" (171).

The landscape of law in which Guantánamo Bay became enmeshed was characterized by an intensely professionalized discourse in which recognition of the detainee's humanity was replaced by debates about whether the detainee did or did not have legal status as an individual. This highly esoteric discourse facilitated the abdication by the general public of its responsibility to demand an ethical and moral course of national action with regard to the detainees. One could say that we outsourced our obligations (civic and moral) to the lawyers and absolved ourselves of our duty to our fellow human beings. Anant Raut (2007) observes perceptively that the only reason a place like Guantánamo "can continue to exist" is that "as a nation we are afraid to admit that we've done something wrong" (B3).

Arbitrary Power over the Body of the Detainee, the Body of the Slave

Western politics is founded on the politicization of "bare life," argues Agamben (1995), noting that habeas corpus privileges the presence of the body and invests it with power. But habeas corpus contains within it a profound contradiction: "the same legal procedure that was originally intended to assure the presence of the accused at the trial and, therefore, to keep the accused from avoiding judgment, turns—in its new and definitive form into grounds for the sheriff to detain and exhibit the body of the accused. *Corpus is a two-faced being, the bearer both of subjection to sovereign power and of individual liberties*" (125). Within Guantánamo Bay, the bodies of the detainees have become hyperpoliticized, not just in the torture to which they have been subjected, but also in the extreme regulations that govern their every movement.

To the slave and the detainee one can apply with chilling appropriateness Frantz Fanon's (2005) phrase "the wretched of the earth." Fanon observes that the colonizer dehumanizes the natives by describing them in zoological terms that strip them of their humanity. The colonizer speaks of the native's "reptilian motions, of the stink of the native quarter, . . . of foulness, . . . of gesticulations" (42). The colonist, notes Fanon, derives his validity from the colonial system (2). The United States, in this historical moment, feels at once profoundly vulnerable and profoundly powerful. Asserting absolute power over the bodies of suspected terrorists is one way that the United States seeks to confirm for itself its capacity to contain and control its enemies.

To give to this total control the sanctity of legality, the Office of Legal Counsel in the Bush administration sought to make a case for why the interrogation techniques (sleep deprivation and waterboarding, for example) it proposed to use on the detainees were not torture and therefore not in violation of the Convention Against Torture and Other Cruel, Inhumane, or Degrading Treatment or Punishment (CAT), which the U.S. government "signed and ratified" in 1984 (Honigsberg 2009, 24). Torture, as defined by 18 USC §§2340–2340A, is "an act committed by a person acting under color of law, specifically intended to inflict severe physical or mental pain or suffering . . . upon another person within his custody or physical control"(qtd. in Bradbury 2005, 2). In an August 1, 2002, memo, the OLC redefined torture: for an act to constitute torture, "it must inflict pain that is difficult to endure. Physical pain amounting to torture must be equivalent in intensity to the pain accompanying serious physical injury, such as organ failure, impairment of bodily function, or even death. For purely mental pain or suffering to amount to torture . . . , it must result in significant psychological harm of significant duration, e.g., lasting for months or even years" (Bybee 2002, 1). Having expanded the domain of permissible techniques, the OLC gave to the Central Intelligence Agency (CIA) virtually unlimited legal authority to inflict severe interrogation techniques on the detainees, resorting to such legal niceties as the difference between "specific intent" and "general intent," and declaring that only if an interrogator acted with the "specific intent to inflict pain" would he or she be guilty of violating a law, but if the interrogator acted "knowing that severe pain or suffering was likely to result from his actions, but no more, he would have acted only with general intent" (Bybee 2002, 3–4) and therefore not be culpable.

In 2005, in response to the growing unpopularity of the administration's policies, the OLC returned to the 18 USC §§2340–2340A definition but chose to apply it liberally. Parsing this definition in the manner of grammar exercise, into "three categories: 'severe physical . . . pain,' 'severe physical . . . suffering,' and 'severe . . . mental pain or suffering'" (Bradbury, 2005, 10, ellipses in original), the Office of Legal Counsel concludes that when examined in light of these three categories independently, waterboarding and sleep deprivation do not constitute torture. Though they may induce physical pain and mental suffering, they do not do so with sufficient severity and over prolonged periods of time to satisfy the statute of what constitutes torture (Bradbury 2005, 10). Such cruelties are justified in the calm and measured language of law, conferring on them a legitimacy that obscures the irrational hostilities and hatreds underlying the legal articulations. Žižek warns that even to discuss and debate torture confers it legitimacy (2002, 103–104), because such discussion allows us to persist in the illusion that we are rational and thoughtful and do not resort to irrational cruelties. The title of Peter Honigsberg's book, *Our Nation Unhinged*, would appear to apply with particular force to the Office of Legal Counsel's justifications for torture.

One might wonder how in a post-concentration-camp world we as a nation would see nothing ironic in our establishment of the detention facilities at Guantánamo Bay. Agamben might assert (and Žižek would concur) that in both spaces, the individual is reduced to a bare minimum of life, *homo sacer*, a person with no rights. One reviewer of this manuscript wondered that we had learned so little restraint despite our knowledge of the horrors of the Holocaust's concentration camp apparatus. I would argue that there is both a logical and an emotional fallacy in regarding these two spaces as similar, other than in the most basic sense. True, in both instances a state and its people constructed an "enemy" and then systematically set about containing and exterminating (in the case of Nazi Germany) this enemy. However, it is precisely because the atrocities of the concentration camps have, in the last fifty years, been rendered hypervisible and readily available (through films and other visual representations, the testimony of Holocaust survivors, and hundreds of thousands of pages of writing), and because we have crafted and enshrined the narrative of our liberatory role in ending that atrocity, that we cannot engage in the type of introspection that might lead us to acknowledge the eerie similarity between the national sentiment that led to the establishment of Guantánamo Bay and that which resulted in the concentration camps. The *externalization* of the Holocaust and the abundance of materials that are at hand to evoke analysis and discussion about it allow us to feel complacent that we will not cross *that* boundary into antipathy and inhumanity. Our outrage has been variously packaged and presented to us for neat and self-satisfied consumption. Andreas Huyssen (2003) observes that "it is no longer possible . . . to think of the Holocaust . . . as a serious ethical and political issue apart from the multiple ways in which it is now linked to commodification and spectacularization in films, museums, docudramas, Internet sites, photography books, comics, fiction, even fairy tales, . . . and pop songs" (18).[19]

Furthermore, even if we were to consider a "connection" between the concentration camp and Guantánamo Bay, it would not necessarily follow that we would therefore be aghast at our own capacity for antipathy and inhumanity. Guantánamo Bay exists for one of two or a combination of both reasons. One could argue that we are perfectly capable of imagining how another would suffer, and it is precisely because of this imaginative capacity that we devise formidable apparatuses of suffering and inflict them upon those we actively choose to target. The moving testimony in May 2008 of Stephen Oleskey and other detainee defense lawyers to the House Subcommittee on Foreign Affairs (Subcommittee on International Organizations, Human Rights, and Oversight) on the horrific conditions that detainees endure at Guantánamo Bay highlights in full measure this tendency. Oleskey (2008) asserts:

> These six and one-third years have seen our client Mustafa Ait Idir beaten to the point of facial paralysis and broken bones and sprayed with pepper spray in unprovoked attacks by guards at Guantanamo. They have seen our client Saber Lahmar's muscles atrophy and his psychological well-being decline precipitously during the nearly two years he has spent confined to an 8′ × 6′ concrete cell in near complete isolation, cut off from human contact, physical activity, and all natural light. And they have seen our client Lakhdar Boumediene—now entering the eighteenth month of his hunger strike against the injustices he and others have suffered at Guantanamo—painfully force-fed twice every single day through a 43-inch tube that is excruciatingly inserted into his nostril and down into his stomach. (2–3)

Jasbir Puar (2005) argues that our ability to inflict cruelty upon certain types of people—those whom we consider barbaric and unlike us—is not "exceptional"; the violation of prisoners at Abu Ghraib is part of a broader culture of abominating human bodies that permeates our society, she observes: "torture is at the very least doubly embedded in sociality: it is integral to the missionary/savior discourse of liberation and civilizational uplift, and it constitutes apposite punishment for terrorists and the bodies that resemble them" (15).

Donald Rumsfeld, first secretary of defense under the George W. Bush administration, railed that the men at Guantánamo Bay are "among the most dangerous, best-trained, vicious killers on the face of the Earth" (qtd. in Gilmore 2002). Gen. Richard Myers, chairman of the Joint Chiefs of Staff until October 2005, said of them: "These are people that would gnaw through hydraulic lines in the back of a C-17 to bring it down, I mean. So these are very, very dangerous people" (Fein 2008, A14). The "suicides" by hanging in June 2006 by three prisoners at Guantánamo Bay were seen by the camp commander as an "act of asymmetrical warfare against us" (BBC News 2006).

(Scott Horton's recent *Harper's Magazine* essay [2010] raises the possibility that these suicides were in fact killings.) The men at Guantánamo Bay are "the wretched" (Fanon 2005) of our national earth; their bodies are at the mercy of an overwhelmingly determined and arbitrary machinery of legal power. While most of the nation is willing to let Guantánamo Bay reside at the periphery of its consciousness, a few hundred lawyers are making it the battlefield for the national soul. They are wresting Guantánamo from its status as "the excised space of the state" (Davidson 2003, 6) and are laboring to ensure that the detainees confined there do not linger indefinitely in a netherworld of abandonment.

Seton Hall law professor Mark Denbeaux (2006) and his team of law students conducted a meticulous analysis of government documents (the Combatant Status Review Board letters) to reveal that even by the government's own data, the individuals held at Guantánamo Bay are in overwhelming number remarkably innocuous. In a report distinguished by its dispassionate and clinical analysis of information, and buttressed by compelling charts, Denbeaux and his team imply that the government's continued holding of the detainees with no prospect of their being released is illogical and arbitrary. Once language is part of an official document, it can take on an importance that has little relation to its inherent worth.

The kind of evidence that the government views as sufficient to determine that a detainee has committed a hostile act is at best laughable, at worst nightmarish in its randomness: "The detainee fled, along with others, when the United States forces bombed their camp" or "The detainee was captured in Pakistan, along with other Uighur fighters" (Denbeaux et al. 2006, 12). Also considered as evidence in proving that detainees were enemy combatants are their "use of a guest house," "possession of Casio watches," and "wearing of olive drab clothing" (17; in bulleted list form in the original). These flimsy conditions constituting the evidence for their being labeled "enemy combatants" are hardly strengthened by the fact that many of the detainees were brought to the U.S. authorities in Afghanistan by bounty hunters responding to strong encouragement by the United States, distributed through flyers, to capture as many Taliban and al-Qaeda supporters as possible.[20] The likelihood of innocent people having been handed over to the United States is extremely high, because "there was little opportunity on the field to verify the story of an individual who presented the detainee in response to the bounty award" (15). The bounty hunter would turn over to U.S. or Northern Alliance soldiers alleged supporters of the Taliban or al-Qaeda and quickly "disappear," so that there was very little possibility of ensuring that the allegations could be supported. Given that "93% of the detainees were *not* apprehended by the United States," one can only wonder at the extent of "mistaken identification" (14). The grim reality is that the lives of hundreds of men are slowly but steadily disintegrating through the corrosive effect of these practices.

Representing the Uighurs: The Legal Dance, the Humanist Project

Denbeaux observes that of detainees at Guantánamo Bay, the government files include the most complete information on the Uighurs. These men belong to an ethnic minority group in China and some parts of Kyrgyzstan and Kazakhstan. They are Chinese Muslims persecuted by the Chinese government, and hence they have fled to neighboring countries such as Afghanistan and Pakistan. The Uighur detainees had been captured in Pakistan by bounty hunters (Denbeaux et al. 2006, 21). What Sabin Willett, lead attorney for the Uighurs, found when he started to inform himself about the Uighur detainees is that a group of eighteen of them had been sold in Pakistan for bounty. They had been taken to Kandahar and turned over to the U.S. authorities there. At Kandahar, the Uighurs were "found to be in the clear" (Willett, interview); nonetheless, they were transported to Guantánamo Bay along with the other prisoners captured in Afghanistan. At Guantánamo Bay they were once again found "to be in the clear by the interrogators" (Willett, interview). However, the Combatant Status Review Tribunals (CSRT) process determined, oddly enough, that five of the Uighurs were *not* "enemy combatants" but that the other thirteen were enemy combatants. Willett observes that all eighteen Uighurs had been captured under identical circumstances, so that no logical basis could explain why the CSRT process had arrived at "a differential finding for them" (Willett, interview). He explained, in an e-mail on March 2, 2011, "We knew it was rigged, and the explanation for the clearances [of some of the Uighurs] had to be that a few decent officers fought the system from within."

Abu Bakker Qassim and A'del Abdu Al-Hakim, the two Uighur detainees whose case Willett and the team of lawyers from his firm took up, had in March 2005 been cleared by the CSRT; however, this crucial piece of information had been "kept secret" by the government" from the court and from the lawyers," Willett clarified (in the e-mail of March 2, 2011). Had Willett not filed in their behalf, their being considered "no longer enemy combatants" (NLECs) would never have been brought to light. As Willett points out, "Even that was false. One can't 'no longer' be an enemy combatant if one never was" (in the e-mail of March 2, 2011). As it was, Willett did not find out, despite his requests to the government for the results of the CSRT determinations, until he actually went to Guantánamo Bay in July 2005 and met his clients for the first time; it was the detainees who informed him that they had been cleared by the CSRT. Willett filed a motion for their immediate release, which the government opposed.

Consequently, a hearing was set for August 1, 2005. What followed with regard to these two detainees reveals the lack of logic and capricious application of law that has marked the government's and the courts' handling of the detainees.[21]

Willett filed the Qassim and Al-Hakim case in the district court in Washington, D.C. On December 22, 2005, Judge James Robertson ruled that though the imprisonment of the two men was illegal, he basically couldn't do anything about it. "'I can't order the military to bring them to court,' is what he said," Willett recalls, "and he dismissed our case. It was a stunning moment. We appealed and filed a motion to expedite the appeals process" (Willett, interview).

Judge Robertson, who presided over the case, observes that it presents two fundamental questions: "Does the government have . . . authority indefinitely to detain non–U.S. citizens at Guantanamo Bay, if they are not enemy combatants? If not, does a district court have the authority to fashion an effective remedy for the illegal detention?" (4). Judge Robertson eventually concluded that the indefinite detention is unlawful. Nonetheless, he made the surprising declaration that though the "habeas statute requires a court after determining the facts 'to dispose of the matter as law and justice require,' . . . the question in this case is whether the law gives me the power to do what I believe justice requires. The answer, I believe, is no" (7). Willett notes that one might explain Judge Robertson's argument in the following way: "I know that the two Uighur men in question are being unlawfully held by the Executive Branch. In the interest of justice, they ought to be released. However, since the only order of release I can give is that they enter the United States and be released here, and because the Executive branch of government has exclusive control of the border, I cannot order that they cross it. Given these alternatives, I must conclude that I have no authority to order their release."

Willett's appeal of Judge Robertson's decision was scheduled to be heard in the Court of Appeals on Monday, May 8, 2006. Willett recalls that on Friday, May 5, he received a phone call from the government's lawyers saying that the two Uighurs had just been sent to Albania. "The government couldn't risk the situation of these two men being made public in Appeals court because it would have shown the untenability of the process" (Willett, interview). Neil Lewis (2006a) writes that a great deal of diplomatic maneuvering preceded the Uighurs' (two of Willett's clients and three others) arrival in Albania: its "willingness to accept the Uighurs solidified [Albania's] standing with the United States and brought it a confrontation with China, which had been its patron during Albania's split from the Soviet Union in the Cold War" (A15). Despite strong protests from the Chinese ambassador in Albania, on "May 7, [2006], Vice President Dick Cheney publicly endorsed Albania's much-hoped-for bid to join NATO" (A15). The Uighurs' having found a safe home in Albania is not unequivocally a cause for celebration. There is little by way of a social or support network for them there, and no one who speaks their language.

The Uighur detainees that remain in Guantánamo Bay continue to face an uncertain future. Though it is now clear that they were wrongly captured, and the Obama administration wishes to relocate them in Virginia (which has an existing Uighur community), political leaders and many members of the general public are unwilling to admit them into their midst. The response of

Republican representative Frank Wolf (in whose district the Uighur community resides and who has, in the past, been sympathetic to the Uighur cause
against China) is typical: "Let them go to some other country" (qtd. in Isikoff
and Hosenball 2009, 10). He is afraid that they may attack Chinese diplomats
in Washington, D.C., and he doesn't wish to inherit that kind of worry.

The situation of the Uighur detainees reveals the complexities of global
politics. These detainees may appear to be the simplest to release and relocate,
but this is certainly not the case. If it is proving this difficult to find a new
home for them, one wonders what the prospects will be for the other detainees who await relocation. Attorney Wells Dixon voices his frustration: "It's
been deeply frustrating for us, because our clients would love to resettle in the
United States or in a country like Canada or a country in Europe. We're talking about people who, at least in the case of the Uighurs, practice a very mod-
erate form of Islam, are pro-democracy, and are capitalists. These are people
who come from an area of western China that they refer to as Turkistan, or
East Turkistan, which is along the former Silk Road. They are traders, entre-
preneurs, so they're very capable of self-sufficiency. They would do very very
well in a Western country. And it's been very deeply troubling for us, and obviously for them, that they remain in Guantánamo, and no country will take
them, particularly when you look at the countries in Europe with large Uighur
populations who have called for the closure of Guantánamo—countries like
Germany, Finland, and Sweden—they will call for the closure of Guantánamo, but they will not open their doors to 17 people who everyone, including
the United States government, acknowledges were picked up by mistake. It's
been very very frustrating for us" (Dixon, interview). (See the Introduction for
the updated situation of the Uighurs. Five remain in Guantánamo Bay as of
June 2010.)

Private Testimony, Public Work

Legal theorist Ronald Dworkin (1986) is deeply optimistic about law's fundamental impulse to transcend the human and empathetic limitations of its
own articulations. He says of those lawyers who push against the constraints
of law's regulations and strictures that "they are chain novelists with epics in
mind, imagining the work unfolding through volumes it may take generations
to write. In that sense, each of their dreams is already latent in the present
law; each dream might be law's future" (409). One could justifiably apply these
words to Gutierrez, Raut, Falkoff, Willett, and Oleskey. They have all made
several public appearances to talk about their detainee defense work. The
venues have included colleges and universities, places of worship, and professional conferences. In addition, they have written editorials and tried in other
ways to communicate to the public the details of and reasons for their involvement in this task. One could see these appearances as evidence of the lawyers'
desire for visibility and renown. One could also consider the lawyers as either

obdurately optimistic or doggedly stubborn in believing that their interventions really count for something. Gutierrez, in particular, insists on engagement, in whatever form possible, to dismantle the culture that gave rise to Guantánamo. She asserts, "I also think there are things people can do to reconnect people in the United States to their own sense of humanity. I think in general our media and our mainstream American culture have really demonized Muslims and Arabs. It is very powerful to go to interfaith services or dinners, to reach out to communities that are targeted in your area and show some form of solidarity or act of kindness, to share, really to share a meal. If someone hasn't sat down and had dinner with someone who is Muslim or Arab, try and spend a month figuring out how to do that. The same thing that happened to the Vietnamese during the Vietnam War, where they became 'gooks' and not human beings, I think Muslims have become detainees and not people. And teach children as well. I think we've all really lost a little bit of our humanity; it's slipped away, both by being perpetrators at Guantánamo and for people who have been victimized" (Gutierrez, interview).

Anant Raut's memoir piece, "Bottomless" (2008), is an eloquent record and reflection of a visit to Guantánamo Bay in which he learns the news of a client's imminent release. The narration is taut and sparse, as if to parallel the constrained circumstances in which they meet and the physical restraints on his client ("Even the 'good' bad guys get shackled" [9]). Raut and his client, Adel, share in the anticipation of freedom, even as they remember the indignities Adel has endured and the time he has lost with his family, and they nervously and excitedly imagine Adel's meeting the five-year-old daughter he has never seen. On the return journey from the detention facility, Raut's paralegal, Nicole, says, "Now I have my law school essay" (14). Raut reflects on her comment, musing, "The only problem, I wanted to say, was that there were almost five hundred more law school essays that needed to be written" (14).

Nicole's comment brings us back to Lauren Berlant's suspicion of the politics of feeling. Nicole has been moved and changed by what she has observed and experienced; she wishes to draw attention to the impact of detainee defense work in her application essay to law school, positioning herself as a worthy candidate for admission. The interaction with Adel has affected her profoundly, one infers, by deepening her appreciation for the complexities of human endurance and illuminating the capacity for man's inhumanity to man. She aims to transmute this intangible gain into the material gain of a law school admission. One could conclude, then, that significant benefits of detainee defense work accrue to the lawyers and paralegals.

Raut's unuttered reflection on Nicole's comment holds multiple significations, contained in the word *problem*. His reference to the five hundred more essays that await writing reminds us of the number of habeas lawyers (and therefore the number of accompanying paralegals) engaged in detainee defense work. Does Raut mean that Nicole would do well to remember that she is not the only one to have had this uniquely transforming experience, and therefore she should realize that her law school essay may not be as special as she wishes it to be? Is he saddened/alarmed/angered/bitter that the five hundred essays on the Guantánamo experience that will be written by paralegals will trivialize the violations suffered by the detainees by repeatedly recasting their suffering as a learning experience for the law school applicants? Does he believe that only by writing about Guantánamo Bay and its detainees can the lawyers and paralegals fulfill their obligation as "witnesses" to an egregious cruelty? And is he impatient for these five hundred law school essays to be written so that law school faculty can absorb the implications of this experience and make the necessary changes to the teaching of law? Or does he hope that the process of writing the essays will impress upon these future lawyers the urgent need to maintain a posture of vigilance: about the law, about potential depredations to the law, and about their own comfortable capitulation to laws that undermine humanity?

Conclusion

Prognosis: *The Future of Empathy in the United States*

On September 22, 2010, Eddie Daniels, antiapartheid activist and fellow prisoner on Robben Island with Nelson Mandela, spoke at the University of Massachusetts Boston about his experience under apartheid and the circumstances that led him to join the resistance movement and subject himself to the dangers of imprisonment. Daniels thanked the world for the fall of apartheid. "Without you, we could not have done it," he said. Though the primary force of the antiapartheid movement came from the oppressed groups and their white allies and from the African National Congress (ANC) membership and its leaders in exile, Daniels reminded the world that we had risen to our moral obligation by divesting our investments in companies doing business with South Africa, banning the country from the Olympic Games and other international sports venues, boycotting its products and academic institutions, and marginalizing it within the global community. South Africa was made a pariah state, and this shame and isolation, implied Daniels, contributed in no small measure to the National Party's leaders' eventual recognition that they would have to accept the reality of negotiating with the ANC to dismantle apartheid.

The fall of apartheid was effected over a long period of time.[1] The boycott and divestment effort took more than two decades to gather sufficient force to extricate the apartheid regime. At the same time, related global phenomena had to occur. Communism had to lose its sway, as Patti Waldmeir (1998) notes; with the fall of the Berlin Wall and the USSR disaggregated, the apartheid government in South Africa saw with relief that the global force of communism would no longer pose a threat to their "Christian" way of life. (The South African Communist Party (SACP) had steadfastly supported the ANC leaders.)

The process of creating a global empathetic movement is fraught with frustrations and setbacks, the more so because such movements usually begin with nonstate players asserting their ethical outrage at violations of human rights. It is the long view that must prevail, because in the struggle to bring down entrenched structures of oppression and arbitrary abuses of power, the adversary has every advantage: control of money, medium, message, and military.

In the context of such a formidable apparatus of power, to display empathy can have profound consequences for livelihood and life, as many have found who courageously assert their empathy for those whom the state deems as "enemies." Albie Sachs is a well-known example of an antiapartheid activist who suffered grievous physical harm (he lost an arm and an eye) from a bomb placed in his car by the operatives of the South African apartheid government while he was in Maputo, Mozambique. Closer to home, former U.S. Marine Corps captain Josh Rushing experienced the displeasure of the Pentagon because of comments he made in the film *Control Room*, in which as a spokesperson for the military during and after the invasion of Iraq, Rushing comes to the realization that *Al-Jazeera*'s coverage of the war is more forthright and respectful of the toll on civilians than that of the American government or its media outlets.

In an interview with the *Village Voice* shortly after the release of *Control Room*, Rushing observed that "in America war has its own branding; when you mention war to Americans, they think of F-16s over the Yankee stadium and sailors kissing their girlfriends in Times Square" (qtd. in Ludden 2004). These images do not communicate the real impact of war, he notes, adding that, by contrast, *Al-Jazeera*'s coverage of war does not leave out the human cost of conflict. "*Al-Jazeera* seems to show all of it and it kind of reminds you how horrible war is. And I think there's some value to this. Anything that slows the fervor for us to go to war is a valuable thing" (qtd. in Ludden 2004). For these remarks as well as for his empathy for the *Al-Jazeera* reporters with whom he came into regular contact while stationed in Qatar, Rushing found himself being criticized by the military, and finally being forbidden to speak with the media. As a result of this order, he ultimately quit the military. His remarks remind us that empathy—ethical or compassionate—can invite censure, opprobrium, or worse.

In the film, Rushing is remarkably honest in expressing his opinion that it causes him more grief when he watches the bodies of dead American soldiers than dead Iraqis—soldiers or civilians. He reflects about his selective empathy, and this capacity to examine himself honestly leads him to move to a position of ethical empathy, where he understands that war can have devastating consequences for all who get caught up in it. He observes, with admirable candor, in an online discussion, "Our empathy is strongest for those who are most similar to us. By understanding we have more in common than in difference with other citizens of the world, our empathy extends more organically to them as well" (Rushing and Ibrahim 2005).

The issue of selective empathy that emerges in Josh Rushing's initial attitude about the casualties of the Iraq War is also at the heart of the scathing criticism that Samantha Power (2001) directs at the Western nations for their indifference to the signals of an impending human rights disaster in Rwanda in 1994. Without mincing words, she accuses the United Nations and Western governments of being "bystanders to genocide." Early in her article that bears that phrase as its title, Power asserts:

> In reality the United States did much more than fail to send troops. It led a successful effort to remove most of the UN peacekeepers who were already in Rwanda. It aggressively worked to block the subsequent authorization of UN reinforcements. It refused to use its technology to jam radio broadcasts that were a crucial instrument in the coordination and perpetuation of the genocide. And even as, on average, 8,000 Rwandans were being butchered each day, U.S. officials shunned the term "genocide," for fear of being obliged to act. The United States in fact did virtually nothing "to try to limit what occurred." Indeed, staying out of Rwanda was an explicit U.S. policy objective. (Power 2001)

She then proceeds to support this damning assessment. What is particularly interesting is Power's characterization of the Congress as "tired of its obligation to foot a third of the bill for what had come to feel like an insatiable global appetite for mischief and an equally insatiable UN appetite for missions" (Power 2001).

Empathy, it would thus seem, is based on expediency or national self-interest. What does not have a direct bearing on national security or national economic superiority does not merit resources and personnel. Anthony Lake, President Clinton's advisor in the National Security Office at the time of the Rwandan genocide, and the person whom everyone expected would be the most attuned to the human dimension of realpolitik (the unrelenting pursuit of national self-interest to the exclusion of all else), regrets his inaction:

> "One scenario is that I knew what was going on and I blocked it out in order to not deal with the human consequences," he says. "Here I'm absolutely convinced that I didn't do that, but maybe I did and it was so deep that I didn't realize it. Another scenario is that I didn't give it enough time because I didn't give a damn about Africa, which I don't believe because I know I do. My sin must have been in a third scenario. I didn't own it because I was busy with Bosnia and Haiti, or because I thought we were doing all we could. . . . I'm as guilty as anybody else, because to the degree that I didn't care about Africa, it would be understandable, but since I was more inclined to care, I don't know why I didn't." (Qtd. in Power 2001)

Lake's interrogation of his inaction is what Power so brilliantly describes as "guilt over an absence of guilt" (2001). That he is willing to own up to his unconscious and unintended but devastating indifference to Africa is a necessary first step toward gaining insight into why he failed to act and why he was not able to recognize as fellow humans the people of Rwanda who were being slaughtered.

It is difficult to know whether the tragedy of our inaction in Rwanda will lead to our heightened awareness of human rights violations, whether ongoing or impending, in the future. It would be unfortunate if we replaced restraint with unthinking intrusion, and worse still if we constructed the invasive intrusion as a rescue mission in which we ride in to "save" the underdog. Of course, we should be ever ready to go out in defense of those who cannot defend themselves. However, as Abdullahi An-Na'im (2003) cautions, we should wait until those who are directly affected by the crisis ask for our help; we should follow the lead of those individuals and groups who are most victimized by the structures of oppression. We should strengthen the resistances they mount and the challenges they launch.

But to clothe our own self-interest with the narrative of helping the oppressed can have unintended consequences. Many feminist scholars, notably Lila Abu-Lughod and Chandra Mohanty, have decried the West's rhetoric of saving Muslim women from oppressive Muslim men. By regarding the burqa as a "body bag" from which the Afghan and Muslim woman needs to be freed, the Western spectator robs the Afghan woman of her capacity for free choice and sees her as life as an unmediated coercion. This constructed empathy for the veiled Afghan woman has, as Ayotte, Husain, Kensinger, and Abu-Lughod have exhaustively documented, become the moral justification for the bombing of Afghanistan: "Following 9/11, it was not only the Taliban as supporters of terrorism, but also the Taliban as oppressors of women, that defined our enemy in the 'war on terrorism.' In the U.S. government's appropriation of the feminist concern with women's oppression, U.S. military action became 'just' in part as the agency of Afghan women's liberation" (Ayotte and Husain 2005, 122). Such a ready embrace of the rhetoric of saving both eclipses the independent choices that Afghan women make and obscures U.S. complicity in having empowered the Taliban during the fight against the Soviets, and the ravages to daily life brought about by U.S. bombing of Afghanistan territory. Thus expedient empathy, as in the U.S. adoption of the discourse of liberating Muslim women, perpetuates representations and forms of knowledge that undermine the agency of Muslim women and feminist organizations such as RAWA—Revolutionary Association of the Women of Afghanistan—who have been resisting the Taliban long before September 11, and justifies aggressive practices of warfare that disrupt already fragile landscapes.

As a nation, we are at a critically important moment in our collective search for a way to move forward that both provides us a sense of who we are as a nation and guarantees our protection as a people. We like to think of ourselves as pluralistic, secular, and welcoming, but all those attributes are fragile at the moment, under attack from our fear of the stranger, our suspicion of the unfamiliar, and our haste in constructing the enemy. At this historical moment, the enemy is Islam and the targets are Muslim men (and to a lesser extent Muslim women). As the lawyers working for Guantánamo Bay detainees say, it is no accident that all those held at Guantánamo Bay are Muslims. The physical remove of Guantánamo Bay from the mainland and the media silence on the domestic detainees has allowed most of the public in the United States to keep the detentions in the background of their consciousness.

But what is impossible to ignore and relegate to the corner of our consciousness is the corrosion of our national psyche made visible by the controversy surrounding the proposed mosque or Islamic center near Ground Zero and the hearings in Congress in March 2011 initiated by Representative Peter King of New York on the "radicalization of Muslims." Presciently, Reza Aslan, in an August 23, 2010, commentary on National Public Radio, powerfully expressed his sense of betrayal. He had naïvely believed that the United States would never make the mistake of European nations; "America's unbreakable dedication to religious liberties would never allow anti-Muslim sentiment to become mainstream" (2010). But, he observes regretfully, it seems that he was wrong. "The same kind of Islamophobia that has made much of Europe inhospitable to its Muslim citizens is now threatening to seize the U.S." (2010). What Aslan fears is the impact of such an atmosphere on the next generation of U.S. Muslim youth; we risk their becoming disaffected and disenfranchised like their European counterparts.

Those who have proposed the mosque at Ground Zero (actually, the proposed location is several blocks away from the site of the fallen towers) are said to lack empathy for those who lost loved ones in the collapse of the twin towers. Yet as Aslan and others have reminded the opponents of the mosque, Muslims, too, were among the dead on September 11. And as Jalal Alamgir (2011) writes, we need hearings not about imagined Muslim radicalization but about ways to integrate Muslims into the fabric of American social and political life. Further, he observes, we need "soul-searching—about the malaise of American news. How can TV coverage become less vacuous and less sensational? How can it be more informative and spur intelligent conversation?" (2011).

The rage and grief we felt immediately after the attacks of September 11, 2001, can, if we allow them, impair our own humanity and cloud our judgment as a people. Frank Bidart's fierce poem "Curse" (2002) enters the attackers' minds and attempts to get a measure of their thoughts as they perpetrated their heinous agenda. Having gained access to their minds, he sees into the crevices of their consciousness, acquiring knowledge of their motivations and leading him to damn them and utter his fiery curse: "May the listening ears of your victims their eyes their / breath / . . . eat like acid / the bubble of rectitude that allowed you / breath." Bidart's rage is formidable, and it is just and fitting.

But one wonders whether the force of his fury is so great as to know no boundaries and accept no end. Is there not the danger that the wrath that engenders his curse can become insatiable, forever seeking to keep itself alive, unwilling to cease its destructive spread? And will we be tempted to craft policy based on such profound anger?

Without giving up our right to furious rage and deep sorrow, we can also find within us the emotions and perspectives that could lead to reconciliations and new friendships. Naomi Shihab Nye (2002) reminds us in her poem "Red Brocade" of the great tradition of hospitality among Arabs, a tradition that may be worth recalling when we are tempted to conflate Arab, Muslim, and terrorist. She writes: "The Arabs used to say, / When a stranger appears at your door, / feed him for three days / before asking who he is, / where he's come from, / where he's headed" (2002). Your hospitality and care of him will revive him and give him the "strength" to answer your questions, she says. But perhaps "by then you'll be such good friends" (2002) that you will not really care about the answers to your interrogation. An act of generosity creates the possibility for true connection, she implies. Will we heed that opening for a meaningful interaction?

Recent manifestations of democratic aspirations by the peoples of Northern Africa and the Middle East have evoked in the American public a mild form of empathy, recognizing their yearning for freedom of expression, for a life of economic opportunity, for dignity. And yet there has been a strong expression of antipathy as well—with doubts that their notion of democracy is the same as ours; what if "Islamic" parties gain ascendancy, we wonder. They are animals unworthy of democracy, we say, pointing to the sexual abuse of journalist Lara Logan by the "mob" in Egypt's Tahrir Square. We are discomforted by our initial empathy for these Muslim Others, and we are therefore quick to seize on reasons for disavowing our nascent empathetic connection. So it would seem that while we may embrace some types of "neighbors," we are unlikely to embrace all neighbors. The challenge that Žižek (2005) poses to us is that we cannot be selective about whom we identify and accept as our neighbor, because we are constituted by all our neighbors as they are constituted by us.

Our leaders have created for us a monstrous enemy, and we have readily acquiesced to their imaginings. Will we finally resist their destructive messages and refuse to be ruled by fear? We are vulnerable, yes, but so are all other nations, all other peoples. Our vulnerability does not give us a right to claim exceptional status and demand exclusive attention from the world. It may take us a while to outgrow our arrogance and narcissism, but unless we do so, the prospects for our future in the world community will be bleak.

Notes

INTRODUCTION

1. Marjorie Garber (2004) provides a useful distinction among empathy, sympathy, and compassion. Empathy, she writes, is "a modern word, although it has a Greek analogue. Coined in the early years of the twentieth century as a translation of German *Einfühlung*, it has come to denote the power of projecting one's personality into the object of contemplation and has been a useful technical term in both psychology and aesthetics. It seems possible that the need for this word arose as the strongest sense of *sympathy* [emotional kinship between equals] began to decline or become merged with *compassion* [akin to pity, where there is a clear hierarchy between those who suffer and those who do not and so dispense their compassion]" (24).

2. Following the Japanese American redress movement, the vacating of the convictions of the three challengers (Gordon Hirabayashi, Minoru Yasui, and Fred Korematsu) of the curfew and the evacuation and internment orders, and the official presidential apology declared by Ronald Reagan in 1988, it is virtually impossible to argue that the Japanese American internment was not racially motivated. Peter Irons, who reopened Korematsu's case in 1983, when evidence came to light that the government lawyers had deliberately suppressed information that would have proved to the Supreme Court justices that there was no reason to doubt the loyalty of the Japanese American community, is only one of numerous scholars who have written conclusively about the racial foundations of Executive Order 9066 that set in motion the processes that tore West Coast Japanese immigrants and Japanese Americans from their homes and placed them in internment camps from 1942 until 1945. See also Jerry Kang's (2004) law review article, which discounts the view that the Supreme Court would have made the morally correct decision if it had been given all the necessary "exculpatory evidence." Kang argues that the Supreme Court was guided by a racist perspective and refused to address the constitutionality of the initial presidential order. Chapters 2 and 3 examine the internment experience in detail.

3. This was in the keynote address that Appadurai delivered for the symposium "In the Life of Cities: Parallel Narratives of the Urban," delivered on March 4, 2011, at Harvard University.

4. Most people can experience only a small portion of the myriad circumstances in which humans find themselves. Moreover, depending on who one is, there are certain circumstances that cannot be physically experienced. A man cannot, for instance, truly experience the pain of labor and childbirth; a white man in the United States cannot experience the visceral fear of a black man surrounded by white policemen. These experiences and their emotions can be absorbed only through linguistic re-creation, through imaginative and complex discourse. Language, then, becomes an important vehicle for the cultivation of empathy.

5. See Greenberg 2009.

6. See also D. Brooks 2009 and Kahan 2006.

7. In 1988, the U.S. government issued a formal apology to the 120,000 Japanese Americans who were interned and provided monetary reparation of $20,000 for each surviving internee (to compensate for wrongful loss of property and freedom). See S. D. Ikeda (2000) for a detailed comparison of the apology letters of George H. W. Bush and Bill Clinton. Ikeda does a close reading of the text of the two letters to assess the relative sincerity of the writers and the degree to which they communicate a genuine sense of national penance. There was also the acknowledgment of error by the six "architects" of the Japanese American evacuation and internment. These were Chief Justice Earl Warren, who declared, "I have since deeply regretted the removal order and my testimony advocating it, because it was not in keeping with our American concept of freedom and the rights of citizens"; Milton S. Eisenhower, the first director of the War Relocation Authority, who expressed his misgivings even as the relocation was going on—"I feel most deeply that when the war is over and we consider calmly this unprecedented [sic] migration of 120,000 people, we as Americans are going to regret the avoidable injustices that may have been done"; and Henry L. Stimson, Francis Biddle, Justice William O. Douglas, and Justice Tom C. Clark (qtd. in Maki, Kitano, and Berthold 1999, 101).

8. See Srikanth 2004, especially chap. 1.

9. I first learned of this story through Anne Erde and Vivian Zamel, who teach ESL courses at the University of Massachusetts Boston. It is available at many sites, one of which is http://www.tikkun.org/article.php/Nye-Gate4A.

10. Sriram sent me the essay in an e-mail dated April 23, 2009.

11. See especially Smith 1976, 5–10.

12. See "Guantánamo Row" 2009.

13. See "Uighurs' Plight" 2010.

14. A selection of law review articles linking internment and the current practices of detention under the global "war on terror" includes Cole 2009, Saito 2010, and Saad Gul 2007.

15. "How to Tell Japs" 1941. See also Minear 2001 for a number of racist cartoons of the Japanese and Japanese Americans that Dr. Seuss drew for the New York newspaper *PM* from 1941 until 1943.

16. Neal Desai, the lead author of the paper "Torture at Times: Waterboarding in the Media" describing the findings of the study, was interviewed by Brooke Gladstone (2010).

17. His observation finds a powerful parallel in Etel Adnan's famous novel *Sitt Marie Rose* (first published in French in 1978) about the early years of the Lebanese Civil War. One narrator bemoans the ethos of group allegiance that inhibits, even prohibits, empathy for the outsider.

18. Beatrice McKenzie's (2006) comprehensive overview of the vast scholarship of gender and race in its relation to the privileges of citizenship provides compelling evidence of the curtailment and forfeiture of citizenship for women and groups of color throughout U.S. history. Up until the 1950s, for instance, Asian American women lost their U.S. citizenship for marrying foreigners, and "unlike white and African American women were never able to regain it" (594). McKenzie's essay also points to scholarship on sexuality laws that define the boundaries of citizenship. Even today, U.S. citizens with foreign same-sex partners cannot sponsor their partners for immigration under the family preference category.

19. In the context of the tension between black women's solidarity with white women along gender lines and their allegiance to black men along race lines, see the brilliant essay by Kimberlé Crenshaw (1992).

20. The presence of power within empathy is one reason that the discourse of empathy is not embraced as a viable means to resolving deep-rooted conflicts, such as the Palestinian-Israeli situation. In this regard, see the collection of essays *Israeli and Palestinian Identities in Dialogue* (Halabi 2004).

21. See "Guantánamo Bay Naval Base" 2011.

22. The Web site http://humanterrainsystem.army.mil/ notes: "The near-term focus of the HTS [Human Terrain System] program is to improve the military's ability to understand the highly complex local socio-cultural environment in the areas where they are deployed; however, in the long-term, HTS hopes to assist the US government in understanding foreign countries and regions prior to an engagement within that region."

23. The refusal by many Israeli soldiers to serve in the occupied territories stems from ethical empathy: they are principally prompted by their distress at the erosion of the ideals on which the Jewish state was founded. See Žižek 2002, 113–114.

24. When David Souter was nominated to the Supreme Court, one of the principal objections to him was that as a single man, he would be unfamiliar with the complexities of parenthood and that, therefore, he would be ill-equipped to rule on cases that called for deep understanding of family matters. In the case of Clarence Thomas, his nomination was seen to provide an empathetic connection to the African American experience. Both perceptions have since been proven to be entirely erroneous.

CHAPTER 1

1. The master of empathy is Nelson Mandela. Given his twenty-seven-year imprisonment by the apartheid regime, there was no reason for him to empathize with his oppressors. But he did. One reason that South Africa was able to effect a relatively bloodless transition to democracy was that Nelson Mandela, despite the lack of power of the African National Congress (ANC) in relation to the ruling apartheid National Party, took the time to understand his adversaries (through learning Afrikaans and studying their literature and music); he was thus able to empathize with the leaders of the apartheid regime by seeing that they, too, loved South Africa but were deeply insecure about the survival of their language and cultural traditions. This insight profoundly affected the course of the negotiations between the ANC and the National Party.

2. Though Tolan's book is set in the Middle East and examines the Palestinian-Israeli conflict, I would argue that this particular situation has direct impact on U.S. foreign policy and is, therefore, highly relevant to this chapter. Those on the right and left would both concur that Israel's special relationship with the United States has significant repercussions for U.S. actions abroad.

3. See Mary Louise Pratt, *Imperial Eyes: Travel Writing and Transculturation* (2008). She speaks of the captivity narrative as the "safe context in which to narrate the terrors of the contact zone" (182), because the captive's return is evidence of the reestablished dominance of the European social, religious, and racial order. While this reaffirmation of the European space is the dominant message of these narratives, my point is that Rowlandson and others use the interstices of their narrative to provide positive "commentary" on Indian spaces.

4. Heather Roberts (2004) writes of Lydia Child that while living in New York in the years 1841–1843, she "took to the streets out of a sense of both personal urgency and moral duty. Her hermeneutic and didactic project in the New York letters was of the profoundest importance personally, politically, and spiritually. She offers her spiritual exegesis of the city as a guide to reforming what she had come to view as a morally disordered society, teaching her readers how to view their city, and one another, through the lens of sympathy" (752).

5. In a related context, on the power of certain kinds of physical landscape to effect profound changes in thinking, Ranen Omer-Sherman (2004) points out that the Israeli writer Amos Oz uses the desert and its continually shifting contours to interrogate supposed certainties and uncertainties. His characters journey into the desert to resist the stranglehold of the Israeli state upon their individual aspirations; once in the desert, they find its harsh and bleak setting, with its howling winds and moving sands, the site of their moral education. Here, they come to realize the Israeli destruction and burial of Arab villages, and gain insight into the ways in which the Israeli state negates and erases both past and present Arab residents of the land. In the desert, Oz's characters learn of the damage done to Arabs by the presence of the nation state of Israel.

6. See the Introduction to this book for an explanation of "empathetic interrogation" that uses the individual in need of empathy as a tool to serve the ends of the empathizer.

7. Twain's critique of war was considered so devastating that his friends advised him not to publish it. He set it aside as something that could be published after his death. "The War Prayer" was published right after World War II.

8. In this regard, see Brenda Wineapple's 2006 article, which says about Stein's response, "Which is another way of saying not to be interested in the atomic bomb in 1946 is an inimitable, annoying, and clever rhetorical device drawing attention to itself and thus of considerable interest to the loving, hating, struggling (i.e., interesting) human being, which is the wonderful, wondrous subject of biography" (43). Stein, according to Wineapple, is ultimately interested in herself, and we literary critics must therefore be interested in her and not shy away from biographical criticism.

9. See Hogan 1996.

10. Japan apologized in 2008 for its wartime coercive use of Korean "comfort women" as prostitutes for the soldiers of the imperial army. Some Korean comfort women felt that the apology did not go far enough. For a sensitive treatment of the relationship between a soldier in the Imperial Japanese Army and a "comfort woman," see Chang-Rae Lee's novel *A Gesture Life* (1999).

11. Moustafa Bayoumi (2008) writes, "On November 5, 2001, the Justice Department announced 1,182 had been arrested, then stopped providing a tally. The average length of detention for post–September 11 detainees was 80 days" (39).

12. See Srikanth 2007 for a comparison of Hamid's novel with Rushdie's *Shalimar the Clown* against the backdrop of a discussion on the viability of South Asian solidarity in the current climate of a U.S.-led "global war on terror."

CHAPTER 2

Acknowledgment: I thank Rita Banerjee for her invaluable help in locating the precise frame numbers on the microfilm reels of the Wayne Collins Collections from which I draw the excerpts included in this chapter.

1. Question 27 asked, "Are you willing to serve in the Armed Forces of the United States on combat duty, whenever ordered?" (Women were required to answer their willingness to serve in the Women's Army Corps.) Question 28 asked whether the internee was willing "to swear unqualified allegiance to the United States of America" and "forswear any form of allegiance or obedience to the Japanese emperor, or any other foreign government, power, or organization" (Castelnuovo 2008, xii). Eric Muller (2006) writes that of the "74,588 internees who filled out the questionnaire, . . . nearly 12% refused to swear allegiance without qualification" (44). Twenty-five percent of the internees answered no to both questions. Resentment at the internment prompted many Nisei to reject the hypocrisy of the government's desire for their labor in the war while denying them their fundamental civil rights; question 28 led both Nisei and Issei to feel that an affirmative answer would suggest that they had previously been loyal to the Japanese emperor. Issei were particularly troubled by question 28, because to answer yes would be to render them stateless, since they were ineligible for U.S. citizenship.

2. See Muller 2006, 51.

3. Wayne Collins microfilm, Wayne Collins Collection, Bancroft Library, University of California, Berkeley, Reel 1, Frame 0125.

4. Digital Densho Archive; interviewers Tom Ikeda and Barbara Takei speak to Tetsujiro (Tex) Nakamura; interview date, September 23, 2009. Densho ID: denshovhntetsujiro-01-0013. http://archive.densho.org/main.aspx. There are twenty-four interview segments with Tex Nakamura. This quotation comes from segment thirteen.

5. Besig was a "transplanted Easterner" to California and was "not licensed to practice law in California" (Kutulas 1998, 204), so he could not himself represent Korematsu.

6. Judge Goodman of the San Francisco District Court ruled in favor of Collins's mass action suit (in April 1949) that the renunciants were U.S. citizens who had given up their citizenship under unusual circumstances of coercion, and so their renunciations had no validity. When the government appealed this ruling, Justice Denman of the Ninth Circuit Court of Appeals agreed with Goodman that the renunciations were made under forced circumstances; but he did not accept the mass suit, and required that other than 1,004 minors whose renunciations were automatically voided, the remaining 3,300+ renunciants would have to file individual affidavits to explain the duress under which they renounced. See Christgau 2009, 180.

7. Digital Densho Archive; interview with Tex Nakamura. Densho ID: denshovhntetsujiro-01-0019. Available at http://archive.densho.org/main.aspx. Interview segment nineteen of twenty-four.

8. Digital Densho Archive, interview with Tex Nakamura. Densho ID: denshovhntetsujiro-01-0009. Available at http://archive.densho.org/main.aspx. Interview segment nine of twenty-four.

9. Collins, in a letter to Attorney General Tom Clark, dated November 1, 1945. This nineteen-page communication alerted Tom Clark that if he did not "take immediate action" to cancel the renunciation, stop the deportation, and effect the release from internment of the hundreds of people whose names appeared on an attached list, then each of the individuals would institute legal proceedings against the government. (From the Wayne Collins Collection.)

10. See, for example, hybrid identities as theorized by Homi Bhabha (1994) and Stuart Hall (1990) and borderland identities as described by Gloria Anzaldúa (1987).

11. The invitation from Doi can be found in Reel 1, Frame 0110. Collins's response is also in Reel 1 and occupies Frames 0110 and 0111. Doi's letter to Collins is dated September 16, 1967; Collins's response to Doi is dated October 20, 1967.

12. See "Transnational Homepages" in Srikanth 2004, 49–97.

13. To Collins, the U.S. citizenship of a person born in the United States is unassailable; one does not even have to speak English to be an American citizen, he observes. In a brief filed with the American consul in Kobe, Japan, on October 3, 1958, in behalf of Kiyoshi Matsuura's application to reinstate his U.S. citizenship, Collins writes, "There is no legal requirement that a native-born citizen must possess a knowledge of the English language. The fact that the appellant's knowledge of English may be somewhat rudimentary is to be attributed to adversity and lack of opportunity to learn it. . . . A great many Americans are illiterate in so far as the English language is concerned. . . . (Only aliens seeking to be naturalized, upon whom our naturalization laws operate, are required to learn a smattering of English in order to become recipients of what actually is nothing more than a 'conditional' citizenship through the naturalization process. No such legal requirement is imposed on the native born. We appear to have the right to be born, to grow up and to die ignorant of our mother tongue English which, itself, is a foreign importation. Perhaps we should all be versed in one or more Indian tongue . . .)." Wayne Collins Collection, Reel 20, Frames 92–96.

14. Letter to Doi, October 20, 1967.

15. Wayne Collins Collection, Reel 1, Frame 0111.

16. Digital Densho Archive; interview with Tex Nakamura. Densho ID: denshovh-ntetsujiro-01-0013. Available at http://archive.densho.org/main.aspx. Interview segment thirteen of twenty-four.

17. The *Amistad* was a Spanish ship that set sail in 1839 from Havana in Cuba to Puerto Principe, also in Cuba. On board the *Amistad* were fifty-three Africans and three white men (including the captain) who were Spanish subjects. There were also documents that claimed that the Africans were slaves and the rightful property of two of the white men, Ruiz and Montez. In fact, the Africans, who were from the Mendi tribe, had been "kidnapped" from their West African home by Spanish slave traders and transported to Cuba, in violation of Spanish laws prohibiting the slave trade. On the journey between Havana and Puerto Principe, the Africans revolted, killed the captain, and demanded that Ruiz and Montez navigate the ship to Africa. Ruiz and Montez tricked the Africans and steered the ship toward the United States, where it ran aground on Long Island. Ruiz and Montez were assisted by Thomas Gedney and Richard Meade, the officers of the ship *Washington*, to regain control of the *Amistad*. The ship was brought to New London, Connecticut, where the Africans and the ship were held as "salvage." Ruiz and Montez claimed that the ship was Spanish property and the Africans their private property as slaves, based on the documents from Cuba. Gedney and Meade demanded a share of the assets of salvage. The U.S. government (under the presidency of Van Buren) argued that the ship and its cargo (including the Africans, who were considered property) should be returned to Spain according to treaty obligations. The Africans argued that they were free men, that the slave trade was illegal in the United States, and that therefore they should be returned to their home in Africa.

18. Wayne Collins Collection, Reel 5, Frames 0042–0051.

19. Wayne Collins Collection, Reel 1, Frames 0079–0080.

20. See Irons 2006. Mitsuye Endo filed a habeas corpus suit, challenging the legality of her detention and asserting that as a citizen whose loyalty had been established,

the government had no right to detain her. The Supreme Court ruled in her favor in December 1944, setting in motion the government's proclamation that it would be dismantling the camps and releasing the internees back into the communities from which they had been evacuated (360).

21. Wayne Collins Collection, Reel 1, Frame 0062.

22. Wayne Collins Collection, Reel 5, Frame 0045.

23. Wayne Collins Collection.

24. See Daniels 2004, 84–86.

25. Wayne Collins Collection, Reel 27, Frame 0184.

26. Letter, February 21, 1946. Wayne Collins Collection.

27. Digital Densho Archive; interview with Tex Nakamura. Densho ID: denshovh-ntetsujiro-01-0020. Available at http://archive.densho.org/main.aspx. Interview segment twenty of twenty-four.

28. See Irons 2006, 352–353. Yasui was turned away from military service eight times. He challenged the curfew orders because they discriminated against U.S. citizens of Japanese ancestry and spent nine months in solitary confinement before his trial. His conviction was upheld by the Supreme Court.

29. See Elliott 2009. Moustafa Bayoumi's nuanced portrait of Sami, an Arab American Marine, also offers a deeply contoured perspective of what it means to be of Arabic ethnicity and fighting in the U.S.-led invasion of Iraq (46–80).

30. See, for instance, McNaughton 2006. Also see Nakamura 2008.

31. See *Takao Ozawa v. United States*, 260 U.S. 178 (1922). Available at http://caselaw.lp.findlaw.com/cgi-bin/getcase.pl?court=US&vol=260&invol=178. See also *United States v. Bhagat Singh Thind*, 261 U.S. 204 (1923). Available at http://supreme.justia.com/us/261/204/case.html.

32. *Acheson v. Murakami*, 176 F.2d 953 (1949). Available at http://174.123.24.242/leagle/xmlResult.aspx?page=3&xmldoc=19491129176F2d953_1890.xml&docbase=CSLWAR1-1950-1985&SizeDisp=7.

33. Digital Densho Archive; interview with Tex Nakamura. Densho ID: denshovh-ntetsujiro-01-0019. Available at http://archive.densho.org/main.aspx. Interview segment nineteen of twenty-four.

34. *Schneiderman v. United States*, 320 U.S. 118 (1943). Available at http://supreme.justia.com/us/320/118/case.html.

CHAPTER 3

1. African Americans might point to the success of the Japanese American redress campaign to make the same charge against the white majority group: that it has been easier to apologize for and make reparations for the wrong done to the internees than it would be to right the centuries-long deleterious effects of slavery and segregation. See Laremont 2001.

2. I am deeply indebted to Greg Robinson for pointing me to the existence of the Kehoe, Means, Edmiston, and Oakes literary treatments of the internment experience.

3. See Yen 2003a, 2003b. The activist organization NCRR (Nikkei for Civil Rights and Redress) played an advisory role in the filming of *Stand Up for Justice*, and one of its members, Janice Harumi Yen, was associate producer.

4. See Grace Hong's (1999) analysis of this piece as evidence of Yamamoto's eventual realization of white denial of property ownership to both blacks and Asian Americans and her desire to make amends for her earlier lack of empathy for Mr. Short. Empathetic

gaps occur even between populations that have had similar experiences of suffering; in this connection, see Srikanth 2006.

5. See also Song 2005, especially chaps. 3 and 4, for a masterful discussion of pessimism, mourning, and melancholy in the Asian American community following the Los Angeles uprising/riots.

6. See Srikanth 2004, chaps. 1 and 4.

7. One of the best literary treatments of this subject is John Okada's 1957 novel *No-No Boy*. Question 27 asked, "Are you willing to serve in the armed forces of the United States on combat duty, wherever ordered?" Question 28 asked, "Will you swear unqualified allegiance to the United States of America and faithfully defend the United States from any or all attacks by foreign or domestic forces, and forswear any form of allegiance or obedience to the Japanese Emperor or any other foreign government, power or organization?" (Chan 1991, 130).

8. That noncitizens and individuals from minority groups are required to lead "perfect lives" is underscored in the film *Sentenced Home* (Grabias 2006), which records the tragic injustice of the U.S. deportation policies on three Cambodian men. Though they have served time for felonies committed as young teens (the men are now in their twenties), in the paranoia and hostility of the post-9/11 climate, their "alien" status (they are not citizens) marks them as automatic targets for deportation to Cambodia, a "home" country they fled nearly twenty years ago and with which they have no connection.

CHAPTER 4

1. The most famous of the rendition ("outsourcing of torture") cases—when individuals suspected of terrorism are apprehended and then taken to prisons (known as black sites) outside the United States where they are subjected to torture—is that of Canadian national Maher Arar. He was seized by U.S. authorities when in transit in 2002 through New York's JFK airport. Erroneously identified as an al-Qaeda member, he was sent to Syria, where he was imprisoned and tortured for several months. Subsequently released by the Syrian authorities because they could find no links to al-Qaeda, Arar returned to Canada and proceeded to sue the U.S. government. Canada commissioned an inquiry into the Arar affair and found that intelligence agencies had spread inaccurate information about Arar, and the U.S. government used questionable tactics in arresting him and transporting him to Syria. The Canadian government cleared Arar's name. See Shane (2006).

2. Gitanjali Gutierrez, attorney at the Center for Constitutional Rights, offered this anecdote in April 2008 during the question-and-answer session following the panel titled "Guantánamo Bay and the Conscience of Asian American Studies" at the annual conference of the Association for Asian American Studies. The detainee had consoled himself in the years between 2001 and 2004 that he was in Guantánamo Bay not because the American people hated him but because there was an irrational ruler in power. His hope was that once the 2004 elections were held, the will of the American people would replace this irrational ruler with someone more humane and reasonable.

3. For numerous articles on Michael Mori and his representation of Australian David Hicks, see http://www.lexisnexis.com/us/lnacademic/results/listview/listview.do? unclassified=false&selRCNodeID=2&docsInCategory=3&treeMax=true&nodeDisplay Name=Legal+News&sort=RELEVANCE&risb=21_T6686515747&cisb=22_T668651 5749&expandable=true&fromClickNode=true. One can access more than a thousand items that refer to Michael Mori's defense of Hicks, in the form of newsprint articles,

news transcripts, magazine and journal articles, and legal news entries. In March 2007, Hicks pleaded guilty to "one charge of material support for terrorism" but pleaded not guilty "to supporting terrorist acts" (White 2007, A01). The circumstances under which the guilty plea was obtained have been challenged by Amnesty International and other critics who allege that torture was used to secure it. Two of Hicks's civilian lawyers, Joshua Dratel and Rebecca Snyder, were not allowed to represent him because one of them refused to sign a document that would have led to the compromising of their ethical responsibilities (White 2007, A01). David Hicks was finally released to Australia in May 2007 to complete his seven-year sentence in an Australian prison.

4. See Lewis 2007. See also "Unveiled Threats" 2007 for excerpts of Stimson's January 11 interview with Federal News Radio, in which he makes his damaging statements.

5. I spoke with Stephen Oleskey in Boston on June 25, 2008. His firm represents six Algerian-born detainees. The six men were arrested by the Bosnian government in October 2001 at the demand of the United States, which claimed that the six were plotting to blow up the U.S. embassy in Sarajevo. Following a three-month investigation by Bosnian police and courts, the men were ordered released by a court in Bosnia for lack of evidence to support the U.S. claims. An international tribunal established by the 1995 Dayton (Ohio) Accords ending the Bosnian war also separately entered an injunction prohibiting anyone from removing the men from Bosnia. Instead of being released, however, the United States insisted that the Bosnians turn over the men to the American military resident in Bosnia as part of the international peacekeeping operation. The men were then shipped to Guantánamo Bay, where they were among the earliest arrivals on January 20, 2002. See http://www.wilmerhale.com/boumediene for details on the *Boumediene* case, named for the lead petitioner named in the habeas petition filed by Wilmer Hale for the six men in July 2004.

6. I first met Sabin Willett on October 5, 2006, at Tufts University. At the time, we had a brief and informal conversation. My longer phone interview of him was conducted on November 3, 2006.

7. I visited the offices of the Center for Constitutional Rights on November 9, 2006.

8. In my interview of Stephen Oleskey, I asked him whether there had been any negative fallout from his firm's corporate clients because of its detainee advocacy. On the contrary, says Oleskey; the corporate clients appreciate the fact that Wilmer Hale is advocating to uphold the applications of the Constitution. He also told me about several corporate clients' reactions to the implication by Cully Stimson, former deputy assistant secretary for detainee affairs at the Department of Defense, that lawyers working pro bono for the detainees were, in fact, receiving funds from questionable sources, and their corporate clients should therefore think about taking their business elsewhere. His corporate clients joked that Wilmer Hale must be very powerful, if the government was trying to put the firm out of business!

9. At a talk delivered at the University of Massachusetts Boston on February 19, 2009. Robbins was invited by the Human Rights Working Group and Al-Nur, the campus arm of the American Islamic Congress.

10. Alan Ray and I had this discussion following my presentation on February 4, 2005, at the University of New Hampshire, where I had been invited by Professor Monica Chiu as part of the speaker series for American Studies. Ray was vice provost of academic affairs at the time of my visit; currently, he is senior vice provost at the University of New Hampshire.

11. Though Katyal provided a spirited defense of Salim Hamdan, Osama bin Laden's driver, and in doing so challenged the many questionable detention practices of

the Bush administration, he is not uncategorically opposed to the exercise of executive power. In fact, there is reason to believe that the Obama administration's floating of the idea of preventive detention—in which certain individuals, suspected of potentially being terrorists, would be held without charge in U.S. prisons—originates in Katyal. See Greenwald 2009. For a valuable discussion of the implications of preventive detention to the American notion of justice, see Greenwald's (2009) interview with ACLU lawyer Ben Wizner.

12. For details of the South African legal battle for mandatory government distribution of the pharmaceutical Nevirapine to prevent mother-to-child transmission of HIV, see Nattrass 2007, especially 95–107. In addition, barrister Geoff Budlender, in a conversation my students and I had with him in Cape Town in January 2008, noted the pride with which lawyers in the years immediately after South Africa's adoption of democracy in 1994 wore their activist credentials. It was an advantage to be known as an activist judge or barrister in those days; the energy of activism had brought down the institution of apartheid, and those who had been trained in that struggle were seen as supremely equipped to lead the nation in its new life. I draw the term *radicalists* from the assertion by attorney Gitanjali Gutierrez of the Center for Constitutional Rights that the lawyers working for the detainees have become "radicalized." When I asked Sabin Willett, one of the pro bono lawyers representing the Uighur detainees, whether this was indeed the case, he appeared uncomfortable with the word, perhaps because of its anarchist overtones. It is not surprising that the detainee lawyers from large corporate law firms would wish to downplay their radical credentials.

13. In August 2008, Kanstroom made the chilling comment to me that the laws surrounding deportation are so rigid and unyielding that he and his student assistants can do no more than render "hospice care" to those caught within the grip of these laws. "All we can do is provide them with humanity."

14. See Levinson 2000: "[Tina] Rosenberg . . . reveals that she may know more about Eastern Europe (and Latin America, about which she has also written sensitive analyses) than her native country when she suggests that because Americans 'worship the self-made man and constantly reinvent ourselves,' they do not 'understand the importance of the past'" (214–215).

15. The full text of the *Rasul v. Bush* (542 U.S. 466 [2004]) ruling can be found at http://supreme.justia.com/us/542/466/case.html. *Habeas corpus* is a Latin phrase that translates literally, according to the *Oxford English Dictionary* (1971), as "thou (shalt) have the body (in court)" (1235). In the realm of law, the right to habeas corpus is deemed fundamental and inviolable to a society recognizing the sacredness of the individual; the first recorded use of the term is in 1231, sixteen years after the signing of Magna Carta. The phrase *writ of habeas corpus* is, according to the *Oxford English Dictionary*, "the prerogative writ . . . requiring the body of a person restrained of liberty to be brought before the judge or into court that the lawfulness of the restraint may be determined" (1235). The defendants in the *Rasul v. Bush* case were two British citizens, Shafiq Rasul and Asif Iqbal, and Australian citizen David Hicks.

Nullifying the administration's argument that constitutional law did not apply in Guantánamo Bay because of the territory's falling outside the limits of U.S. sovereign power, the Supreme Court noted that for all practical purposes the United States "exercises 'complete jurisdiction and control' over the Guantanamo Bay Naval Base, and may continue to exercise such control permanently if it so chooses." Furthermore, the Supreme Court ruling states categorically that "aliens held at the base, no less than American citizens, are entitled to invoke the federal courts' authority." With references to the sanctity of the principle of habeas corpus and its origins in Magna Carta (1215), the majority opinion emphasizes that "application of the habeas statute to persons detained at the base is consistent with the historical reach of the writ of habeas corpus." Before Rasul and Iqbal could make an appearance in court to challenge the validity of their detentions, a diplomatic agreement between Britain and the United States resulted in their return to Britain, where they were found to be entirely innocent and released.

16. See "Torn Fabric of the Law: An Interview with Michael Ratner" 2005.

17. See Hamilton 2005. See also the CCR archives for the use of Guantánamo Bay to isolate Haitian refugees who were HIV-positive. Available at http://ccrjustice.org/ ourcases/past-cases/haitian-centers-council%2C-inc.-v.-sale.

18. Eugene Gressman and colleagues (2007) note the "unusual array of amici that included retired military officers, retired federal appellate judges, former prisoners of war, and Fred Korematsu" (512, footnote 167) for *Rasul v. Bush*.

19. Both our fascination with and revulsion for torture was problematically featured in the Coney Island "Water Board Thrill Ride" exhibit by Steve Powers, in which visitors to the exhibit paid money to peer through a window and saw robotic figures undergo waterboarding in a room that looked like a cell at Guantánamo Bay. Powers, a creative artist and Fulbright winner, believes that the exhibit, because of its provocative nature, will force people to discuss an issue that they've been silent about. Powers asks, "'What's more obscene, . . . the official position that waterboarding is not torture, or our official position that it's a thrill ride?'" See Kaminer 2008.

20. Andy Worthington's *Guantánamo Files* (2007) gives the details of how numerous men were captured and turned over for bounty. The Pakistani police force are also implicated in turning over hundreds of men to the U.S. military in order to collect bounty.

21. *Qassim v. Bush*, No. 05–0497 (D.D.C. 2005). The full text of Judge Robertson's ruling can be found at http://obsidianwings.blogs.com/obsidian_wings/files/show_case_ doc8.pdf.

CONCLUSION

1. See Borstelmann 2005; Nesbitt 2004; Thörn 2006; and Waldmeir 1998.

References

Aaltola, Mika. 2005. "The International Airport: The Hub-and-Spoke Pedagogy of the American Empire." *Global Networks* 5, no. 3 (July): 261–278.

Agamben, Giorgio. 1995. *Homo Sacer: Sovereign Power and Bare Life*. Palo Alto, CA: Stanford University Press.

———. 2005. *State of Exception*. Translated by Devin Attell. Chicago: University of Chicago Press.

Ahmed, Akbar S. 2003. *Islam under Siege: Living Dangerously in a Post-honor World*. Cambridge, UK: Polity Press.

Alamgir, Jalal. 2011. "The Congressional Hearings That Are Really Needed." *Huffington Post*, March 11. Available at http://www.huffingtonpost.com/jalal-alamgir/the-congressional-hearing_b_834682.html.

Alsultany, Evelyn. 2007. "Selling American Diversity and Muslim American Identity through Nonprofit Advertising Post-9/11." *American Quarterly* 59 (3): 593–622.

Ammons, Elizabeth. 2000. "*Uncle Tom's Cabin*, Empire and Africa." In *Approaches to Teaching Stowe's* Uncle Tom's Cabin, edited by Elizabeth Ammons and Susan Belasco, 68–77. New York: Modern Language Association of America.

An-Na'im, Abdullahi Ahmed. 2003. "Introduction: Expanding Legal Protection of Human Rights in African Contexts." In *Human Rights under African Constitutions: Realizing the Promise for Ourselves*, edited by Abdullahi Ahmed An-Na'im, 1–29. Philadelphia: University of Pennsylvania Press.

Anzaldúa, Gloria. 1987. *Borderlands: La Frontera*. San Francisco: Aunt Lute Books.

Apess, William. 1997. "Eulogy on King Philip, as Pronounced at the Odeon, in Federal Street, Boston." In *A Son of the Forest and Other Writings*, edited by Barry O'Connell, 103–139. Amherst: University of Massachusetts Press.

Aslan, Reza. 2010. "European Islamophobia Finds a Home in the U.S." *All Things Considered*. National Public Radio (August 23). Available at http://www.npr.org/templates/story/story.php?storyId=129381552.

Ayotte, Kevin J., and Mary E. Husain. 2005. "Securing Afghan Women: Neocolonialism, Epistemic Violence, and the Rhetoric of the Veil." *Feminist Formations* 17, no. 3 (Fall): 112–133.

Baldwin, James. 1953. "Everybody's Protest Novel." In *The New Partisan Reader, 1945–1953*, edited by William Phillips and Philip Rahv, 326–332. New York: Harcourt.

Bauer, Ralph. 2003. *The Cultural Geography of Colonial American Literatures: Empire, Travel, Modernity.* Cambridge: Cambridge University Press.

Bayoumi, Moustafa. 2008. *How Does It Feel to Be a Problem? Being Young and Arab in America.* New York: Penguin.

BBC News. 2006. "Guantanamo Suicides 'Acts of War.'" June 11. Available at http://news.bbc.co.uk/2/hi/5068606.stm.

Bearden, Russell E. 1999. "One State's Reaction to Wartime Internment." *Journal of the West* 38, no. 2 (April): 14–21.

Belasco, Susan. 2000. "The Writing, Reception, and Reputation of *Uncle Tom's Cabin*." In *Approaches to Teaching Stowe's* Uncle Tom's Cabin, edited by Elizabeth Ammons and Susan Belasco, 21–37. New York: Modern Language Association of America.

Berlant, Lauren. 2002. "The Subject of True Feeling: Pain, Politics, and Privacy." In *Left Legalism/Left Critique*, edited by Wendy Brown and Janet Halley, 105–134. Durham, NC: Duke University Press.

Bhabha, Homi. 1994. *The Location of Culture.* London: Routledge.

Bidart, Frank. 2002. "Curse." *Threepenny Review* (Spring). Available at http://www.threepennyreview.com/samples/bidart_sp02.html.

Blum, Lawrence. 1999. "Race, Community, and Moral Education: Kohlberg and Spielberg as Civic Educators." *Journal of Moral Education* 28 (2): 125–143.

———. 2004. "The Poles, the Jews and the Holocaust: Reflections on an AME Trip to Auschwitz." *Journal of Moral Education* 33, no. 2 (June): 131–148.

Boltanski, Luc. 1999. *Distant Suffering: Morality, Media, Politics.* Cambridge: Cambridge University Press.

Boraine, Alex. 2000. "Truth and Reconciliation in South Africa: The Third Way." In *Truth v. Justice: The Morality of Truth Commissions*, edited by Robert I. Rotberg and Dennis Thompson, 141–158. Princeton, NJ: Princeton University Press.

Borer, Tristan Anne. 2003. "A Taxonomy of Victims and Perpetrators: Human Rights and Reconciliation in South Africa." *Human Rights Quarterly* 25, no. 4 (November): 1088–1116.

Borstelmann, Thomas (Tim). 2005. "Squeezing White Supremacy." Review. *Diplomatic History* 29, no. 3 (June): 569–572.

Bow, Leslie. 2001. *Betrayal and Other Acts of Subversion: Feminism, Sexual Politics, Asian American Women's Literature.* Princeton, NJ: Princeton University Press.

Bradbury, Steven G. 2005. Principal Deputy Assistant Attorney General of the OLC, memo to John A. Rizzo, Senior Deputy General Counsel of the CIA (May 10). Available at http://luxmedia.com.edgesuite.net/aclu/olc_05102005_bradbury_20pg.pdf.

Brittain, Victoria, and Gillian Slovo. 2004. *Guantánamo: Honor Bound to Defend Freedom.* London: Oberon Books.

Brooks, David. 2009. "The Empathy Issue." *New York Times*, May 28. Available at http://www.nytimes.com/2009/05/29/opinion/29brooks.html.

Brooks, Peter. 2003. "Law, Therapy, Culture." In *Cultural Analysis, Cultural Studies, and the Law*, edited by Austin Sarat and Jonathan Simon, 245–256. Durham, NC: Duke University Press.

Brown, Wendy. 2002. "Suffering the Paradoxes of Rights." In *Left Legalism/Left Critique*, edited by Wendy Brown and Janet Halley, 420–437. Durham, NC: Duke University Press.

Brown, Wendy, and Janet Halley. 2002. "Introduction." In *Left Legalism/Left Critique*, edited by Wendy Brown and Janet Halley, 1–38. Durham, NC: Duke University Press.

Bruner, Jerome. 2002. *Making Stories: Law, Literature, Life*. Cambridge, MA: Harvard University Press.

Butler, Judith. 2001. "Giving an Account of Oneself." *Diacritics* 31, no. 4 (Winter): 22–40.

Bybee, Jay S. 2002. Assistant Attorney General, memo to Alberto R. Gonzales, Counsel to the President (August 1): 1–50. Available at http://www.washingtonpost.com/wp-srv/nation/documents/dojinterrogationmem020020801.pdf.

Castelnuovo, Shirley. 2008. *Soldiers of Conscience: Japanese American Military Resisters in World War II*. Westport, CT: Greenwood Press.

Center for Constitutional Rights. 2006. *Articles of Impeachment against George W. Bush*. New York: Melville House.

———. n.d. "Mission and History." Available at http://ccrjustice.org/missionhistory.

Chan, Sucheng. 1991. *Asian Americans: An Interpretive History*. New York: Twayne.

Chen, Tina. 2005. "Towards an Ethics of Knowledge." *MELUS* 30, no. 2 (Summer): 157–173.

Child, Lydia Maria. 1991. *Hobomok and Other Writings on Indians*, edited by Carolyn Karcher. New Brunswick, NJ: Rutgers University Press.

Chin, Frank. 1981. *The Chickencoop Chinaman; The Year of the Dragon: Two Plays by Frank Chin*. Seattle: University of Washington Press.

Christgau, John. 1985. "Collins versus the World: The Fight to Restore Citizenship to Japanese American Renunciants of World War II." *Pacific Historical Review* 54, no. 1 (February): 1–31.

———. 2009. *Enemies: World War II Alien Internment*. Lincoln: University of Nebraska Press.

Coetzee, J. M. 1999. *Disgrace*. New York: Penguin.

Cole, David. 2009. "Out of the Shadows: Preventive Detention, Suspected Terrorists, and War." *California Law Review* 97 (July): 693–750.

Collins, Donald E. 1985. *Native American Aliens: Disloyalty and the Renunciation of Citizenship by Japanese Americans during World War II*. Westport, CT: Greenwood Press.

Creef, Elena Tajima. 2000. "The Gendering of Historical Trauma in Internment-Camp Documentary: The Case of Steven Okazaki's *Days of Waiting*." In *Countervisions: Asian American Film Criticism*, edited by Darrell Y. Hamamoto and Sandra Liu, 163–174. Philadelphia: Temple University Press.

Crenshaw, Kimberlé. 1992. "Whose Story Is It, Anyway? Feminist and Antiracist Appropriations of Anita Hill." In *Race-ing Justice, En-gendering Power: Essays on Anita Hill, Clarence Thomas, and the Construction of Social Reality*, edited by Toni Morrison, 402–441. New York: Pantheon Books.

Crow, Charles L. 1987. "A MELUS Interview: Hisaye Yamamoto." *MELUS* 14, no. 1 (Spring): 73–84.

Crozier, W. Ray, and Paul Greenhalgh. 1992. "Beyond Relativism and Formalism: The Empathy Principle." *Leonardo* 25 (1): 83–87.

Daniels, Roger. 2004. *Prisoners without Trial: Japanese Americans in World War II*. New York: Farrar, Straus and Giroux.

Davidson, Robert A. 2003. "Introduction: Spaces of Immigration 'Prevention': Interdiction and the Non-Place." *Diacritics* 33, no. 3/4 (Fall/Winter): 3–18.

Davis, Kimberly Chabot. 2008. "White Book Clubs and African American Literature: The Promise and Limitations of Cross-Racial Empathy." *Literature Interpretation Theory* 19:155–186.

Davis, Thadious M. 2003. *Games of Property: Law, Race, Gender, and Faulkner's* Go Down, Moses. Durham, NC: Duke University Press.

De Kok, Ingrid. 1998. "Cracked Heirlooms: Memory on Exhibition." In *Negotiating the Past: The Making of Memory in South Africa*, edited by Sarah Nuttall and Carli Coetzee, 57–72. Cape Town, South Africa: Oxford University Press.

Denbeaux, Mark P., with Joshua Denbeaux, David Gratz, John Gregorek, Matthew Darby, Shana Edwards, Shane Hartman, Daniel Mann, and Helen Skinner. 2006. "Report on Guantanamo Detainees, a Profile of 517 Detainees through Analysis of Department of Defense Data." Available at http://papers.ssrn.com/s013/cf_dev/AbsByAuth.cfm?per_id=543402.

Dinerstein, Joel. 2009. "'Uncle Tom Is Dead!': Wright, Himes, and Ellison Lay a Mask to Rest." *African American Review* 43, no. 1 (Spring): 83–98.

Dorfman, Ariel. 2007. "Afterword: Where the Buried Flame Burns." In *Poems from Guantánamo: The Detainees Speak*, edited by Marc Falkoff, 69–72. Iowa City: University of Iowa Press.

Douglass, Frederick. 1990. *The Heroic Slave*. In *Three Classic African-American Novels*, edited by William L. Andrews, 23–71. New York: Penguin.

Dworkin, Ronald. 1986. *Law's Empire*. Cambridge, MA: Harvard University Press.

———. 2009. "Justice Sotomayor: The Unjust Hearings." *New York Review of Books*, September 24. Available at http://www.nybooks.com/articles/archives/2009/sep/24/justice-sotomayor-the-unjust-hearings/?page=1.

Edmiston, James. 1955. *Home Again*. New York: Doubleday.

Elliott, Andrea. 2009. "Complications Grow for Muslims Serving in the U.S. Military." *New York Times*, November 8. Available at http://www.nytimes.com/2009/11/09/us/09muslim.html?_r=3&pagewanted=1.

Esaki, John (director). 2004. *Stand Up for Justice*. DVD. Visual Communications.

Esmeir, Samera. 2006. "On Making Dehumanization Possible." *PMLA* 121, no. 5 (October): 1544–1551.

Estes, Donald H., and Mathew T. Estes. 1999. "Letters from Camp: Poston—The First Year." *Journal of the West* 38 (April): 22–33.

Falkoff, Marc, ed. 2007. *Poems from Guantánamo: The Detainees Speak*. Iowa City: University of Iowa Press.

Fanon, Frantz. 2005. *The Wretched of the Earth*. New York: Grove Press.

Faulkner, William. 1990. *Go Down, Moses*. New York: Vintage International.

Fein, Bruce. 2008. "Prosecute or Free." *Washington Times*, December 9, p. A14.

Felman, Shoshana. 2002. *The Juridical Unconscious: Trials and Traumas in the Twentieth Century*. Cambridge, MA: Harvard University Press.

Gadamer, Hans-Georg. 1989. "Destruktion and Deconstruction." In *Dialogue and Deconstruction: the Gadamer-Derrida Encounter*, edited by Diane P. Michelfelder and Richard E. Palmer, 102–114. Albany: State University of New York Press.

Garber, Marjorie. 2004. "Compassion." In *Compassion: The Culture and Politics of an Emotion*, edited by Lauren Berlant, 15–29. New York: Routledge.

Gehring, Petra. 2008. "The Jurisprudence of the 'Force of Law.'" In *Derrida and Legal Philosophy*, edited by Peter Goodrich, Florian Hoffman, Michel Rosenfeld, and Cornelia Vismann, 55–71. New York: Palgrave Macmillan.

Ghosh, Amitav. 1994. *In an Antique Land*. New York: Vintage Books.

Gilmore, Gerry J. 2002. "Rumsfeld Visits, Thanks U.S. Troops at Camp X-Ray in Cuba." U.S. Department of Defense. Available at http://www.defense.gov/news/newsarticle .aspx?id=43817.

Glaberson, William. 2008. "A Conviction, but a System Still on Trial." *New York Times*, August 10, p. A27. Available at http://www.nytimes.com/2008/08/10/ washington/10gitmo.html.

Gladstone, Brooke. 2010. "Newspapers and 'Waterboarding.'" Interview with Neal Desai. *On the Media*. National Public Radio (July 9). Available at http://www.onthemedia .org/transcripts/2010/07/09/03.

Grabias, David (director). 2006. *Sentenced Home*. Sentenced Home Productions.

Greenberg, Jan Crawford. 2009. "Obama Seeks 'Common Touch' in his Supreme Court Nominee." ABC News (May 25). Available at http://abcnews.go.com/Politics/ story?id=7668848&page=1.

Greenwald, Glenn. 2009. "Backlash Grows against Obama's Preventive Detention Proposal." *Salon*. Available at http://www.salon.com/opinion/greenwald/2009/05/25/ obama/.

Gressman, Eugene, Stephen M. Shapiro, Kenneth S. Geller, Timothy S. Bishop, and Edward A. Harnett. 2007. *Supreme Court Practice*, 9th ed. Bethesda, MD: Bureau of National Affairs.

Gross, Terry. 2007. Interview with Mohsin Hamid. *Fresh Air*. National Public Radio (April 3).

"Guantánamo Bay Naval Base." 2011. *New York Times*, April 25. Available at http:// topics.nytimes.com/top/news/national/usstatesterritoriesandpossessions/guantana mobaynavalbasecuba/index.html.

"Guantánamo Row: Cross Purposes." 2009. *The Economist* (May 30). Available at http:// www.economist.com/node/13743286.

Gudridge, Patrick O. 2005. "The Constitution Glimpsed from Tule Lake." *Law and Contemporary Problems* 81:81–118.

Gul, Saad. 2007. "Return of the Native? An Assessment of the Citizenship Renunciation Clause in Hamdi's Settlement Agreement in Light of Citizenship Jurisprudence." *Northern Illinois University Law Review* 27, no. 2 (Spring): 131–169.

Gurujal, Gretchen. 2002. "First Novel Is Small but Strong." *AP Weekly Features*, December 16, Lifestyle section. Available at http://web.lexis-nexis.com.eresources .lib.umb.edu/universe/document?_m=73e47983e4b921b144dabfed74c2bc6a& _docnum=6&wchp=dGLbVtz-zSkVA&_md5=fcb26324f099bc61d6410e74e6fe 0a47.

Guterson, David. 1995. *Snow Falling on Cedars*. New York: Vintage Books.

Habermas, Jürgen. 1993. *Justification and Application: Remarks on Discourse Ethics*. Cambridge, MA: MIT Press, 1993.

Halabi, Rabah, ed. 2004. *Israeli and Palestinian Identities in Dialogue*. New Brunswick, NJ: Rutgers University Press.

Hall, Stuart. 1990. "Cultural Identity and Diaspora." In *Identity: Community, Culture, and Difference*, edited by Jonathan Rutherford, 222–237. London: Lawrence and Wishart.

Hamid, Mohsin. 2007. *The Reluctant Fundamentalist*. Orlando, FL: Harcourt.

Hamilton, Rebecca J. 2005. "Review of *Guantánamo: What the World Should Know*." *Harvard Human Rights Journal* 18 (Spring): 299–300.

Hartman, Saidiya V. 1997. *Scenes of Subjection: Terror, Slavery, and Self-Making in the Nineteenth Century*. New York: Oxford University Press.

Hayashi, Brian Masaru. 2004. *Democratizing the Enemy: The Japanese American Internment*. Princeton, NJ: Princeton University Press.

Henderson, Lynne N. 1987. "Legality and Empathy." *Michigan Law Review* 85, no. 7 (June): 1574–1653.

Hersey, John. 1989. *Hiroshima*. New York: Vintage Books.

Hoffman, Martin L. 2000. *Empathy and Moral Development: Implications for Caring and Justice*. Cambridge: Cambridge University Press.

Hogan, Michael J. 1996. "The Enola Gay Controversy: History, Memory, and the Politics of Presentation." In *Hiroshima in History and Memory*, edited by Michael J. Hogan, 200–233. Cambridge: Cambridge University Press.

Hong, Christine. 2009. "Flashforward Democracy: American Exceptionalism and the Atomic Bomb in *Barefoot Gen*." *Comparative Literature Studies* 46 (1): 125–156.

Hong, Grace Kyungwon. 1999. "Something Forgotten Which Should Have Been Remembered: Private Property and Cross-Racial Solidarity in the Work of Hisaye Yamamoto." *American Literature* 71, no. 2 (June): 291–310.

Honigsberg, Peter Jan. 2009. *Our Nation Unhinged: The Human Consequences of the War on Terror*. Berkeley: University of California Press.

Horton, Scott. 2010. "The Guantanamo 'Suicides.'" *Harper's* (March): 27–37.

"How to Tell Japs from the Chinese." 1941. *Life*, December 22: 81.

Huyssen, Andreas. 2003. *Present Pasts: Urban Palimpsests and the Politics of Memory*. Stanford, CA: Stanford University Press.

Ikeda, Stewart David. 2000. "The Art of Apology: Grading the Ex-Presidents on their Internment Lessons." IMDiversity.com. Available at http://www.imdiversity.com/Villages/Asian/history_heritage/ikeda_internment_apology.asp.

Irani, George E. 1999. "Islamic Mediation Techniques for Middle East Conflicts." *Middle East Review of International Affairs* 3, no. 2 (June): 1–17.

Irons, Peter H. 1983. *Justice at War: The Story of the Japanese-American Internment Cases*. New York: Oxford University Press.

———. 2006. *A People's History of the Supreme Court*. New York: Penguin.

Ishigo, Estelle. 1972. *Lone Heart Mountain*. Los Angeles: Anderson, Ritchie, and Simon.

Isikoff, Michael, and Mark Hosenball. 2009. "Next Stop Nowhere." *Newsweek* 153, no. 22 (May 23): 10. Available at http://www.newsweek.com/2009/05/22/next-stop-nowhere.html.

"Issei, Nisei, Kibei." 1944. *Fortune* 29, no. 4 (April): 1–20. Available at http://archive.densho.org/Core/ArchiveItem.aspx?i=denshopd-p141–00019.

Johnson, James Weldon. 1995. *The Autobiography of an Ex-Colored Man*. Mineola, NY: Dover.

Kahan, Don. 2006. "Yale Law School Commencement Remarks," May 22. Available at http://www.law.yale.edu/documents/pdf/kahanrevised.pdf.

Kakutani, Michiko. 2002. "War's Outcasts Dream of Small Pleasures." *New York Times*, September 10, p. E6.

Kaminer, Ariel. 2008. "Coney Island Sideshow Has Guantanamo Theme." *New York Times*, August 6, p. E1. Available at http://www.nytimes.com/2008/08/06/arts/design/06wate.html.

Kang, Jerry. 2004. "Denying Prejudice: Internment, Redress, and Denial." *UCLA Law Review* 51 (April): 933–1013.

Kang, Laura Hyun-Yi. 2002. "The Desiring of Asian Female Bodies: Interracial Romance and Cinematic Subjection." In *Screening Asian Americans*, edited by Peter X. Feng, 71–99. New Brunswick, NJ: Rutgers University Press.

Kanstroom, Daniel. 2007. *Deportation Nation: Outsiders in American History.* Cambridge, MA: Harvard University Press.

Kaplan, Amy. 2003. "Homeland Insecurities: Reflections on Language and Space." *Radical History Review* 85 (Winter): 82–93.

Karcher, Carolyn. 1991. "Introduction." In *Hobomok and Other Writings on Indians*, edited by Carolyn Karcher, ix–xxxviii. New Brunswick, NJ: Rutgers University Press.

Kawano, Kelly. 2002. "A Conversation with Julie Otsuka." Available at http://www.randomhouse.com/boldtype/0902/otsuka/interview.html.

Kehoe, Karon. 1946. *City in the Sun.* New York: Dodd, Mead.

Khan, Mahvish Rukhsana. 2008. *My Guantánamo Diary: The Detainees and the Stories They Told Me.* New York: Public Affairs.

Kim, Elaine H. 2000. "Home Is Where the *Han* Is: A Korean-American Perspective on the Los Angeles Upheavals." In *Asian American Studies: A Reader*, edited by Jean Wu and Min Song, 270–290. New Brunswick, NJ: Rutgers University Press.

Klein, Rick. 2006. "Deal Made on Detainee Questioning." *Boston Globe*, September 22, pp. A1, A8.

Knight, Jessica. 2006. "Representing Internment: Ambivalent Visibility in Miné Okubo's Citizen 13660." Paper delivered at the Midwest MLA convention, Chicago, IL, November 9–12. Available at http://blog.lib.umn.edu/manu0014/gwmh/knight_GWMH_Paper.doc.

Kolker, Carolyn. 2005. "Justice at Bay." *American Lawyer* (May): 95–100.

Koshy, Susan. 2002. "South Asians and the Complex Interstices of Whiteness: Negotiating Public Sentiment in the United States and Britain." In *White Women in Racialized Spaces: Imaginative Transformation and Ethical Action in Literature*, edited by Samina Najmi and Rajini Srikanth, 29–51. Albany: State University of New York Press.

Kutulas, Judy. 1998. "In Quest of Autonomy: The Northern California Affiliate of the American Civil Liberties Union and World War II." *Pacific Historical Review* 67, no. 2 (May): 201–231.

———. 2006. *American Civil Liberties Union and the Making of Modern Liberalism, 1930–1960.* Chapel Hill: University of North Carolina Press.

Langdell, Cheri Colby. 2004. *Adrienne Rich: The Moment of Change.* Westport, CT: Greenwood.

Laremont, Ricardo René. 2001. "Jewish and Japanese American Reparations: Political Lessons for the Africana Community." *Journal of Asian American Studies* 4, no. 3 (October): 235–251.

Lee, Chang-Rae. 1999. *A Gesture Life.* New York: Riverhead Books.

Lefebvre, Alexander. 2008. *The Image of Law: Deleuze, Bergson, Spinoza.* Stanford, CA: Stanford University Press.

Levinson, Sanford. 2000. "Trials, Commissions, and Investigating Committees: The Elusive Search for Norms of Due Process." In *Truth v. Justice: The Morality of Truth Commissions*, edited by Robert I. Rotberg and Dennis Thompson, 211–235. Princeton, NJ: Princeton University Press.

Lewis, Neil. 2006a. "Freed from Guantanamo but Stranded Far from Home." *New York Times*, August 15, p. A15.

———. 2006b. "Judge Sets Back Guantanamo Detainees." *New York Times*, December 14, pp. A32.

———. 2007. "Official Attacks Top Law Firms over Detainees." *New York Times*, January 13. Available at http://www.nytimes.com/2007/01/13/washington/13gitmo.html.

Ludden, Jennifer. 2004. "Josh Rushing's Surprise Role in 'Control Room.'" *All Things Considered*. National Public Radio (October 20). Available at http://www.npr.org/templates/story/story.php?storyId=4135294.

Ludwig, Mark. 1990. "Introduction." In Mary Rowlandson, *The Captive: The True Story of the Captivity of Mrs. Mary Rowlandson among the Indians and God's Faithfulness to Her in Her Time of Trial*. Tucson, AZ: American Eagle.

Mahler, Jonathan. 2008. *The Challenge: Hamdan v. Rumsfeld and the Fight over Presidential Power*. New York: Farrar, Straus and Giroux.

Maki, Mitchell, Harry L. Kitano, and Sarah Megan Berthold. 1999. *Achieving the Impossible Dream: How Japanese Americans Obtained Redress*. Champaign: University of Illinois Press.

Mamdani, Mahmood. 1996. "Reconciliation without Justice." *Southern African Review of Books* (November/December): 3–5.

———. 2002. "Amnesty or Impunity: A Preliminary Critique of the Report of the Truth and Reconciliation Commission of South Africa." *Diacritics* 32, no. 3/4 (Fall/Winter): 33–59.

Marks, Jonathan H. 2006. "9/11 + 3/11 + 7/7 = ? What Counts in Counterterrorism?" *Columbia Human Rights Law Review* 37 (Spring): 559–626.

Massaro, Toni M. 1989. "Legal Storytelling: Empathy, Legal Storytelling, and the Rule of Law: New Words, Old Wounds." *Michigan Law Review* 87 (August): 2099–2127.

Mathur, Shubh. 2006. "Surviving the Dragnet: 'Special Interest' Detainees in the US after 9/11." *Race and Class* 47, no. 3 (January): 31–46.

McCoy, Alfred W. 2006. "The Myth of the Ticking Time Bomb." *The Progressive* 70, no. 10 (October): 20–24.

McKenzie, Beatrice. 2006. "Gender and United States Citizenship in Nation and Empire." *History Compass* 4, no. 3 (May): 592–602.

McNaughton, James C. 2006. *Nisei Linguists: Japanese Americans in the Military Intelligence Service during World War II*. Washington, DC: U.S. Government Printing Office.

Means, Florence Crannell. 1945. *The Moved-Outers*. Boston: Houghton Mifflin.

Mielke, Laura L. 2004. "Sentiment and Space in Lydia Maria Child's Native American Writings, 1824–1870." *Legacy* 21 (2): 172–192.

Minear, Richard. 2001. *Dr. Seuss Goes to War: The World War II Editorial Cartoons of Theodor Seuss Geisel*. New York: New Press.

Muller, Eric L. 2006. "The Japanese American Cases—A Bigger Disaster Than We Realized." *Howard Law Journal* 41 (Winter): 1–71. Available at http://papers.ssrn.com/sol3/papers.cfm?abstract_id=881099.

Mura, David. 2005. "Asian and Japanese Americans in the Postwar Era: The White Gaze and the Silenced Sexual Subject." *American Literary History* 17, no. 3 (Fall): 604–620.

Nakamura, Kellie Y. 2008. "'They Are Our Human Secret Weapons': The Military Intelligence Service and the Role of Japanese-Americans in the Pacific War and in the Occupation of Japan." *The Historian* 70, no. 1 (Spring): 54–74.

Naqvi, H. M. 2009. *Home Boy*. New York: Shaye Areheart Books.

Nattrass, Nicoli. 2007. *Mortal Combat: AIDS Denialism and the Struggle for Antiretrovirals in South Africa*. Durban, South Africa: University of KwaZulu-Nattal Press.

Nesbitt, Francis Njubi. 2004. *Race for Sanctions: African Americans against Apartheid, 1946–1994*. Bloomington: Indiana University Press.

Newman, Katherine. 1986. "Review of *The Ethnic Image in Modern American Literature 1900–1950*." *MELUS* 13, no. 1/2 (Spring/Summer): 135–142.

Ngai, Mae M. 2004. *Impossible Subjects: Illegal Aliens and the Making of Modern America*. Princeton, NJ: Princeton University Press.

Noujaim, Jehane (director). 2004. *Control Room*. DVD. Noujaim Films.

Nussbaum, Martha C. 2001. *Upheavals of Thought: The Intelligence of Emotions*. Cambridge: Cambridge University Press.

Nye, Naomi Shihab. 2002. "Red Brocade." *Nineteen Varieties of Gazelle*: Poems from the Middle East. Available at http://asitoughttobe.com/2010/02/27/saturday-poetry-series-presents-naomi-shihab-nye/.

———. 2007. "Gate 4-A." *Tikkun* (July/August). Available at http://www.tikkun.org/article.php/Nye-Gate4A.

Oakes, Vanya. 1955. *Roy Sato: New Neighbor*. New York: Julian Messner.

Okada, John. 1977. *No-No Boy*. Seattle: University of Washington Press.

Okazaki, Steven (director). 1991. *Days of Waiting*. DVD. Center for Asian American Media.

Okubo, Miné. 1946. *Citizen 13660*. New York: Columbia University Press.

———. 2004. "Statement of Miné Okubo before the Congressional Committee on Wartime Relocation and Internment (1981)." *Amerasia Journal* 30 (2): 15–18.

Oleskey, Stephen. 2008. "City on the Hill or Prison on the Bay? The Mistakes of Guantanamo and the Decline of America's Image." Testimony before the House Subcommittee on Foreign Affairs (May 6). Available at http://www.wilmerhale.com/files/upload/Oleskey_TestimonybeforeHouse.pdf.

Omer-Sherman, Ranen. 2004. "'A Disgrace to the Map of Israel': The Wilderness Journey of the Citizen-Soldier in Amos Oz's *A Perfect Peace*." *Journal of Modern Literature* 27, no. 3 (Winter): 97–115.

Omori, Emiko (director). 1999. *Rabbit in the Moon*. DVD. Wabi-Sabi.

Oren, Tasha G. 2005. "Secret Asian Man: Angry Asians and the Politics of Cultural Visibility." In *East Main Street: Asian American Popular Culture*, edited by Shilpa Davé, LeiLane Nishime, and Tasha Oren, 337–361. New York: New York University Press.

Otsuka, Julie. 2002. *When the Emperor Was Divine*. New York: Anchor Books.

Oxford English Dictionary. 1971. Compact ed. New York: Oxford University Press.

Packer, George. 2006. "Knowing the Enemy: The Anthropology of Insurgency." *New Yorker*, December 18, pp. 60–70.

Parker, Alan (director). 1990. *Come See the Paradise*. DVD. Twentieth Century Fox.

Patterson, Anita Haya. 1998. "Resistance to Images of the Internment: Mitsuye Yamada's Camp Notes." *MELUS* 23, no. 3 (Fall): 103–127.

Peters, Julie Stone. 2005. "Law, Literature, and the Vanishing Real: On the Future of an Interdisciplinary Illusion." *PMLA* 120, no. 2 (March): 442–453.

Power, Samantha. 2001. "Bystanders to Genocide." *The Atlantic* (September). Available at http://www.theatlantic.com/magazine/archive/2001/09/bystanders-to-genocide/4571/1/.

Pratt, Mary Louise. 2008. *Imperial Eyes: Travel Writing and Transculturation*, 2nd ed. New York: Routledge.

Puar, Jasbir. 2005. "On Torture: Abu Ghraib." *Radical History Review*, no. 93 (Fall): 13–38.

Raut, Anant. 2007. "Why I Defend 'Terrorists': An Open Letter to a Pentagon Critic from a Lawyer Representing Five Men at Guantanamo." *Chicago Sun-Times*, January 21, p. B3. First published as "Why I Defend 'Terrorists.' An Open Letter to Cully Stimson, Deputy Assistant Secretary of Defense for Detainee Affairs." *Salon*, January 17.

————. 2008. "Bottomless." *Catamaran: South Asian American Writing* 8:8–15.

Rich, Adrienne. 1986. *Your Native Land, Your Life: Poems*. New York: Norton.

Riechmann, Deb. 2006. "White House, Senate Resolute on Detainee Legislation." *Boston Globe*, September 17, p. A25.

Roberts, Heather Leland. 2004. "'The Public Heart': Urban Life and the Politics of Sympathy in Lydia Maria Child's *Letters from New York*." *American Literature* 76, no. 4 (December): 749–775.

Roberts-Miller, Patricia. 2002. "John Quincy Adams's Amistad Argument: The Problem of Outrage; Or, the Constraints of Decorum." *Rhetoric Society Quarterly* 32, no. 2 (Spring): 5–25.

Rostow, Eugene V. 1945. "Our Worst Wartime Mistake." *Harper's* 191, no. 1144 (September): 193–201.

Rowlandson, Mary. 1990. *The Captive: The True Story of the Captivity of Mrs. Mary Rowlandson among the Indians and God's Faithfulness to Her in Her Time of Trial*. Tucson, AZ: American Eagle.

Rushing, Josh, and Hassan Ibrahim. 2005. "Film: Control Room." *Washington Post* Live Online, January 24. Available at http://www.washingtonpost.com/wp-dyn/articles/A27078–2005Jan21.html?nav=rss_liveonline/entertainment.

Saito, Natsu Taylor. 2010. "Internments Then and Now: Constitutional Accountability in Post-9/11 America." *Duke Forum for Law and Social Change* 2 (71): 71–102.

Sanders, Jessica (director). 2005. *After Innocence*. DVD. American Film Foundation.

Scarry, Elaine. 1996. "The Difficulty of Imagining Other People." In *For Love of Country: Debating the Limits of Patriotism*, edited by Joshua Cohen, 98–111. Boston: Beacon Press.

————. 2010. *Rule of Law, Misrule of Men*. Cambridge, MA: MIT Press.

Schaffer, Kay, and Sidonie Smith. 2004. *Human Rights and Narrated Lives: The Ethics of Recognition*. New York: Palgrave Macmillan.

————. 2006. "Human Rights, Storytelling, and the Position of the Beneficiary: Antjie Krog's *Country of My Skull*." *PMLA* 121, no. 5 (October): 1577–1585.

Shaffer, Robert. 1998. "Cracks in the Consensus: Defending the Rights of Japanese Americans during World War II." *Radical History Review* 72:84–120.

Shane, Scott. 2006. "Torture Victim Had No Terror Link, Canada Told U.S." *New York Times*, September 25, p. A11.

Shiekh, Irum. 2011. *Detained without Cause: Muslim Stories of Detention and Deportation in America after 9/11*. New York: Palgrave Macmillan.

Shuman, Amy. 2006. "Entitlement and Empathy in Personal Narrative." *Narrative Inquiry* 16 (1): 148–155.

Simpson, Caroline Chung. 2001. *An Absent Presence: Japanese Americans in Postwar American Culture, 1945–1960*. Durham, NC: Duke University Press.

Slaughter, Joseph. 2007. *Human Rights, Inc.: The World Novel, Narrative Form, and International Law*. New York: Fordham University Press.

Smith, Adam. 1976. *The Theory of Moral Sentiments*, edited by D. D. Raphael and A. L. Macfie. New York: Oxford University Press.

Song, Min. 2005. *Strange Future: Pessimism and the 1992 Los Angeles Riots*. Durham, NC: Duke University Press.

Sontag, Deborah. 2006. "A Videotape Offers a Window into a Terror Suspect's Isolation." *New York Times*, December 4, pp. A1, A22.

Spanos, William V. 2005. "Humanism and the *Studia Humanitatis* after 9/11/01: Rethinking the *Anthropologos*." *Symploké* 13 (1–2): 219–262.

Srikanth, Rajini. 1998. "Ram Yoshino Uppuluri's Campaign: The Implications for Pan-Ethnicity in Asian America." In *A Part, Yet Apart: South Asians in Asian America*, edited by Lavina Dhingra Shankar and Rajini Srikanth, 186–214. Philadelphia: Temple University Press.

———. 2002. "Ventriloquism in the Captivity Narrative: White Women Challenge European American Patriarchy." In *White Women in Racialized Spaces: Imaginative Transformation and Ethical Action in Literature*, edited by Samina Najmi and Rajini Srikanth, 85–105. Albany: State University of New York Press.

———. 2004. *The World Next Door: South Asian American Literature and the Idea of America.* Philadelphia: Temple University Press.

———. 2006. "When Empathy Disappears: The Disconnect between African American and Asian American Muslims." *Works and Days: Intellectual Intersections and Racial/Ethnic Crossings* 24 (47/48): 89–117.

———. 2007. "South Asia and the Challenge of Intimacy in the 'Global War on Terror.'" *South Asian Review* 28 (1): 5–23.

Starn, Orin. 1986. "Engineering Internment: Anthropologists and the War Relocation Authority." *American Ethnologist* 13, no. 4 (November): 700–720.

Stauffer, John. 2005. "Frederick Douglass and the Aesthetics of Freedom." *Raritan* 25, no. 1 (Summer): 114–136.

Stefancic, Jean, and Richard Delgado. 2005. *How Lawyers Lose Their Way: A Profession Fails Its Creative Minds.* Durham, NC: Duke University Press.

Stein, Gertrude. 1973. "Reflection on the Atomic Bomb." In *Reflection on the Atomic Bomb: Volume 1 of the Previously Uncollected Writings of Gertrude Stein*, edited by Robert Bartlett Haas, 161. Los Angeles: Black Sparrow Press.

Stephenson, Anne. 2002. "'Divine' Gently Drives Home History." *USA Today*, October 3, p. 8D.

Stowe, Harriet Beecher. 1981. *Uncle Tom's Cabin.* New York: Bantam Books.

Suzuki, Peter T. 1986. "The University of California Japanese Evacuation and Resettlement Study: A Prolegomenon." *Dialectical Anthropology* 10, no. 3/4 (April): 189–213.

Tajima, Renee E. 1989. "Lotus Blossoms Don't Bleed: Images of Asian Women." In *Making Waves: An Anthology of Writings by and about Asian American Women*, edited by Asian Women United of California, 308–318. Boston: Beacon Press.

Thörn, Håkan. 2006. *Anti Apartheid and the Emergence of a Global Civil Society.* New York: Palgrave Macmillan, 2006.

Thorpe, Jessie. 2003. "Book Review: A Divine 'Emperor.'" United Press International (January 28). Available at http://www.upi.com/Odd_News/2003/01/28/Book-Review-A-Divine-Emperor/UPI-44601043771689/.

Todorov, Tzvetan. 1996. *Facing the Extreme: Moral Life in the Concentration Camps.* New York: Henry Holt, 1996.

Tolan, Sandy. 2006. *The Lemon Tree: An Arab, a Jew, and the Heart of the Middle East.* New York: Bloomsbury.

"Torn Fabric of the Law: An Interview with Michael Ratner." 2005. *Mother Jones* (March 21). Available at http://www.motherjones.com/politics/2005/03/torn-fabric-law-interview-michael-ratner.

Treat, John Whittier. 1995. *Writing Ground Zero: Japanese Literature and the Atomic Bomb.* Chicago: University of Chicago Press.

Tritter, Daniel F. 2005. "In the Defense of Fred Korematsu: *Vox Clamantis in Deserto Curiarum.*" *Thomas Jefferson Law Review* (Spring): 255–316.

Turner, Brian. 2005. *Here, Bullet.* Farmington, ME: Alice James Books.

Twain, Mark. 1923a. "To the Person Sitting in Darkness." In *Europe and Elsewhere*, edited by Albert Bigelow Paine, 250–273. New York: Harper and Brothers.

——. 1923b. "The War Prayer." In *Europe and Elsewhere*, edited by Albert Bigelow Paine, 394–398. New York: Harper and Brothers.

"Uighurs' Plight: After a Court Gambit Fails, Chinese Muslims at Guantanamo Still Need Help Resettling." 2010. *Washington Post* (March 3): A16. Available at http://www.lexisnexis.com.ezproxy.lib.umb.edu/hottopics/lnacademic/.

"Unveiled Threats." 2007. *Washington Post* (January 12). Available at http://www.washingtonpost.com/wp-dyn/content/article/2007/01/11/AR2007011101698.html.

Upchurch, Michael. 2002. "The Last Roundup." *New York Times*, September 22, sec. 7, col. 1, p. 14.

Vandergrift, Kay E. 1993. "A Feminist Perspective on Multicultural Children's Literature in the Middle Years of the Twentieth Century." *Library Trends* 41, no. 3 (Winter): 354–377.

Vogler, Candace. 2004. "Much of Madness and More of Sin: Compassion, for Ligeia." In *Compassion: The Culture and Politics of an Emotion*, edited by Lauren Berlant, 29–59. London: Routledge.

Volpp, Leti. 2000. "Blaming Culture for Bad Behavior." *Yale Journal of Law and Humanities* 12 (Winter): 89–116.

——. 2002. "The Citizen and the Terrorist." *UCLA Law Review* (June): 1575–1599.

Waldmeir, Patti. 1998. *Anatomy of a Miracle: The End of Apartheid and the Birth of the New South Africa.* New Brunswick, NJ: Rutgers University Press.

Walker, Alice. 1981. "Advancing Luna—and Ida B. Wells." In *You Can't Keep a Good Woman Down*, 85–104. New York: Harcourt, Brace, Jovanovich.

Walker, Samuel J. 2005. "Recent Literature on Truman's Atomic Bomb Decision: A Search for Middle Ground." *Diplomatic History* 29, no. 2 (April): 311–334.

Ward, Ian. 2003. *Justice, Humanity, and the New World Order.* Hampshire, UK: Ashgate.

Weglyn, Michi. 1976. *Years of Infamy: The Untold Story of America's Concentration Camps.* New York: Morrow.

Weiner, Isaac A. 2009. "Displacement and Re-placement: The International Friendship Bell as a Translocative Technology of Memory." *Material Religion* 5 (2): 180–204.

West, Robin. 1993. *Narrative, Authority, and Law.* Ann Arbor: University of Michigan Press.

White, Josh. 2007. "Australian's Guilty Plea Is First at Guantanamo." *Washington Post*, March 27, p. A01.

Willett, Sabin. 2006. "The Innocent Man at Guantanamo." *Boston Globe*, September 27, p. A11.

Wineapple, Brenda. 2006. "The Politics of Politics; or How the Atomic Bomb Didn't Interest Gertrude Stein and Emily Dickinson." *South Central Review* 23, no. 3 (Fall): 37–45.

Worthington, Andy. 2007. *The Guantánamo Files: The Story of the 774 Detainees in America's Legal Prison.* London: Pluto Press.

Wright, Richard. 1989a. "How Bigger Was Born." In *Native Son*, vii–xxxiv. New York: Harper and Row.

——. 1989b. *Native Son.* New York: Harper and Row.

Yagoda, Ben. 2001. *About Town: The New Yorker and the World It Made.* Cambridge, MA: Da Capo Press.

Yamada, Mitsuye. 1983. "Invisibility Is an Unnatural Disaster: Reflections of an Asian American Woman." In *This Bridge Called My Back: Writings by Radical Women of*

Color, edited by Cherríe Moraga and Gloria Anzaldúa, 35–41. Latham, NY: Kitchen Table Women of Color Press.

———. 1998. *Camp Notes and Other Writings*. New Brunswick, NJ: Rutgers University Press.

Yamamoto, Hisaye. 1988a. "The Legend of Miss Sasagawara." In *Seventeen Syllables and Other Stories*, 20–34. Latham, NY: Kitchen Table Women of Color Press.

———. 1988b. "The Wilshire Bus." In *Seventeen Syllables and Other Stories*, 34–39. Latham, NY: Kitchen Table Women of Color Press.

———. 2001. "A Fire in Fontana." In *Seventeen Syllables and Other Stories*, 150–158. New Brunswick, NJ: Rutgers University Press.

Yen, Janice Harumi. 2003a. "Historic Lazo Docu-Drama Completes Filming." Nikkei for Civil Rights and Redress. Available at http://www.ncrr-la.org/news/1_24_03/4.html.

———. 2003b. "Who Was Ralph Lazo?" Nikkei for Civil Rights and Redress. Available at http://www.ncrr-la.org/news/7_6_03/2.html.

Zernike, Kate. 2006. "Top Republicans Reach an Accord on Detainee Bill." *New York Times*, September 22, pp. A1, A14.

Žižek, Slavoj. 2002. *Welcome to the Desert of the Real*. London: Verso.

———. 2004. "From Politics to Biopolitics . . . and Back." *South Atlantic Quarterly* 103, no. 2/3 (Spring/Summer): 501–522.

———. 2005. "Neighbors and Other Monsters: A Plea for Ethical Violence." In *The Neighbor: Three Inquiries in Political Theology*, edited by Slavoj Žižek, Eric L. Santner, and Kenneth Reinhard, 134–197. Chicago: University of Chicago Press.

Index

Rajini Srikanth is Professor of English at the University of Massachusetts Boston. She is the author of *The World Next Door: South Asian American Literature and the Idea of America* and the coeditor (with Sunaina Maira) of *Contours of the Heart: South Asians Map North America* and (with Lavina Dhingra Shankar) of *A Part, Yet Apart: South Asians in Asian America*.